For the Norwegians in our family and those who live with them & love them.

MaryBeth 9/25/2013
Almaurade Cohen

THE ART OF COMPASSION

Thanks to my mom, Mabel Clara Nelson Almaurade
1905-1994

THE ART OF COMPASSION

A biography of

SIGRID UNDSET

Nobel Laureate for Literature

Yola Miller Sigerson

To order additional copies of this book, contact:
Xlibris Corporation
1-888-795-4274
www.Xlibris.com
Orders@Xlibris.com
36055

CONTENTS

Books By Sigrid Undset...11

I   In The Beginning (1882-1893)..13

II   Youth (1898-1904)...29

III   "Become Something, Darling . . ." (1904-1909)...........46

IV   Love—"Not Pale, Tired, Grey-weather Dreams" (1909-1912) 55

V   Marriage (1912) 78

VI   Ski (1913-1916) 93

VII   Sinsen (1916-1918) 105

VIII   Lillehammer (1919)..116

IX   *A Woman's Point of View* (1919) 127

X   *Kristin Lavransdatter* (1920-1922) 136

XI   Happy Times (1921-1924) 155

XII   *The Master of Hestviken* (1924-1928) 170

XIII   The Nobel Prize (1928) 179

XIV   The Thirties (1929-1940)..189

XV   War (1940) 205

XVI   America (1940-1945) 217

XVII   The Occupation (1940-1945) 234

XVIII The Long Loneliness is Over (1945-1949) 256

Notes 277

Endnotes 279

"I was never able to feel that other people's troubles were no concern of mine."

(from a letter to Marjorie Kinnan Rawlings)

ABOUT THE AUTHOR

Yola Miller Sigerson was the lighting designer for the Original Ballet Russes when Sol Hurok brought it to America; Production Stage Manager for Broadway musicals written and directed by George S. Kaufman; Co-producer with Cheryl Crawford of *Flahooley*, and associated with E. Y. Harburg, Joseph Losey and Leopold Stokowski on a number of stage productions.

She organized and staged close to a hundred pageants and public events at Madison Square Garden, New York's Central Park, the Hollywood Bowl, and other major arenas throughout the country, and produced a series of concerts with Leonard Bernstein, Benny Goodman, Artie Shaw and other classical, jazz and folk music artists at Carnegie Hall.

Her children's play, *The Big Rock Candy Mountain*, a folk musical written with Alan Lomax, was produced at Joan Littlewood's Theater Workshop in London.

In 1971 she moved with her family to London, where she researched and wrote *Clara*, a biography of Clara Wieck Schumann.

The Art of Compassion was researched in Norway, London, and the United States.

ABOUT SIGRID UNDSET

Sigrid Undset received the Nobel Prize for Literature in 1928. She was the third woman to be so honored.

Kristin Lavransdatter and *The Master of Hestviken*, her highly erotic, meticulously researched depictions of life in medieval Norway have been translated into almost every language, and enraptured readers all over the world are still naming their children after her unforgettable characters, yet there is no comprehensive biography of her, (to my knowledge)—not even in Norwegian. There are many studies of her work, and some memoirs have been published, but no "portrait of her progress through life," as Edmund Gosse defined biography, has appeared.

Undset constantly probed the seemingly irreconcilable multiple roles demanded of women as individuals, wives, and mothers, and she was fervently outspoken about their need for sexual fulfillment. Her great artistry, psychological insight, and compassion for human fallibility enabled her to treat ordinary people with a kind of dignity and respect not found elsewhere in literature, and her sensitive stories about working women are as eloquent as her medieval novels.

A prolific journalist, Undset's deep concern with moral and ethical considerations in her many articles on political and social issues gave her a reputation as a provocative thinker. Her campaign against Nazi Germany earned her an early position on Hitler's list of enemies of the Reich. She escaped when his forces invaded her country and spent five years in the United States working for his defeat.

Her feud with Knut Hamsun, in 1915, and excerpts from her book, *A Woman's Point of View* (published in 1919 but not available in English), are especially relevant to feminist discussions today.

At Undset's request, her family has, until recently, protected her private life from public scrutiny, but I have been fortunate in establishing excellent relationships with surviving relatives and friends. Her Norwegian and

American publishers have been most helpful, and lengthy interviews with Alfred A. Knopf and her editors have provided many personal insights and anecdotes. Letters to Willa Cather, Marjorie Kinnan Rawlings, Hudson Strode and Dorothy Day as well as quotes from her books that were not available in English appear here for the first time.

BOOKS BY SIGRID UNDSET

Norwegian	English	
1902		*Fru Marta Oulie* (novel)*
1908		*Den lykkelige alder* (*The Happy Age*)* (short stories)
1908		*I graalynseninegen* (*In the Gray Light of Dawn*)* (play)
1909	1936	*Fortaellinegen om Viga-Liot og Vigdis* (*Gunnar's Daughter*) (novel)
1910		*Ungdom* (*Youth*)* (poetry)
1911	1921	*Jenny* (novel)
1912		*Fattige skjebner* (*Poor Fates*)* (short stories)
1959		*Simonsen* and *Selma Brøter* in *Four Stories*
1914		*Vaaren* (*The Spring*)
1915		*Fortaellinger om Kong Arturo g ridderne av det runde bord* (*Tales of King Arthur and the Knights of the Round Table*)*
1917	1938	*Splinten av troldspeilet* (*Images in a Mirror*) (two stories)
1918		*De kloge jomfruer* (*The Wise Virgins*) (short stories)
1959		*Tjodolf* in *Four Stories*
1919		*Et kvinde-synbspunkt* (*A Woman's Point of View*)* (articles on women's rights)

KRISTIN LAVRANSDATTER (novel) (Three Volumes)

1920	1923	*Kransen* (*The Bridal Wreath*)
1921	1925	*Husfrue* (*The Mistress of Husaby*)
1922	1927	Korset (*The Cross*)

1923		*Tre sagaer om Islaendinger* (*Three Sagas of Icelanders*)*
1925		*Sankt Halvards liv, död og jertegn* (*Saint Halvard's Life, Death and Miracles*) (Biography)

THE MASTER OF HESTVIKEN (novel) (Two Volumes in Norwegian)
1925   *Olav Audunssøn I Hestviken*
1927   *Olav Audunssøn og Hans Born*

THE MASTER OF HESTVIKEN (Four Volumes in English)
       1928   *The Axe*
       1929   *The Snake Pit*
       1929   *In The Wilderness*
       1930   *The Son Avenger*

1933   1934   *Etapper* (*Stages on the Road*) (essay)

THE WINDING ROAD (novel) (Two Volumes)
1929   1931   *Gymnadenia* (*The Wild Orchid*)
1930   1932   *Den brennende busk* (*The Burning Bush*)

1930   *Das Weihnachtswunder* (*The Miracle of Christmas*)*
1931   *Begegnungen und Trennungen* (*Meeting and Parting*)*
                     (essays)
1932   1941   *Christmas and Twelfth Night*
1932   1933   *Ida Elisabeth* (novel)
1933   1934   *Ny raekke* (*Stages on the Road II*) (essays)
1934   1935   *Elleve aar* (*The Longest Years*) (autobiographical novel)
1936   1937   *Den trofaste hustru* (*The Faithful Wife*) (novel)
1937   1934   *Norske helgener* (*Saga of Saints*) (essay)
1938   1939   *Selvportretter og landskapsbilleder* (*Men, Women and Places*) (essays)
1939   1940   *Madame Dorthea* (novel)
1949   1942   *Tilbake til fremtiden* (*Return to the Future*) ?
1947   1942   *Lykkelige dager* (*Happy Times in Norway*) (children's book)
1943   1943   *Sigurd and His Brave Companions* (children's book)
1945   1945   *True and Untrue and Other Norse Tales* (children's book)
1951   1954   *Caterina av Siena* (*Catharine of Siena*) (biography)
1952   *Artikler og taler fra krigstiden* (*Tales and Articles from the War Years*)*
1957   1945   Introduction to Twelve Stories by Steen Steensen Blicher, (Princeton Press)

---

*   Not available in English, (translation of title for identification only)

CHAPTER I

IN THE BEGINNING
1882-1893

Although she has always been considered Norwegian, Sigrid Undset was born in her maternal grandfather's house in Denmark. In her autobiographical novel, *The Longest Years** she described her first memory as "a perpetual basking in sunshine on warm ground."[1] The sky was always blue in the little town where she was born. The square in front of her grandfather's house had "a vast, deserted look for the houses surrounding it were small and low."[2] Morning, noon and night dairy carts rattled past, bearing churns and milkmaids, and the pumps where the women washed their clothes went all day long.

"The air of the old town had a strange smell peculiar to itself—the acrid odor of filth and all the offal incidental to daily life, and a manifold and powerful scent of all the luxuriant growth and flowering in the little yards and gardens where the mould had been fertilized by many centuries of human occupation . . . The bad smell from the outhouses was allayed by the strange, keen fragrance of vine leaves, for most people had trellised vine on their warmest wall, and one of the local excitements was always—will the grapes ripen this year?"[3]

Sigrid's grandfather, Peter Andreas Gyth, who was the Chancery Councilor of Kalundborg, was a prosperous lawyer and estate manager and the long, one-storied Gyth residence, which stood behind two huge, sweet-smelling lime trees, was the grandest in town. Originally, the Gyth family had migrated

---

* Published in Norwegian by H. Aschehoug & Co. in 1934; and in English by Alfred A. Knopf in 1935.

from Scotland to Norway, but in 1772, they moved to Denmark and there they remained. By the time Sigrid was born their ancestral home had lost much of its splendor. It was still imposing on the outside, but each occupying generation had remodeled the interior to suit its needs, and the once graciously proportioned rooms had been cut up and rearranged so many times, that only the Councilor's study and the drawing room with its brown flowered wallpaper were still intact.

Her grandfather had married Clara Petrea Worsøe, the daughter of Dean Vilhelm Adolf Worsøe, a Lutheran clergyman, and for a number of years they had had a happy life together, but eight days after the birth of their sixth child, on a sad Christmas Eve, the Councilor's wife died and, as was customary in those days, her oldest unmarried sister came to keep house for him.

Sigrid's grandfather was an impressive looking man. He was tall and broad, with steel-grey eyes and an imposing head, and he believed himself to be just as important as he looked. He was devoted to his children, but because he had never been exposed to overt expressions of affection, he was incapable of relating to them with anything more than formal courtesy. Morose and taciturn, he was always occupied with business. He left their upbringing to his sister-in-law, and reserved the evening mealtime for correcting their manners and instructing them on proper behavior. Each day, when they had had their supper, and he had seen his family safely settled in the drawing room, he would close the windows and blinds, lock the doors, and go to his study not to be heard from again until the following morning—and as soon as he was out of the way, his sister-in-law would reverse the procedure. It was too early to go to bed and she liked to see what was going on in town.

In Norwegian, the word for mother is "mor" and sister is "søster." One's mother's sister is "Moster." When Moster Signe Dorthea Worsøe came into the Gyth household, she was considerably older than the children's mother had been. She was an exceptional housekeeper, extraordinarily capable with her hands, sharp of tongue and impulsive. Sigrid described her mental activity as that of "a cat springing and digging its claws into things alive and dead."[4] Although she was the daughter of a rationalist clergyman who had fought for enlightenment and common sense against prejudice and superstition, Moster Signe was quick to judge and unable to forgive. She could annihilate a person with a down putting remark and had an apt adage ready for most situations. Uninterested in "extenuating circumstances," she could be extremely judgmental of anyone except her father, whom she credited with saintly virtues, but as Sigrid discovered many years later, "his former parishioners took a considerably less optimistic view of his prospects in eternity."[5]

Moster Signe cared for her brother-in-law and his children with devotion. Sigrid's mother, Anna Charlotte,* who was the oldest, was eleven when her aunt came to live with them. She was small for her age, delicately beautiful, and extremely intelligent, and she immediately became her aunt's favorite. Not concerned with being fair, the liberties which Moster Signe allowed her niece had no limits. Determined to have her admired by all for the exceptional creature that she believed her to be, she indulged Charlotte at the expense of the other children, used her own savings to buy beautiful clothes for her, and saw to it that she got a university education—a rare privilege for a woman in those days. Charlotte was exceptional, but the special treatment her aunt granted her made her willful and self-centered.

At the University of Copenhagen, Charlotte met Ingvald Martin Undset, a brilliant Norwegian archeologist, who was doing research in Denmark. They fell in love, and in July, 1881, when she was 26 years old, he asked for her hand in marriage. Her father had been looking for a more prosperous bridegroom, but he didn't oppose their union. Archeology was a respectable occupation. Ingvald had already received considerable recognition for his work, and the Councilor knew that his daughter would not be easy to please.

Moster Signe was delighted with Charlotte's choice. Ingvald came from a good family. He was handsome and kind, and planned to take Charlotte on his field trips to act as his secretary and do drawings of his findings—and that was the kind of life she approved of for her favorite niece.

Outfitted with the most elegant trousseau that her father and aunt could provide, Charlotte accompanied her husband to Rome immediately after the wedding. Ingvald wanted to explore the beginning of the Iron Age in Italy. They planned to go on from there to Greece and expected to be away for at least two years.

Charlotte had married an interesting man. Although Ingvald came from a long line of well-to-do farmers, of Osterdale, his father, Halvor Undset, had chosen to become a warden at a prison labor camp near Trondheim. He had married Ollegaard Kristine Dahl, from that area, and Ingvald, who was their first child, was born on November 9, 1853. Halvor was a deeply religious man. ("It was somehow frightening that a man could '*love*' God as grandfather did," Sigrid wrote),[6] and he wanted his son to study theology,

---

*   Born May 30, 1865

but Ingvald wanted to be an archeologist. As a boy, he and his friend Henrik Mathiessen,* had prowled around the Nidaros Cathedral in Trondheim, and the Elgesaeter Augustinian Cloister in Trøndelag, and they had promised each other that they would one day decipher the ancient inscriptions on their walls and floor tiles. Ingvald was sent to Frederik's University in Christiania** but since they didn't offer a degree in archeology, he studied classical history and took courses in the runic alphabet and whatever else they taught that could be useful, and continued his studies on his own. He became an assistant to Professor Rygh and after eight months of study at the museum in Copenhagen, he got a job at the Antiquities Collection of the museum in Christiania. For the next few years he attended international archeological conferences wherever they were held in Europe, and by sleeping on benches in railroad stations and saving on food, he was able to do research in Vienna, Prague, Belgium, Germany and Russia. In June 1881, he completed his thesis on *The Iron Age in Northern Europe* and received a doctoral degree. It was then that he returned to Copenhagen to marry Charlotte, and they left for Rome.

Seven months later, while digging in Etruscan graves, he developed a severe case of malaria (which was endemic in that part of the world), and when the Italian doctors could not reduce his fever, Charlotte, who was expecting their first child, brought him to her father's house in Kalundborg.

Sigrid, the first grandchild (on both sides), was born on May 20, 1882. She was alert and healthy and Moster Signe immediately "proclaimed her an infant prodigy and insisted that every person to whom the child (as instructed) waved from her perambulator was to feel flattered and lucky."[7] In a letter to a friend, Ingvald described his daughter as "a future beauty . . . with strong lungs and a violent, energetic temperament."[8]

Although he was still ailing, Ingvald returned to Rome shortly after Sigrid was born. It was too risky to take their daughter and Charlotte stayed home. He had a relapse in Venice but managed to complete his work and get to Greece before he collapsed and had to return to Kalundborg.

Sigrid was a year old when her father came home. She was a precocious child and Ingvald lost no time in beginning her training as an archeologist. Before she had much of a vocabulary, she could say "blunt-edged axe" and

---

*   Later an outstanding archeologist.

**   Founded in 1050, the largest city in Norway was called Oslo. After a fire in 1624, it was rebuilt by King Christian IV and named Christiania. Its name was changed back to Oslo in 1925.

"shaft-hole axe" and he allowed her to play with his priceless artifacts. One of her favorite toys was a little terra-cotta horse from Troy which the famous Heinrich Schliemann had given her father. Everyone was shocked that he permitted her to play with it, but it amused him to think that his little girl's damp, pudgy hands were patting a toy that a Trojan child had played with thousands of years before. "It was a rash impulse on his part," Sigrid wrote, "as the marks of cement on the horse's legs will testify to all time."[9]

After some months at home, Ingvald was sufficiently recovered to leave for Germany and he didn't return until after his second daughter, Ragnhild, was born.* He was sick all the time he was away and it was obvious that he would have to abandon his field trips. He moved his family to Norway and continued his research at the university in Christiania.

They rented a house in West Aker, an undeveloped area on the outskirts of Christiania, and furnished their first home. Since Charlotte wanted it to be elegant, they bought a dining room table, sideboards and straight-backed, cane-bottomed chairs of light oak, and spent the greatest part of the money that her father had given them on their drawing room. Unable to resist a collection that had won a design prize at an exhibition, they splurged on a group of small, fragile chairs and causeuses** upholstered in golden-yellow silk, tufted with glistening buttons, and trimmed with fringe, tassels, and *passementerie* which were beautiful to look at but neither practical nor comfortable to sit on—and made do with painted beds and plain wooden chairs and wardrobes in the bedrooms.

When they moved to Christiania, Sigrid was two and her sister was an infant. "That children are normally jealous of a new arrival is an exaggeration," Sigrid wrote later.

> *It may be true in the case of sickly children or children who are too dependent, or where circumstances are so straitened that an addition to the family directly affects the children's welfare, but a healthy child, with a fair share of initiative, sufficiently well situated to suffer no diminution of comfort, is by no means ungratefully disposed towards the little creature which occupies the attention of its mother and the other controlling powers, enabling it to make the most of many emancipated moments.*[10]

---

*   April 12, 1884

** Tête-à-tête sofas meant for two.

Those were noble sentiments as hindsight, but Sigrid was extremely jealous of her younger sister. For the first years of her life, "almost everything she took it into her head to do—except making a little pig of herself"[11]—had been received with applause and she had learned to expect praise and admiration from all. It is understandable that she would have problems when another being entered her territory.

Long after Ragnhild could talk quite well, Sigrid wrote, she continued to get her way with cute little baby expressions and if these failed, she could cry so charmingly that the grown-ups couldn't resist her. Sigrid "could only cry when she was angry or afraid—and then she howled at the top of her voice, with a swollen, discolored face and a running nose, and her smooth nut-brown hair was plastered in damp wisps about her red and tear-stained cheeks."[12] When her little sister pulled all of the chenille braid and tassels off a table that the Danish aunts had made, her mother said, "It's extraordinary what a mania that child has for pulling things to pieces,"[13] but if Sigrid had done that, she was sure she would have gotten a spanking. When her sister was troublesome, Sigrid "took it with calm resignation"—except when she did something which made her "fly up and go for her."[14] ("Go for her" meant biting her, a habit which Sigrid developed at this time.)

In Lutheran Norway almost all pleasures were considered sinful and children were brought up to expect dire punishment for misbehaving. When they were small, Sigrid's mother told them stories about two little girls called Mette-Lene and Agate. They understood that Mette-Lene was supposed to be little sister, and Agate was herself. Agate always begged or screamed until she got what she wanted. For this, she was often made to stay home when the nurse took her sister out in the pram, and something nice inevitably happened while they were out to make Agate sorry that she had been forced to stay home. They would meet a nice Count who would give Mette-Lene a lovely little white poodle with a pink ribbon on his neck, and when Agate saw it, "you may be sure she regretted" having been bad. "When Agate wouldn't go out, whining and saying it was such nasty weather, Mette-Lene was always willing to be trundled out well tucked up in her comfortable pram."[15]

It is not hard to see why Sigrid disliked these stories. Goody-goody girls disgusted her. Later, when she started to read, she found saccharine children's books, like Louisa May Alcott's *Little Women* "insufferably mawkish"[16] and books like *Our Sons' and Daughters' Moral Education* or *Our Children's Teeth* (with pictures of Danish children with rows of hideously decayed black teeth—and charming Italian and Spanish children with teeth as white as pearls) extremely irritating. She preferred the books she found in her mother's library, "about scarlet fever and measles and woolen trousers and bad habits,"[17] and one called *Hygiene for Women* which helped her find out about a lot of things that occupied her mind a good deal at that time.

Her father's stories were more to her liking. His main character was a lineman on the railroad who had three birch rods—one was kept in pickle brine, one was stuck all over with pins, and one had razor blades attached to it—which he used to punish naughty children. The children in her father's stories were *really* naughty—not little girls who wouldn't go for a walk with their mother because their mittens tickled them. They did appalling things. There were always three sisters. "Malene seldom did anything wrong . . . . that was little sister, naturally. Kamelia was a good deal more enterprising and was rewarded on occasion with the rod that had the pins in it"[18]—so she was Sigrid. The third was Dromedary, who could "destroy a big locomotive as easy as anything"[19] and burnt down a hotel when she played with matches—and she deserved the birching she got with the razor blades.

Moster Signe and Sigrid's aunts also told stories like that, but when Sigrid told a story it was usually about a time when she would go to "Kamerica" and marry a captain, or about King Belte and his family who had fabulous foods to eat—which she enjoyed describing in great detail.

After the Undsets moved to Norway, they were able to visit their father's family in Trondheim. Her Danish relatives lived in the sleepy little town where only "thundershowers and the keen fragrances of vine-leaves were able to obliterate the acrid odor of offal," but Trondheim was a large city on the northwestern coast of Norway which was "saturated with bitter and provocative scents of balsam-poplar, wet timber, and salt fish."[20] People who came from Trondheim were particularly proud of it. Even her father, who had traveled and could laugh at "those who disliked Paris because it bore so little resemblance to their Norwegian or Danish hometown, or who found fault with the Italians for having no whey cheese and for not going in for a spring cleaning in the Norwegian style three times a year"[21]—still remained loyal enough to Trondheim to find it far superior to Christiania.

Her Danish grandfather was a religious man, but not like her Norwegian grandfather. In Kalundborg, the children were punished if they did something wrong, but in Trondheim there were always ministers and lay "readers" visiting the family, and the children had to listen to endless sermons about being good.

When Sigrid was four, the family moved to 10 Lyder Sagens Street which was near West Aker but much nicer. Charlotte was pregnant again and they needed a larger apartment. Sigrid and Ragnhild had had no children to play with in West Aker, but this house seemed to be crawling with children of every size. The Undset's apartment was on the second floor of a large square structure which stood in the middle of a garden. Iron steps led up to the front door and on the day that they moved in, children were hanging upside-down from the iron railing, chasing each other in the garden, running in and out of the downstairs apartment, and playing games on an ice chest that stood in the entryway.

Sigrid's mother had never been one to indulge in hugging and kissing. She made their clothes but she wasn't a good cook, and domestic chores bored her. High strung, and often preoccupied, she preferred working with her husband to playing with her children. Her family was not neglected, they had a maid to care for them and one to help with the housework, but their home lacked warmth.

In contrast, Anna Winter-Hjelm, the mother of the ten children who lived downstairs was always cheerful and relaxed and seemed to want nothing more than to be with her children—and she made a larger-than-life impression on Sigrid.

The Winter-Hjelms had a veranda with a broad flight of steps that led to their part of the garden, and in the summer "unceremoniously and without being invited, youngsters of the street made a highway of their rooms—in at the veranda and out by the back door."[22] One or two were usually staying for dinner. They sprawled on the sofas and beds, were permitted to browse through the books and play with whatever they chose, and Mrs. Winter-Hjelm looked on with pleasure. Born in Germany of French stock, she was small and round and, according to Sigrid, "so lovely that no one on earth could look at her without being made happy. It was not merely that she was beautiful, but her beauty seemed to be simply a mold in which her mind and nature found expression."[23] Her black wavy hair was tied in the back with a ribbon in a style that was uniquely her own. "One could not say what her mouth was really like, because its expression was so animated, constantly changing . . . . It was her eyes, however, that made one feel she belonged to a species apart . . . they were so dark as to appear positively black, but always gentle . . ."[24]

Sigrid's mother was well educated and worked hard, but she was never self-effacing. Mrs. Winter-Hjelm was not an intellectual but she "gave of herself as a prodigal who never thinks of where the wealth comes from."[25]

Otto Winter-Hjelm, like Sigrid's father, was the center of attention in the family. He was the conductor of the Oslo Philharmonic Society Orchestra, an organist, composer, music critic and close friend of Edvard Grieg. He was very tall and extremely thin, and he had thick reddish hair and a beard tinged with grey. When the children disturbed him at work, he would grab the first child he could get hold of—not bothering to ascertain who had been at fault—but the children were not afraid of him because he rarely punished them. He was a creative gardener and grew exquisite roses of many varieties.

The Winter-Hjelms had many friends—musicians, teachers, writers, artists, and students who were often preparing for concerts—and they held open-house gatherings on Sundays to which the children were always welcome. Sigrid loved to be there. They were not dour, gloomy people. They did not feel that life was "bound to be a rotten business."[26]

Norway, in 1886, was a sparsely populated agricultural country with a comparatively small number of educated people. The Undsets were well-educated, and university professors, painters and archeologists visited them often, but although they could be amusing, there seemed to be few occasions for laughter in their home. The bohemian atmosphere in their neighbors' house provided an oasis of pleasure free from stress, and there is no doubt that Anna Winter-Hjelm became the model for Sigrid's concept of the ideal woman.

On March 7, 1887, when Sigrid was five years old, her mother gave birth to another daughter whom they named Signe.

There was no school for girls near Lyder Sagens Street and they were tutored at home. When she was six, Sigrid could read and write—but girls were expected to know how to cook and sew—and sewing proved to be torture. She was given a piece of white muslin with threads pulled out lengthwise and crosswise and told to go under four threads and over four threads to make a nice, even running stitch. After she did this, her mother explained, she would learn backstitch, chain stitch, herringbone stitch, and finally hemstitch which was so fine it was almost invisible. It was hard to count the fine threads, the needle kept going into the wrong lace, the thread tangled, and when she pulled it, it came out of the needle. She couldn't rethread it and her mother was annoyed when she had to do it for her. Each time she did one wrong, her mother ripped it out and told her to start over, and after struggling for what seemed like an eternity, the cloth was a mess and she had only four acceptable stitches. When she had mastered that, she was told, she would be given canvas and Berlin wool in many lovely colors and she would learn cross-stitch embroidery so that she could make "a pot holder as a Christmas present for her grandmother, a pincushion for her aunt, and penwipers of felt embroidered with chain stitch and backstitch and silver beads—for papa, her grandfathers and godfathers."[27]

When her old aunt was Sigrid's age, or not much older, she had embroidered a little landscape with a Roman temple and a mountain with trees growing on its side and a town at the top that looked like a pen-and-ink drawing. It was hanging over her mother's writing table—and that fine sampler that hung framed and glazed in Aunt's bedroom was made by Sigrid's mother when she was still at school. Sigrid was sure she would never be able to do "a piece of embroidery worthy of framing and glazing, not even a penwiper for either of her grandfathers."[28] She couldn't even fill in the background after her mother had done the figure.

She "toiled and moiled and perspired over her sewing"[29] until she burst into tears, but she never seemed to be able to do it right. Her mother shook her. She wasn't trying. How could she be so clumsy? What kind of wife would she make? Girls had to know how to use their hands. She kept at her until, in a fury of frustration, Sigrid grabbed the beautiful little sewing box that her godfather had sent her, (which smelled of sandalwood and contained a silver thimble, a needlecase, and a pair of scissors), and scratched and tore at its blue, satin lining until it was ruined. Then, "howling with all the force of her lungs,"[30] she ran from the room and cried until she fell asleep from exhaustion. (One would think that she would hate sewing after that, but she did beautiful handwork all of her life, and enjoyed it thoroughly.)

Sigrid wrote often about things that were considered unmentionable. One day, she related in a matter-of-fact way, she was walking down Lyder Sagens Street when she noticed a little boy who had "something sticking out of the front of his breeches. Shouting 'Look out! Here comes the watercart!' he ran into the road with shuffling steps . . . sending out a thin jet of water which left a dark zigzag track in the dust."[31] She was sad when she discovered "that all little boys could do that but girls could not. It was a decided disadvantage when they played railway train, for instance, because boys could fill an old saucepan and pretend it was machine oil."[32]

By the time she was eight, her father was too sick to make the trip to work each day and they moved to a ground floor apartment on Keyser Street in the center of town where she was able to go to school. Not any school, but a very special private school which was run by Ragna Nielsen who was a divorced woman and a militant fighter for women's rights. It was the only co-educational institution for children in the country, and members of the Storting,* journalists, artists, and intellectuals of the Left sent their children there. Sigrid was enrolled to start in September but before that they were going to Drøbak in the hope that the sea air would be good for her father.

One morning, Sigrid went out to play near the water. She was building a sand castle when a boy whom she had seen in town came over to watch her.** Other children told her that he had lost his mother, that he lived with his father and a housekeeper in Christiania, and that he was visiting an aunt and uncle

---

*   Norwegian parliament.
**   In *The Longest Years* she called him Olaf.

who had no children. Although it was unusual for boys of his age to play with girls, he came to watch her each morning and after a few days, he began to join her games. He was taller and broader than she was, his hair was almost white, his eyes were bright blue—and she liked him very much. He often brought apples which they shared. Since they were usually green, the two had frequent stomachaches, but her mother assured her there was nothing to worry about since it was "a good way to cleanse one's insides."[33] He came with pockets full of string, and taught her all kinds of knots, and when he wound the string around her fingers and they touched, "she always had the same sweet and happy feeling . . . and she could see that Olaf liked it too."[34]

One day he asked her what school she went to, and when she told him that she was enrolled at Ragna Nielsen's he was shocked.

> *"That's the Liberal school," he said, "and they have boys and girls together! Is your father a liberal?*
> *She had to admit that he was. "Isn't your father the same?" she asked despondently.*
> *"Are you crazy! He's a captain. No sailors are Liberals!"*[35]

When the summer was over, Sigrid started school. She found Mrs. Nielsen very attractive. She admired her silver grey hair which was pulled up in a bun on the top of her head, and she liked her fluffy bangs. She always wore light grey or dark dresses with white inserts at the neckline that gave her short, trim figure a look of authority, and although she was strict, she was fair. When she was angry "a deep flush spread over her face as a warning that one had better be careful,"[36] but Sigrid preferred her to the teachers who were gentler but couldn't control their students.

School was hard to get used to. She was starting in the third grade and most of the children had been there from the beginning. Her mother had taught her without textbooks. She had learned to read with a history of Norway, and to keep her from becoming "one-sided," she had alternated with a history of Denmark. She knew about Agamemnon and Clytemnestra, Cassandra and Orestes, Norse, Lapp, and Hans Christian Andersen's tales, but she had read none of the stories that were in the school readers. Her handwriting was dreadful, her arithmetic poor, and she hated to declaim, with expression, the poems they had to learn by heart.

Her parents had taught her Scriptures but she was permitted to repeat them freely as she understood them. In school there was one acceptable version and no other would do. She could read maps and her knowledge of geography was far beyond that of her schoolmates, but she had never had to memorize names of towns, rivers, and mountains with no information to help her remember them. Her answers were often correct but because they were not presented in the format that was required, she provoked laughter. Most of the children had already formed their friendships and she was an outsider, but she preferred it to studying with her mother.

The school differed with popular opinion on many subjects and although she agreed with most of what they stood for, no allowance was made for any variance from their positions. Most of what she was taught about Norwegian history, for instance, which was stated as fact, was questioned by her father. It was either incorrect, in his opinion, or simply guesswork. Even if something was known with certainty, he maintained, someone might make a discovery someday which would throw a new light on the question. No such doubts could ever be raised in school. Although many of their opinions were more radical than those of other institutions, the school's insistence on conformity was just as rigid.

It wasn't only school that made her feel different. She didn't seem to be able to fit in anywhere. She had asked for either skis or a bobsled for Christmas and was overjoyed when she got a bobsled from her parents and skis and a pair of skates that had belonged to her father, from her Trondheim grandfather—but when she went out to display her treasures, her friends told her that her skates were old-fashioned, the bobsled was the kind that only babies used because it had an iron back on it, and the skis (which were her greatest joy) were laughable. Skis had to be the same thickness all the way, with no steering edge which turned up sharply at the point—and the right kind of ski poles to have were broom handles with a loop through a hole which served as a handle. Her skis were handmade and especially designed by her grandfather. They were long and narrow, with a steering edge and they turned up at the rear as well as in front—and he had made ski poles for them that were tapered to fit the hand. The children made such fun of her presents that she was ashamed to take them out.

When she complained to her father, he said that city people didn't know anything about how skis ought to be made. When he first came to Christiania, "people scarcely know whether to put skis on their feet or on their backsides. Imagine them trying to teach an Osterdale man what skis ought to be like! . . . If you're so silly as to pay attention to people who criticize what they don't know anything about, I shall be very disappointed in you."[37]

Clothes were a problem too. When they had lived on Lyder Sagens Street it hadn't mattered what they wore, as long as their clothes were not torn or dirty when they went out to play. Sundays, of course, they wore their best. Little girls slept on a coil of hard braids after their hair was washed on Saturday night so that it would have a nice wave when it was combed out loose on Sunday. On those days, the Undset girls had the prettiest dresses. They were white, and trimmed with lace. Their aunts sent them with white cotton stockings in different patterns. But Sigrid was growing so fast, that sometimes she had outgrown her dress before it arrived. Ragnhild would get it and her mother would make her one of her own design. Once, her mother fell in love with a Kate Greenaway dress she had seen in a London magazine. It was a pretty white muslin with tiny flowers but it came down to her ankles and had a high waist and none of her friends dressed like that.

At school, the children wore dark wool and semi-stiff tartan dresses with pleats that hung from a yoke and sleeves that were full on top and tight on the arm. They were belted below the hips which made them blousy at the waist, and they had rows of black velvet ribbon on the skirt, belt, cuffs and yoke. Sigrid wanted, desperately, to have such a dress but her mother said they were ungainly and ugly. She bought her knitted skin-tight boys' shirts and breeches and made her short skirts to wear over them. Such clothes, she said, were warm and easier to play in than fussy dresses and white, lace-trimmed pants that never stayed clean. Other parents eventually saw the advantage of such attire and it became a fad, but only after Sigrid had borne the ridicule of her classmates.

Charlotte Undset believed that if her hair was cut, it would grow dark and lose its sheen and that it was healthier for it to hang free so the air could get at the roots. Sigrid's hair hung loose and when she bent her head forward it was all over her face. Her teacher complained. When Sigrid reported this to her mother, she said, "Tell your teacher that I find her remarks impertinent."[38]

Most children carried their books in a satchel, but Charlotte believed that one arm would become permanently longer than the other due to the weight of the books, so Sigrid carried hers in a knapsack. Not an ordinary one, of course, but an old one that her father had as a boy. It was made of ugly green leather and had hearts and designs all over it.

Sigrid loved to read and during the next few years Holberg, Cooper and Marryat were her favorites. Ibsen, Bjørnson and Lie didn't interest her yet, but she adored popular romances and Wild West stories. She was told that "they made one think of foul smells and tainted water that had been forgotten in a carafe,"[39] but she read all she could get. She enjoyed listening to her mother read Shakespeare and Heine to her father although she didn't understand much of it, and once when her father promised to give her two crowns if she read all six volumes of *A History of the World*, she accepted the challenge. It took two years but she earned the crowns. Browsing through her grandfather's books in Trondheim, she had discovered a collection of Icelandic tales called *Njal's Saga* and she read and reread them many times.

As her father's health continued to deteriorate the atmosphere at home became depressing. Charlotte did everything she could do to keep up their spirits, and the huge crates filled with presents that arrived from Trondheim and Kalundborg each Christmas (which always included a goose from Charlotte's brother Leopold who had married Ingvald's sister Kirsa) helped tremendously.

One Christmas day, Charlotte sent the two older girls out for fresh air while she prepared the goose. It was cold and windy and Sigrid didn't want to go, but as usual, Ragnhild in her sweet and gentle way, went cheerfully. When they had walked half a block, she announced that she was going to visit her girlfriend and disappeared into a house, and Sigrid was feeling sorry for herself as she headed for the Palace Park alone. She was thinking of the rare roast beef dinner they were going to have at the Winter-Hjelms' house later in the week (her mother's roast beef was always grey and overcooked) when she ran into Olaf. He was visiting his grandmother for the day and offered to take her down the hill in his new bobsled. She had often wondered if she would ever see him again after that summer in Drøbak, and here he was. They had a delightful afternoon and she arrived home flushed, elated, and prepared for a reprimand for being late, but as usual, her mother surprised her.

Pleased with her daughter's red cheeks and happy face, she didn't seem angry at all. She pointed out how good a little bit of fresh air could be for a child—and that was it.

Sigrid never forgot how thrilling it was to sit close to Olaf on that sled, but other encounters in those days bothered her—the kind that children have to endure: A derelict in the park who wanted to show her "a funny thing"—a delivery boy who said rude words—the man who wanted her to go down to the basement with him to show him where her father kept the coal—or the fat man who looked like a toad and brought cakes for her and Ragnhild when they visited their father at Grefsen Bad,* and then wanted them to kiss him. Some of these encounters may have been innocent, but she had developed a fear of strange men "who catch little girls and do something cruel to them . . . one feels a groping paw or someone pressing up behind one—and the sense of shame and impotence is so unbearable, one feels . . . homicidal towards these people who can never leave one in peace."[40]

---

* A health spa.

That spring, the movement for Norway's independence from Sweden was gaining momentum and everyone was taking sides.* The pupils in Sigrid's school were ardently pro-independence, and on the 17th of May they participated in a demonstration in favor of the immediate separation of the two countries. A counter-demonstration of those who were loyal to the Union with Sweden confronted them.

Sigrid was coming out of a candy store with some girlfriends when she met a group of boys who were carrying Union flags. Her school carried "clean" flags (without the Union symbol). A skirmish developed with the pro-Union students shouting "traitors!" and the Nielsen group yelling "liberty for Norway!" Sigrid, who was carrying a "clean" flag, was as militant as the rest until she caught sight of Olaf. He was looking very handsome in a blue sailor suit and cap and he was carrying a big Union flag. Unable to face him, she turned onto a side street and walked away as fast as she could, but her cowardice embarrassed her and she mentioned the incident to her father. He empathized with her discomfort and explained that it wasn't easy to have a mind of one's own. If you went against the status quo your life could be lonely.

The day came when they knew that her father would not live much longer. He was physically weak but his mental capacities weren't diminished, and pressed for time, Charlotte devoted herself to helping him record the information he had gathered. When Charlotte had to go out, Sigrid sat with him. Although she was too young to understand what life could be like without him, she hung around his wheelchair hungry for any time they could have together. He could explain things better than anyone and she could share her thoughts with him more easily than with her mother. When he had a good

---

* At the end of the 9th century, the Viking King Harald the Fair Hair had united the Norse into one nation, but after the plague swept Europe in 1334, Norway was so depleted of manpower that she was forced to come under Danish rule During the Napoleonic wars, Denmark sided with France and when the French were defeated, Sweden, which had fought against them, was given Norway as part of the postwar settlement. The Norwegians had not been consulted and they threatened to revolt. On May 17, 1814, Sweden agreed that Norway could have its own constitution if it became "Sweden's self-ruling partner under a common king" and May 17th was celebrated as Constitution Day. The Norwegians were never comfortable with that arrangement, and when Sigrid was growing up, a strong movement for complete independence developed. (The Union was dissolved in 1905 and Norway became an independent country.

day, she read him the things he wanted to hear, but when he was too sick to concentrate, she entertained him with Wild West stories.

He died on November 3, 1893, six days before his 40th birthday.

When he was working, his salary had been seventy-five hundred kroner a year, but after he died, his family received a pension of eight hundred. It was too little to live on. Charlotte was not trained to do anything to add to their income, and her family had to help her. She sold their furniture and Ingvald's library,* and they moved again, this time to a smaller place on Observatory Street. Mrs. Nielsen gave the girls scholarships, which was a great relief to Charlotte, but Sigrid found it hard to be a "charity case."

It was a frightening time. Sigrid would never get over the loss of her father but, always attuned to contradictions in human behavior, even when they were her own, she wrote that despite her sorrow and fears for the future she had not been able to suppress her delight with her new mourning dress.

> *"It was made from fine, light woolen material, quite in the fashion, with a yoke and trimmed with many rows of black mohair braid. The doctor's wife had asked to be allowed to see to this and had presented all three little girls with their fine frocks."* [41]

"Their home put you in mind of a bell whose clapper had fallen out," [42] she wrote in another context, and it certainly applied to their situation after her father died. She was eleven years old, but her childhood was over. She was the oldest, and her mother was not able to carry the burdens alone.

---

* In 1953, at the 100th anniversary of his birth, his granddaughter, Sigrid Braatøy, compiled a bibliography of his work. The list contained 154 published titles including articles on Italian prehistory, the Hungarian Bronze Age, Troy and Mycenæ, Hallstatt and La Tene, German prehistory, Mexican artifacts, the Gokstad ship and other Norse archeological finds, the Trondheim Cathedral, Kvart archeology, runes, woodlocks, Norse four-leaf clover buckles, floods in North Italy in 1882, and a railroad accident in Baden. His most popular work, *From Akershus to the Acropolis*, which was published in 1892, is still of interest today.

CHAPTER II

YOUTH

1898-1904

At sixteen, Sigrid was tall and slender. She had a high bosom, a narrow waist, sensitive hands, and pretty feet. Her mother had taught her to hold herself erect, and with her long, thick braids wound several times around her head, she had the majestic air of her imposing Danish grandfather. Beautiful in an unusual way, one's first impression was one of arrogance, but that lasted only until one noticed her huge, thoughtful, wide-apart grey eyes and tremulous mouth—and her vulnerability was revealed.

In a neighborhood where the residents tried to out-do each other in displaying their affluence, her family lived in poverty. Charlotte Undset was well educated and spoke German and French fluently, but there was little that she could do to supplement her tiny pension. She tried translating from French, but her Norwegian was too Danish to be acceptable. She could have moved to Denmark (she claimed she didn't because she had promised her husband she would raise the children in Norway) but to return to her father's house as a dependent was not her style. Her situation made it necessary to accept financial aid from him, but she would not permit him to see her struggle. Her position was painful and she made each contribution from home last as long as possible. She gave up the few friends she had and turned all her attention to her children. It had never been easy to get along with her—her nature was not geared to making sacrifices—and their poverty didn't make it any easier.

By the time she was a senior in middle school Sigrid agreed with Ragna Nielsen on many subjects, but she took exception to the didactic way in which opinions were forced upon her. She wanted to think for herself. She needed freedom to explore, and it took courage to question Mrs. Nielsen's "rights" and "wrongs." To protect herself from the ridicule of the students who didn't question anything, she acquired a haughty manner which, coupled with her superior intellect, did not endear her to her classmates.

"My schoolmates thought I imagined myself to be somebody, to be 'different' and they set about to make me see how unpleasant life ought to be made for anyone who is different from others." She lived, she said, "like a porcupine who bristled when approached—not to attack—but for self-defense."[1]

Lessons were slow and boring and she did little work spending most of the time with her chin propped on her hand sketching or reading a hidden book. It didn't make it easier for her that her sister Ragnhild had inherited their mother's petite prettiness, or that she was outgoing, flirtatious and popular. *She* had no problem about what to believe. Happy to accept the prevailing point of view, she was a diligent student and appeared to be loved by all.

Sigrid found the boys of her age immature and the girls' gossip inane, and she had few friends. In fact, her only real friend was Emma Münster[*] whose father was a geologist and a radical deputy in the Storting. Emma wanted to be a doctor and she too found her classmates boring. The girls shared a passion for botany and went on excursions in to the countryside to collect specimens. They tramped through brambles, waded in brooks, got wet and dirty, and smoked endless numbers of cigarettes, and together, they started a magazine called *The Four Leaf Clover* for which they wrote most of the material.[2]

As Sigrid approached the last semester in middle school, she had a number of important decisions to make. If she wanted to qualify for a university she would have to spend two more years at Ragna Nielsen's, and that seemed a waste of time. When she was interested in a subject she liked to explore it thoroughly, and there was much that she wanted to learn, but the snail's pace with which subjects were taught at school made them unbearably boring. She had always taken it for granted that she would go to college, and her mother assured her that if she wanted to go, she would find a way to send her, but their economic situation was so desperate, and it was so painful to watch her mother struggle to feed them, that Sigrid felt it was her duty to find a job.

Norway was an agricultural country and there were few professions open to women. Most who had to work became servants or farm girls and those who were lucky enough to have gotten an education became teachers or nurses. If

---

[*]   Emma became a doctor and practiced medicine in a remote fishing village in Westland, but they kept in touch. In 1914, she married a doctor who was seventeen years her senior and had three children. She died during the flu epidemic of 1918 at the age of thirty-six.

she went to a university, none of the professions that interested her would be available to her and she would end up teaching—and that didn't appeal to her. Besides, she knew that her mother would have to go to relatives for help, and being "a charity case" was as unacceptable to her as it was to her mother. Her Aunt Clara had gone to a secretarial school and was working in an office, and she decided to do the same. Since she didn't want to work in an office forever, she planned to spend evenings trying to become an artist, but when she showed her work to her father's friend, Theodor Kittelson, (who was a painter and illustrator of Norse tales), he discouraged her. He thought she had talent, but didn't recommend art as a career for anyone who had to depend on it for a living.* So, if art was out, she decided to work at becoming a writer.

Later, she claimed that she left school because of Ragna Nielsen's dogmatism, which had taught her "boundless skepticism,"[3] but that was surely not her primary reason for leaving school. Their financial situation was so bad that she really had no choice.

At secretarial school, it was harder than ever to make friends. The students came from poor, uneducated families and she had little in common with them. She continued to go on tramps with Emma, but Emma was studying hard and had little time for recreation. Sigrid's sisters were busy with their school friends and she felt more isolated than ever.

Norway's battle for independence from Sweden was growing stronger and in an effort to foster better understanding between the two nations the Norwegian newspaper *Urd* offered to match students of similar ages and special interests who might want to become pen pals. Sigrid registered, listing her background and ambitions, and received a letter from Andrea Hedberg of Malmø, Sweden.

Andrea was the daughter of a book dealer and four months older than Sigrid. She was an avid reader, wrote poetry, and planned to become a writer. The sponsors of the program believed they would have much in common. The girls exchanged photographs and autobiographical information, and began a correspondence which lasted forty-two years. More stimulating than diaries, their letters served as sounding boards for their ideas and aspirations and, during Sigrid's formative years, they provided an opportunity for a kind of intimacy that she was incapable of having in any other way.

Because they didn't' meet face-to-face, it was easy to confide in each other. A catalyst of immeasurable importance in her development, their correspondence sustained her when her loneliness and frustration seemed

---

*   This incident was described later in her story *Florida Waters*.

unbearable, forced her to clarify her thoughts, cut her down to size when her opinion of herself became too inflated, and challenged her to "make something of herself."

The first letter from Sigrid was written on July 16, 1898, when she was still attending secretarial school. Addressing her new friend as "Dear Dea," she wrote that she was fond of reading and listed a number of her favorite Swedish books. She liked the theater, but not balls, preferred small gatherings "where people knew each other" to large parties, was "indescribably unmusical and vain," but believed that she had a good head. Of her sisters, she wrote:

> *Ragnhild is 14, very clever, flighty, the best in her class, looks quite nice, is liked by everyone because she shows her claws only when she is home . . . Signe is 11, tall for her age, slender, blonde and grey-eyed and the beauty of the family . . . Ragnhild is fond of balls and hiking trips and plays the comedienne and the prima donna . . .*

In her second letter she discussed more books, described the art exhibitions she had seen, asked if Dea liked to be cuddled, (Sigrid did, but didn't know many people from whom she would care to accept it), and urged her friend to send her samples of her writing. "I find it hard to write comedy," she confided. She planned to start a correspondence with one of Ragnhild's boyfriends who had moved to Sweden. Her sister didn't want to answer his letters because she thought he wasn't a bit gifted, didn't understand art or politics, and didn't like to go to balls. She had other boyfriends who were sweeter and more gifted, she said, but Sigrid thought she was just a little teenage flirt.[4]

By the third letter, they were discussing poetry and questioning the meaning of life. About religion, Sigrid wrote:

> *Priests, yes, there are good and nice people among them, but Christian Tolerance, the Church, our Common Mother, etc., those ideas I was cured of when I studied for my confirmation. Our excellent Pastor Arnesen certainly closed the door of heaven for us. Closed it with double locks for everyone who allowed himself to have the smallest difference with the Norwegian State Church.*[5]

Her mother did not attend church, Sigrid continued, but she had taught her daughters to say their prayers and they were confirmed when they came of age. On holidays, the Undsets sang hymns, but they were uplifting, inspiring songs, unlike the threatening ones they were taught in school. She didn't like to think that God was watching every move she made, ready to pounce on her if she did anything wrong. She couldn't picture Him as an "irascible, vindictive magistrate of whom one had to be continually aware." Surely, He had more important things to do. On the other hand, "Pastor Arnensen's God was like a self-satisfied Norwegian bourgeois" and he didn't appeal to her either.

When her father's health had deteriorated, her grandfather had comforted her mother by saying that "everything God sends us is a good gift. Good fortune or bad, health or sickness, life or death, one has to have Faith and accept God's gifts in the spirit in which they are given," but her mother said she "wanted nothing from a God who have his Grace only to the humble."[6]

Dea wrote that she yearned to fall in love and Sigrid wrote,

> *My ideal is perhaps not as high as yours. I would only love and be loved as a sinful child of earth loves and is loved. But if he were proud and manly and faithful—then he could gladly beat me if he wanted to—as long as he didn't give up loving me. The idea that after death there should be nothing more than sisterly love is quite horrible . . .* [7]

Sigrid, who was to write some of the most passionate love scenes in literature, and who would spend her life fighting for a woman's right to enjoy sexual pleasure without social opprobrium, was, at the age of sixteen, bemoaning a sexless heaven!

She gushed over a famous actress who always wore violet (which just happened to be her favorite color too), whom she and her friends often followed on the street, but she didn't fawn on the actress the way the others did, and she didn't, like the others, "think that she is as interested in us as we are in her."[8] She asked if Dea would like to see some of her writing.

In February, a few months before her seventeenth birthday, Sigrid got a job in the Christiania office of the German Electric Company (Allgemeine Elektrizitätz Gesellschaft) as a typist. Her secretarial skills were not exceptional, (she had not been able to pass the final examination) but she had a phenomenal memory and was so organized and calm in a crisis that she soon became indispensable. Although she could not get used to routine work and "disliked being at everyone's beck and call," she was fascinated by the women she worked with. She visited them in their boarding houses and pensions, went to theaters and restaurants with them, and accumulated impressions and experiences which made it possible for her to write about working women with great empathy later on.

The office was dark and it had no view of the street. On weekends, Ragnhild was usually with her friends or dressing for parties. Her friends weren't mature enough to interest Sigrid, and Sigrid was too self-conscious to seek her equals. When her sister left all dressed up and ready for an entertaining evening, Sigrid curled up with a book, or tried to write. Sometimes her mother persuaded her to accompany her sister but those efforts were so unrewarding that she preferred to stay home.

Writing at home was not easy. She had no privacy. The sitting room was small and used by the whole family and she shared a bedroom with one of her sisters. After she began to earn some money they moved away from the center of town and she was able to have a room of her own. Well, not entirely her own. It was too small to sleep in and Ragnhild tutored pupils there during the day, but in the evenings it was all hers.

She painted the walls blood red, and her desk, a large bookcase, and some rattan chairs bright green. She had a beautiful "farmer's chair" on which "she wished Dea could sit while they drank tea, smoked cigarettes, and talked," and an old faded corner couch on which she draped an Italian carpet. Books, flowers, ceramics and pictures from her mother's collection, as well as a Botticelli print that she bought for herself, completed the décor. She found it cozy and beautiful.[9]

Besides exchanging views about love, art and literature, she and Dea practiced their writing skills on each other with long descriptions of nature, their moods, and their observations of life. Sigrid's father had made the past so alive for her that she was planning to write a book about people who lived in the year 1340. She would call it *Svend Trøst*. It was about "two unhappy young people caught in an unhappy love and an unhappy marriage." Her greatest desire was to become an author: "A real female artist not a pen-pushing lady . . . not a giver-outer of books." If that was to be her fate, she would rather die in her office chair."[10]

She described the people she worked with. Her boss Brunn, "the screaming ape" had horrible manners but was so "unconsciously comic" that he was almost sweet. One of the secretaries irritated her all day with her naïve self-satisfied selfishness and lack of considerations for others."[11]

Of an outing with "some very nice girls" she wrote:

> . . . it was disgusting . . . that hot bedchamber air that sometimes comes up in young girls. They were very moral young women, just as moral as you or I and used no bad words, but the conversation and jokes were all about 'him.' This unpleasant great 'he' that one puts up

cabals for—happiness, everything has to do with 'him.' He appears
on the edge of all conversations even though not any of the girls are in
love with a definite person. How idiotic and disgusting. It's a thing one
puts under the bed together with another unmentionable item—until
a priest or mayor legalizes it and puts it into some kind of eternity.
But as long as it is still in a corner or under the bed, people will joke
about it and wonder about it—more or less delicately . . . When it is
legitimate and put on the altar, then it can be spoken about freely; and
respect for the great mystery's Holy Grail goes to Hell.[12]

The office was exposing her to more than the lives of working girls. She was becoming aware of the magnitude of human endeavor. She was impressed with the numbers of shoes and clothes and machines out there that were being created by people. She had just discovered how water was being used to make electricity. It was one gigantic fairy-tale. She suffered from teen-age blues. She was "incredibly down about living and not living." She felt she was "standing in a corner while life passed her by." She took the same roads to and from work each day and looked at the same three faces year in and year out. "I don't have the ability to live," she wrote, "because I don't have the ability to meet people and find pleasure in the things that others enjoy. I don't enjoy dancing, walking with girlfriends on Drammenvein* or being with gentlemen."[13]

When Dea wrote that she was going to Dresden to stay with relatives and study languages, Sigrid asked her to greet the Sistine Madonna for her and let her know if it looked "like a box of chocolates." She didn't like Raphael very much but adored Botticelli. She believed that learning languages was very important. It was wonderful to be able to read authors in the original and avoid the explanations of literary historians. One could listen to the speech of the time and hear the dead speak. She was struggling through Shakespeare and Chaucer in the original. Had Dea read the letters of Heloise and Abelard?[14]

When she was depressed and worried that her life was slipping away and she had nothing to show for it, she buried herself in research. On February 25, 1901 she wrote:

Since I come into little contact with other people and people easily
give me the impression of being superficial, I spend too much time by
myself. My mother has worked hard for her children. Ragnhild's interests

---

* A main street in Oslo.

*are, apart from mathematics and physics, simply to go on sleigh rides
and dances with boys from the gymnasia, but when one is constantly
examining oneself, and when one sees things differently than the school,
clergymen, doctors, teachers, etc., then it is quite natural that one tells
oneself, 'You are too good to wear yourself out on an office chair.' Then
the devil comes in and says, 'become something, darling—become a
painter, an actor, an author.'*

She was researching the Middle Ages and she was enchanted with the
folk songs of the period. Not the English ones which were "obviously written
by men." They were "full of swooning ladies whose only crime was that they
were not ready to fall upon a young man's neck as soon as he declared his
love." They patiently bore being abandoned for years, and the unfaithfulness
of their honorable knights, without complaining. On the day before their
marriages to horrible men they dared not run away with their true loves
because "it was not fitting."

German folk songs were all about people who "loved but tried to forget.
It hurt but they pretended that it didn't matter." The ones she liked the most
were the Danish ones. "They were not written to become literature. Therefore
there was no good or evil—angels or devils—just men and women." They had
wonderful lyrics and the freshest profoundest descriptions of characters." It
was not easy to find source materials for the period she wanted to write about
and these songs were treasures. She warned Dea not to discuss her discovery
with anyone and sent her a Danish folksong about a girl named Kristin.[15]

Although she had befriended several of the women in her office, and
was going out more often with her peers, she was still spending most of her
evenings engrossed in her research and writing.

On June 23rd, she wrote, "I have read too much and lived too little. I'm
nineteen years old and still haven't learned to love life."

She was reading Shakespeare's *Venus and Adonis* in English and loving it,
but the books that Dea recommended she found

> *. . . too heartily well meant . . . to idealized . . . construction not
> real. They admire their characters too much to be able to understand
> their feelings. The ladies have to love artists or doctors who fall in love
> with them at first sight—have dreamed of them always, and are full
> of the terrible nonsense that people who love each other have to know
> each other totally and share everything completely . . .*

To respect that which one doesn't understand in another is sufficient for love . . . I think most marriages fail because they want to know each other too well—one looks for an ideal wonder and love dies when they see each other in shirts and underpants and corsets and stockings—what, unfortunately, people call reality. Perhaps you considered your acquaintance of last year in the same way . . . I long to live life because I need it to create art. I won't write books about dreamed-of figures that flow out into blue ideals. Writing ladies nearly always betray their own sex . . . When they moralize they take the point of view of the man and they want the man to be the same idealized person that men demand from a woman—but a woman's nature is different from a man's. It's more personal. Her idea of honor is related to faithfulness to one's body. Many men sacrifice their honor for the concept of honor—but most women have a private honor and don't care so much about accepted ideas of honor.

Selma Lagerlöf looks at life through a woman's soul and her work shines. She is too noble to plagiarize a man . . . If only women would try to find themselves and not compete with men or accept what they say about what is eternal in woman—what they ought to be—and not be too frightened to admit that we belong to the order of mammals who suckle their young.[16]

Slowly, her novel about the Middle Ages was taking shape. She enclosed a synopsis and asked Dea to tell her what she thought of it. It was about the marriage of two young lovers. Their love carries them "beyond all consideration" before they get married, but they are merely children and not "comfortable in marriage." Agnete is "deadly tired." She doesn't understand what her husband wants and longs for a man with whom she can find peace and rest. She knows that her husband, who loves her, would gladly do anything to make her happy, but he is a boy and doesn't understand how to reach her. Neither can give up the other and their love destroys them.[17]

The inability of people to understand each other's needs and their reluctance to make sacrifices for each other, even with the greatest love and the best intentions, (a problem she was encountering with her mother and sisters) is a theme that Sigrid explored, over and over again, and finally dealt with masterfully in *Kristin Lavransdatter*. It is amusing that her female characters are "deadly tired" at his time. Tired of waiting for love as she was, perhaps?

Having discussed her work, she didn't find it difficult to switch to complaints about her sister Ragnhild. She got along fine with Signe, who was five years younger, but Ragnhild, who was much closer to Sigrid in age, was a constant irritant. In *The Longest Years*, Sigrid wrote that it is an "exaggeration to say that children are normally jealous of a new arrival," but her feelings about Ragnhild were so intense that she was never able to be completely rational about her. Physically, Sigrid resembled her Danish grandfather. She was tall and tried to maintain a "stately bearing." She didn't want to seem coy and flirtatious like the women in her office with their curls and cheap perfumes, but wearing her hair wound around her head like a crown, which she thought made her look distinguished, simply made her seem unapproachable. Although she had found it difficult to make friends at school, there had always been the possibility that she would find her intellectual equals as she grew older, but her job had taken her away from academic circles and she was floundering in her search for a direction in her life.

Ragnhild was cheerful and fun-loving, and not interested in "finding herself." She was flirtatious and manipulative and dedicated to outshining her brilliant older sister. Since she couldn't win that battle with her intellect, she tried to do so by being charming and popular. In pictures of the period Sigrid is much prettier and more interesting looking, but she envied Ragnhild her easy-seeming conquests—and their mother's constant prodding for her to be more like her sister confused Sigrid. She was never sure whether what she believed to be her virtues were not, in fact, faults. Since she would not stoop to competing with Ragnhild on her level—she wouldn't even make an effort to learn to dance—she withdrew and stubbornly clung to the very behavior that was making her miserable.

To Dea, she described her sister as a "narrow, silk-soft, little phenomenon," "very neat with her clothes," "like a little cat," "gracious and singing like a bird."

She had playing eyes and a rose mouth that never said anything but lovable things, but her small innocent-looking hands were fast as a boy's, and everyone "danced to her pipe." She had an incredible faculty to make people feel happy if they could make her happy. She could do anything. She had begun to take classes at the university and was getting high grades. She was seventeen years old and was "reading math with an older teacher, and French with a bank clerk." The pupils she tutored always brought her flowers, and all of her friends adored her. Their father's old colleagues greeted her in the corridors, and as if that were not enough, she danced like an elf, embroidered beautifully, and found time to help her mother in the house. "Mama says she is the only one who helps her."[18]

Ragnhild had begun to do some tutoring to help with the family finances. Sigrid had been their main support for two years—yet Ragnhild was the one who was getting her mother's praise for being "the only one who helps."

One day, Sigrid confided, she had arranged to meet her sister at the university after work. It was very cold and it was raining hard, and Ragnhild kept her waiting in a doorway for almost an hour. When she finally arrived, she explained that she was late because her hair was a mess and she hadn't been able to get her hat and veil to look right. She was so grateful when Sigrid took her out, she said, that she wanted to be sure she looked her best. "I am always pleased to buy her a cup of chocolate on a cold day or some ribbons, or gloves, or shoes for a ball, and when she hugs and kisses me and says, 'it is beautiful that we can be so much to each other,' it *is* beautiful."[19] (They were a close family, and despite the sibling rivalries, they *did* love each other.)

"The one thing I fear," Sigrid wrote a few months before her twentieth birthday, "is to be affected. Insincerity is where most authoresses go wrong . . ." She enclosed a picture of herself so Dea could see how good looking she was. She knew, she continued, that she had a strong figure and pretty hands, but was aware of her shortcomings. Her face was too round and she "went down on her heels." She had constant arguments with her mother about the kind of clothes she should wear. Sigrid felt that modern styles and bright colors didn't suit her. She preferred plain black dresses with old-fashioned stiff linen collars and large cuffs edged with lace, a silver brooch in her hair, and a rose pinned to her chest—but her mother kept after her to wear more youthful colors. "She can't understand that it is a virtue of necessity. I can't satisfy myself with styles from books and exhibitions. I can see that a red dress is beautiful, but not for me." It hurt her to hear dance music because she was too old now to learn how to dance, and if she couldn't dance beautifully, she didn't want to dance at all. Her mother believed that she had a natural antagonism against dancing and having a good time, and when she told her that she loved a Florentine bust in a gallery, her mother actually believed that she didn't want young men to admire her and flirt with her.

> My Lord, because the art students and cadets and engineers and bookkeepers and idiots that I have met so far have not given me the desire to see them again after being with them for five minutes, Mama believes that I'm longing for a plaster head in a gallery. All I demand is a little spirit and wit and grace in a man's foot—he can be as ugly as sin.[20]

She longed to meet someone whom she could love but none of the young men interested her, and she was terrified that if she were ever lucky enough to meet such a wonderful man, he would probably not want her.

Dea fell in love frequently and when the romances came to an end, she wrote to Sigrid about them. "Don't marry," Sigrid advised, "unless you are so much in love that you would rather be with your friend in Hell than alone in Heaven . . . In marriage, happiness is usually bought for that which is one's most precious property or even worse, for another's most precious property . . . Most women become stupid after marriage. They sacrifice their own interests for those of their husbands and children and are left with little to sustain themselves."

Sigrid intended to keep trying to become what she had it in her to become, and if she failed, it would be nobody's fault but her own. "Not God's, the devil's, my forefathers', my mother's, my father's, my grandfather's or anyone else's living or dead."

When Dea complained that it would be nice if the men she met would behave towards others as one wished others to behave toward them, Sigrid countered that it was important to behave towards others as one wished others to behave to oneself, but in the end, one had to be responsible for oneself.[21]

She was free with advice, but Dea's problems with boyfriends only underlined her own lack of opportunities. Everyone seemed to be able to find someone who could love them. What was wrong with her? Why couldn't she? Her sisters were very popular and were constantly falling in and out of "love" but as Sigrid made no effort to meet people, she was still spending most of her evenings alone. Nevertheless, she wasn't as lonely as she wanted Dea to believe. She was discovering how engrossing intellectual pursuits could be, and she was deriving incredible excitement and pleasure from her research and writing.

On April 23rd, Dea sent her some poetry she had written. Sigrid wrote that she thought she had talent and an ability for rhyming, but that it came too easily.

You don't think out what the theme is. It is not personal enough. 'Your most shining star,' etc. is not very personal. Don't write a line, not a word, not a comma that you haven't thought out, that you don't know the meaning of, that doesn't belong. 'You shall offer the king your reddest blood.' What do you mean by that? 'To sacrifice blood for a king?' Who does that in our time? A German woman for example, should teach her child to sacrifice blood for a whim of Kaiser Wilhelm's? Blood of her own blood? I would prefer to see my son shot as a revolutionary. Then at least he died for a cause that he had thought through—that he believed in—a son who dares to die for what he believes to be right—him I would be proud of. For heaven's sake, Dea, don't think twice but 10 times before you write and remember that it is worse to strengthen the children of mankind in their old authorized wrong opinions than to preach new ideas for them to examine and explore.

She begged Dea not to be angry, but she had to be honest. Inspiration, she continued, was fine, but one had to think it over carefully before using it. It was very difficult "to timber an action so that it could unfold and live." When one was interested in a minor character, it was necessary to keep that person in his right place so he didn't come too far forward. It was better to describe a character through his actions than by his inner feelings. "One line should be as clear as ten were before you cut and pruned and added what gives breadth to a character . . ." One should not "paint with other's colors."

Sigrid was planning to use Kalundborg surroundings for her medieval story. She wanted "flesh and blood people and overwhelmingly passionate lovers." They would "have to have nerves working in the half-dark places of their instincts," without sounding modern. It would take place in 1339. The woods were mostly oak then. The reader would have to know where it took place, how people looked, what they wore, their weapons and clothes and saddles, houses, people and children . . . and why they acted as they did. "What may seem violent to us was natural in everyday life to them."

She planned to be so familiar with the 14th century that she would be able to describe the daily life. Language was another problem. She couldn't hope to duplicate the speech of the period, but she was trying to find a way to give it "an aged tone" and avoid words and phrases that were not in use at the time. It was difficult to hit on the right old-world sound and still not sound pompous or affected. She tore up more than she kept, but she was beginning to have small bits that pleased her. She planned to avoid actual historical events so that she would be freer to move her characters around—and she worried about who would want to publish it after she finally got it right.[22]

She spent the summer in a *pensione* while her mother and sisters went on a holiday. The people bored her but she forced herself to make friends. She couldn't write but she spent the time researching medieval literature.

By October, she had the first draft of her novel finished and she sent it to Dea with a new photograph of herself. She was twenty years old. In the picture she is standing. Her hair hangs loose to below her hips, and she is wearing one of those black dresses with a starched white collar that she found so attractive. She is obviously trying to look seductive and "interesting"—but all she manages to accomplish is a pathetically affected and theatrical pose.*

She waited anxiously for her friend's verdict and just before Christmas it arrived. The day had started badly. She had quarreled with her mother before leaving for work. At the office she slammed a glass door which shattered and she had to pay for replacing it. When she got home, her sister told her that her mother had cried all day and was worried about her nervousness. But all was forgotten when she opened Dea's letter. She had only good things to say about the novel.

"I wish I had lived 100 years ago and had been married off with an honorable, pious and hard-working young man—a good citizen who took care of his job and his own," she wrote in her next letter to Dea. "Then I could have twins, a spinning wheel, a piano, a white hat and keys at my waist."[23] (Now that she had received confirmation of her ability as a writer, she was eager to get the rest of her life in hand!)

She had been feeling like "a wingless ant," she wrote in May. "Flies do not get into containers easily and it is still harder to get them out," but she hadn't gotten "a chicken-step ahead" with her personal life. She hated people who complained about poverty and she hated the kind of pity she used to get in school, but people who preached about living within one's means were harder to bear. She was working on a story abut "a little business woman with artistic pretensions who can do nothing but worry about money, money, money." She yearns for a prince to take her out of it all. "The prince arrives and he is a bore. Not even a bad person—just a bore." She becomes ill and "he comforts himself by marrying a light little gay person."[24] That "light little gay person" was to be a stock character in many of Sigrid's stories.

Most of the girls she knew had boyfriends. How did they find them? Some of their beaux were really quite nice. If the girls didn't respond to them at the first meeting, the young men didn't give up. They pursued them. Why did no one pursue her? It was her own fault. She was too critical. She judged people too harshly. Ragnhild thought that everyone she knew was "sweet." Ragnhild would graduate soon as would get a job teaching. Signe was going to go to secretarial school. As soon as they were earning some money she would be free. Perhaps she would travel.

---

*   The photograph is available.

"Mama says I am the kindest, sweetest, most wonderful person and that God has something extra in His fat hands for me," she wrote to Dea. "It is nearly as encouraging as having my whole fortune placed in long-term securities with some suspect banking house."[25]

She had been corresponding with Dea for almost five years, but they had not met. They made endless plans to do so, but could never work out the details. Sigrid did not want her friend to see the way she lived, and she could not afford to go to Sweden, but in April, she earned some extra money taking shorthand notes at public meetings, and she was finally able to visit Dea. Too excited to sleep, she stayed up nights making herself a white, lace-trimmed dress (by hand) for the long awaited occasion.

Their meeting was a thrilling but sobering event. Dea was prettier, wiser, and more mature than she had pictured her. The middle-class comfort in which she lived was luxurious compared to Sigrid's, and her social life seemed positively glamorous. She had many interesting friends and several of the young men were extremely attractive. Dea's sisters and brothers were older than she was, and their friends were more mature than Sigrid's acquaintances. She enjoyed the visit tremendously, but she came home considerably subdued. Dea was more successful with the opposite sex than she had realized. In fact, she was far better off in every way, and yet, she couldn't be dismissed as "a light gay little person."

"I've decided to be more natural," she wrote when she got back.

"I'm ashamed now when I think of how often I have been sentimental and affected and untruthful with you. I wasn't that way willfully. You can't imagine how fond I got of you when I listened to you reading your verses to me with your sweet serious voice. You are the first woman or many whom I have met who really wants to become an artist.

On the boat, she had returned to two youthful faults, she added, "seasickness and trying to write poetry."[26]

Mrs. Undset rented a house in Strømmen for the summer, and Sigrid had to walk twenty minutes to get to the station, ride fifty minutes on the train, and walk ten minutes from the station to the office. "I heartily hope that we have good weather," she quipped.[27]

Her visit with Dea strengthened her desire to "make something of herself," and she worked harder on her novel. She was reading folk songs in Danish, English and German—Keats, Heine, Byron's *Don Juan* (which she found difficult), Edgar Allan Poe, "whose poems are masterpieces," and many Scandinavian writers.[28]

Once, Dea asked why she didn't have more of a message in her stories and she answered that books were better without messages. She had never learned to like what she called "preaching literature . . . I don't believe I have a gift for the pious."

Her office moved to a more cheerful quarters and she could see the street.

> *I look out all day at all of those people and speculate about why I can never meet anyone who really interests me. Who really warms me personally when I get close. It is as if life has no use for me. Mama and my own are fond of me, but not for myself. They would love me just as much if I were the opposite of what I am. I stay up nights examining all that I feel is good and admirable in me and I grieve. It couldn't buy me a single human being's love. You have often told me that you are fond of me and I believe it too, but I don't know if you would continue to be if we were near each other always. I think of all that we have both been disappointed in. We demand that things should happen as we dream.*[29]

Sigrid's complaints about never going out or meeting people were exaggerated to some degree. She had certainly not met anyone she could fall in love with, and that was obviously very much on her mind, but she was not as much of a recluse as she wanted her friend to believe. She had a delightful sense of humor and an incredible amount of information and knowledge, and although she lacked opportunities to meet new people, she was good company when she did.

Dea wrote that her sister was getting married to a foreigner.

"It may be better that they don't speak the same language," Sigrid answered. "They will not be able to speak their love to pieces. Speech has no doubt killed more love than silence."[30]

Sigrid cleaned her room before Christmas and reread all of Dea's letters. Surely it was their mutual suffering that had kept them writing to each other, she wrote to her friend. "Had one of us ever been happy, perhaps the whole thing would have died. Now I don't think that will happen."

Apologizing for having reacted only to those of Dea's experiences that echoed her own, Sigrid promised to pay more attention to Dea's problems in the future. She understood Dea better since their meeting, she continued, and realized that she had not responded enough to the things that were troubling her. That good intention, however, only lasted until the next sentence when she was back to her own concerns again.

The other day, she wrote, the head of her office told the bookkeeper that she was so innocent that he didn't dare say a rough word in front of her. "I *am* uncertain, clumsy, shy, introverted and given to dreams, but Mama is

wrong when she thinks I'm not suited for life . . . Above everything else, I
wish to live. It's only that I won't live a life I would look down on." Life could
be richer than most people dreamed of, and she'd rather die than settle for
one that was shabbier than her "most pale and tired grey-weather dreams."
"I don't eat the porridge I have spit into, as we say in Norwegian."

Her salvation, she hoped, would come as an author. Her medieval novel
was almost finished and she was in a better mood. It would soon be spring.
"The green isn't visible yet but the flowers are beginning to come up. We
have nothing yet, but we have everything ahead of us. That is the one good
thing about our situation."[31]

There were debates in the Swedish press about free love and Dea asked
Sigrid how she felt about it. Sigrid wrote that she believed that people who,
for one reason or another, couldn't get married, should live together if they
loved each other, but they had to be ready to take the consequences. (As birth
control methods were illegal, she was not only referring to the disapproval
of the community—but the much more serious consequences of raising an
illegitimate child in that atmosphere.)

On May 28th, she wrote to Dea that she had just read an anonymous book
called *Woman Created by Man* (in its 5th edition) which was provoking much
pro and con discussion in the press in Norway, and that she had sent her
opinions about the book to *Aftenposten* before going to work one morning.
Her comments appeared on May 12rh, 1904 and Sigrid had the pleasure of
seeing her name in print for the first time.[32]

The fight for Norway's independence was accelerating and the newspapers
of both countries were full of it, but there is no reference to it in their
correspondence. Their countries had opposing interests and it was more
tactful to avoid the subject.

Then, at the end of May, she got a letter that took her breath away. *Dea was
getting married*. She was marrying a Professor Leonard Forsberg, who taught
agricultural economics in Akarp, (near Malmø). Completely unprepared for
the news, Sigrid found it hard to congratulate her friend with the warmth
that she should have felt. Addressing her as "My Own Dear Girl," she wished
her "the best."

"Bless your seven rooms," she wrote, "yourself, your fiancé, parents, sisters,
brothers, wonderful sister-in-law, and brothers-in-law . . . Do you remember
what I wrote at Christmas? That we will go on writing to each other even if
one of us is happy?" She begged not to be forgotten, and asked if Dea planned
to continue their correspondence.[33]

After that there are no letters for three years.

CHAPTER III

"BECOME SOMETHING, DARLING . . ."
1904-1909

Dea's marriage electrified Sigrid. It drove her to make more of an effort to improve her social life, and because she wasn't sure that she would succeed, she tried harder to become an author. That was something within her control. She rewrote her medieval novel, and when it was finished, she got all dressed up in a big flower-trimmed hat, a new blue dress and silk stockings, and "trembling with apprehension" took it to Peter Nansen, an editor at Gyldendal, one of the two major publishing houses in Norway.

The interview was short, A. H. Winsnes reported in his book, *A Study in Christian Realism*. Mr. Nansen took her manuscript and told her to return in a month. The month passed slowly, but when she came back, he gave her a friendly pat on the shoulder and told her not to try her hand at any more historical novels. They were not her line. Why didn't she try something modern?*

"I came home, my mind in a whirl and wrote *Mrs. Marta Oulie*. That, I felt, should be modern enough," she later recalled.[1]

Finished in the spring of 1906, she submitted it to Aschehoug, the larger of the two major publishing houses, and on June 8th, Andreas Jynge turned it down. Although he found it "promising for a debutante," he felt that "everyday stories of marriage and infidelity were not longer interesting."[2] Discouraged, but not beaten, she took her sisters' advice and sent it to the dramatist Gunnar Heiberg. He was impressed and convinced Aschehoug to publish it.

---

* That medieval novel was rewritten and published twenty years later as *The Master of Hestviken*.

*   *   *

Mrs. Marta Oulie appeared in 1907, when Sigrid was 25 years old. It begins: "I have been unfaithful to my husband. I write it down and sit and stare at the words." Written in the form of a diary, it is the confession of a young woman who, through a series of flashbacks, describes how she met her husband, their life together, the birth of their four children, her infidelity, and its affect on all of them.

Her husband, Otto, is a businessman, good looking and prosperous. When they met he had a nice apartment with a plush sofa, a console mirror, a piano and a potted plant. She was 22 and had never been kissed. She was an honor student and had always had contempt for businessmen, but his kisses inflamed her and she married him.

She was a schoolteacher when they met, and she continues to teach after their marriage. They furnish a nice apartment "with a Turkish corner"[3] and their first years together are happy ones. They spend a weekend in Paris and she does the Can-can for him in their hotel room. Before their third child is born she stops teaching. Shortly after that her cousin Henrik, who moved to England when she married, comes back to Norway and becomes her husband's business partner. They have many intellectual interests which her husband doesn't share. Otto admires her superior intellect and is proud of her efforts for women's rights and better education, just as he admires everything else that is his—his children, his friend Henrik, his parents, his brothers and sisters, his home, his garden and his summer cottage . . . but he no longer stimulates her. She no longer feels like doing the Can-can for him. She "lets things happen" and "almost innocently" she and Henrik drift into an affair. Henrik was as eager to have it as she was—but she couldn't say that he started it. "She had taken him . . .

> *It was a natural drive that broke in her—brutal, impossible to satisfy—and she, the proper little miss who had quietly cared for her children, became an evil and dangerous animal who could create damage. It wasn't simply vanity. It was something deeper . . . She could think of nothing but love. She was shameless. It was enough that her children had food and clothes. She lay with her lover two rooms away from where they slept. It wasn't Henrik that she thought about, actually he meant no more to her than the mirror on her dressing table,*

  Not published in English.

it was love that occupied her mind. Love was everything. Nothing else mattered.[4]

Otto can't conceive of *his* wife being unfaithful and notices nothing. When her fourth child is born, she knows it is her lover's but her husband is so blind that he chooses that child as his favorite. Before they were married Otto told her that he had had other women. He wanted everything to be open and aboveboard, but she didn't tell him when she became unhappy in their relationship, nor did she ask him what *his* needs were—and now, she doesn't tell him that the child is not his.

Otto develops tuberculosis and goes to a sanatorium and she regrets her duplicity. Her husband had always been devoted to her and the children as if they were "his creditors,"[5] while she had behaved dishonestly. She tries to establish a more loving relationship with him but his letters "which arrive as regularly as Tuesdays and Saturdays"[6] are disappointingly matter-of-fact and businesslike. He dies and she feels "like the shirt in the fairy tale that has had tallow spilled on it. The more one tries to clean it, the dirtier it gets."[7] She recalls an incident that occurred when she first started to teach. A little girl was knocked down by a beer truck which had driven over her hand, and while Marta and the other teachers were trying to stanch her gushing blood, the child kept pleading, "Let me see my hand. I want to see what happened to my hand."[8]

Marta realizes that it was sex that had attracted her to Henrik, and since she doesn't love him, she decides against marrying him. She goes back to teaching and will bring up her children alone.

*   *   *

Sigrid was doing something new when she described a woman's desire for sexual gratification, but she was also saying that women had to be honest and that marriage was a serious commitment and could not be taken lightly.

Marta's sin was not her yearning for, nor her enjoyment of sex, but her dishonesty (she sneaked her relationship with Henrik, never told Otto of her unhappiness, never tried to find out what his needs might have been, and never told him that his favorite child was not his). In Lutheran Norway, enjoying sex (even for a man) was considered sinful, and women who did were thought to be no better than whores. That a woman could yearn for physical pleasure, that it was healthy for her to do so, and that she had the right to refuse to legitimize her relationship with Henrik when he was ready to "do the right thing by her" after her husband died, preferring to take responsibility for herself and her children, was not an acceptable way for a woman to behave.

"When the strong sex was the only one on the literary scene," the reviewer in *Nationaltidende* wrote on December 27, 1908,

> . . . *women were usually treated with varied and sometimes too much regard . . . recently a whole school of female authors have tried to make up for lost time . . . and what has appeared has, after all, not been a gain for literature . . . Mrs. Marta Oulie . . . is of course, a modern woman who has passed her exams with outstanding honors, and later got married. But as often happens, free education does not seem to be the best education for marriage . . . She betrays her husband and his partner and friend . . . Her husband gets sick and dies of TB and she is filled with repentance that poisons her every day and hour.*
>
> *It is, perhaps, not necessary to point out that Mrs. Marta Oulie, although told in quite a lively way, is as superficial and unnecessary a work as a large amount of her predecessors' and followers'.*

The rest of the reviews were in the same vein, but Sigrid knew it was only to be expected.

Shortly after her book appeared, she received an announcement from Dea that she had given birth to a daughter. It was the first letter from her friend in three years, and Sigrid answered at once. "I hope you get all the pleasures in the world out of your little Elizabeth," she wrote, "and she, little pussycat, gets it from the world."[9]

By now Sigrid had some male friends. It is doubtful that they were meaningful relationships and they were probably not sexual, but she was trying to reach out. She wrote of an engineer who had worked in her office, who moved to America just when she thought they were beginning to care for each other, and a seaman, with whom she may have had a romance, appears in several stories.

In Sigrid's story, *My Favorite Aunt,*[*] a young woman visits her family in Denmark in the hope of renewing the acquaintance of a seaman who had moved there. Her grandaunt notices her disappointment when she is unable to locate him and tries to arrange a match for her with the local minister.

---

[*] Published in *Mademoiselle Magazine* during World War II, and as "Min Tante Og Presten Hennes" in *Artikler Og Taler Fra Krigstiden* published by H. Aschehoug & Co. in 1952.

First the eccentric old lady praises Pastor Røddinge, then she says that she has decided to give the furniture which her niece had been promised, to him, because she likes him so much. Then she invites him to tea and suggests that the two young people go out to see her garden. When they are in the garden, she locks the gates and disappears. Her niece finds the pastor attractive, and although her aunt's efforts are embarrassingly obvious, she is beginning to enjoy the situation when he, in great discomfort, explains that he is engaged to be married.

The story was written good-naturedly, years after the event, but it must have been painful if it was based on an actual experience.

Dea was delighted with *Mrs. Marta Oulie* and asked for permission to translate it. Sigrid wrote that she would enjoy forwarding her request to her "dear publisher." He was being very nice to her since 531 books had already been sold and the book was just out.* He considered it a successful debut and had already agreed to publish and had already agreed to publish her next book which was to be called *The Happy Age.*** It was a collection of short stories about women and children. It was much bigger than her first book, she wrote, and contained one story that was "very daring for Norway." Full of enthusiasm, she explained that she had three other books she was longing to write and, to impress Dea even more with her newly acquired position as a published writer and woman of the world, she added that the doctor had told her that her heart was weakened from too much tobacco and no sleep. "I'd better hurry, I guess. I'm still happy about my unexpected luck. I got six hundred crowns for the new book which surely makes me feel good after my past circumstances."[10]

*   *   *

The Happy Age appeared a year after *Mrs. Marta Oulie*. The stories are about young women, like herself, who are always "on the outside" and haven't had the good fortune to get much out of life. They struggle to find out what they want to do with their lives as they enter the work force and are compelled to live away from home in sordid little *pensiones* where they have to prepare their own meals and establish new rules for their social behavior. In the title story, Charlotte and Uni come from poor but intellectual families and have "ideals." Charlotte commits suicide and Uni works hard at becoming an

---

* 531 copies may seem little, but Norway had a population of four million people and a large percentage of them were illiterate and living in remote rural areas.

** Not available in English.

actress. Just when she achieves some success, she gives up her career, marries, and starts a family. She is not happy and will never know if she married because she loved her husband and wanted children, or because she feared that she lacked the talent to succeed.[*]

The Stranger (which was indeed "very daring for Norway") was a more interesting story. The description of the *pensione* in which the impoverished Edele Hammer, another girl "with ideals," is going to live, is brilliant. The dark hallway with its smell of female underclothes and stale perfume—the sausage hair-do on the bare-necked, well-corseted, plump, little pink-and-white lady who hasn't vacated Edele's rooms yet—her library books on the powder-strewn dresser—the rhinestone jewelry, hairpins, brooches and combs with tangled blonde hair still clinging to them—all—including the prints of Psyche and Napoleon that flank the mirror above the dresser—presage Sigrid's unequalled way of putting the reader into a time and place whether it be a farm, a *pensione* for working women, or a castle in the Middle Ages.

Edele works in an office and has been going out with a well-to-do architect but he has never tried to make love to her. She believes that he doesn't want to rush her because he is considerably older, and she is stunned when he tells her that he plans to marry a widow who has a son. Why did he choose an older, less attractive woman when he could have had her? What was it that made some women more attractive to men?

Determined to get something out of life, she turns to Aagaard, a handsome young man who lives in her *pensione* and brings shopgirls to his room. She feels a bit silly when he asks her to sit on his lap, but she does, and eventually she allows him to make love to her. She "knows that it should have been disgusting," but she likes it more each time they are together and soon she can think of nothing but making love. She decides that sex is what love is all about and they plan to marry until she visits the architect and his new wife and is reminded how stimulating life can be when one is with a person who shares one's interests.

The story falls apart after that, but it is well written up to that point—and Sigrid's handling of a young woman's yearning for love, and her lack of guilt when she discovers the magic of sex, must surely have shocked Norwegian sensibilities.

The best of the collection is a very short little gem of a tale called *A Half Dozen Handkerchiefs*. Worthy of inclusion in any anthology of great short

---

[*]   Sigrid continued Uni's story in *Images in a Mirror* which was published in 1917.

stories, it is about a nine-year-old girl who wants to take dancing lessons. In a very few pages Sigrid manages to sum up, poignantly, how poverty forces parents to hurt their children—and she introduces the first of her male characters who does not mean to be cruel but cannot deny himself his little pleasures.

*   *   *

More successful than her novel, the stories established Sigrid's reputation. In a state of euphoria, she applied for a travel stipend from the Theodor Henrichsen Fund which was set up to help artists and writers. Signe had just gotten a job in an office and Ragnhild was teaching school. Free at last, she planned to give up her job in the spring, and travel until her royalties were exhausted—whether she got the stipend or not. She had started a third book, but she would finish it at her grandfather's house in Denmark. Then she planned to go to Germany, Italy and France. She wrote to Dea to ask if she could visit her on her way to Kalundborg. Dea was delighted and urged her to come.

"I can't tell you how I am looking forward to going out straight and free," she wrote,

> 'Happy and light but poor in property,' as the folk song goes. Not that I am so happy and light but maybe that will come. I leave my job as of the 1st or 15th of May—if only I can get a travel stipend. Other authors swear I'll get one, but I want to see it before I'll believe it. I have had offers for translations from Germany and have given Rhea Sternberg the right to translate 'The Stranger.' It could be a long time before she gets it placed. I have a one-act play* which I will try to place with Fahlstrøm where they have that wonderful actress Mrs. Wettergreen. Not at the National Theater—they keep things for years before they do them and they don't have a good actress for the part. I don't expect to have an audience for years. One gets that by either writing crap or being completely deaf to criticism and if one does always what one thinks is right, and if one lives long enough and is persistent enough, and if one has talent, of course, one will come through finally. Learn from criticism? Oh dear. D. K. wrote a review. She was kind but

---

* Her play, *In the Grey Light of Dawn*, was, like *Mrs. Marta Oulie*, about infidelity—except that this time it was the husband who was unfaithful.

*didn't understand it at all. Nevertheless, I can thank her for helping
to sell books.*

*I have embroidered a tablecloth for my mother (English embroidery)
for Christmas. It is one-and-a-half meters long. Thank god, I've finally
put the animal in the wash.*[11]

On March 8th, she wrote,

*There were comments about books of the year in Samtiden from a
strict critic and I got a long and thorough-going review. I'm called the
most important and characteristic of all the latest young authors. When
I began to write about what was under my nose—I found something
quite new without quite understanding it. Christiania has been written
about only by outsiders who have criticized our poor provincial city . . .
I am not writing about Christiania now and I'm afraid the critics will
not accept it and send me back to my specialty.*

She had many chores to do for herself before she left but she managed to
embroider another tablecloth and napkins for Ragnhild "who has just announced
that she is secretly engaged*—while skiing and running around to lectures with
her beloved, not thinking of serious things like tablecloths and napkins."[12]

At the end of May, she resigned from the office. After ten long years she was
finally free. Her sense of accomplishment was tonic. Working nights instead
of running around to boring entertainments had been lonely, but it had paid
off. She was twenty-seven years old and doing what she enjoyed most, and
she was free to keep at it—forever. Five years earlier, when her manuscript
had been turned down, she hadn't despaired, she just kept at it, and now
she had two books in print, another contracted for, and the beginning of a
reputation as a writer.

Her send-off from the office was emotional. She described it to Dea on
June 3, 1909.

*Roses in a crystal bowl at the typewriter from the workers. A
farewell note with a piece of jewelry from the head of the company . . .
a dinner in a private room of a restaurant with the ladies, and endless
goodbyes . . .*

---

* Ragnhild must have changed her mind because she didn't marry until
March 1921.

Finally after ten years I am my own master and it looks like my luck will completely overwhelm me. I was prepared to travel out into the world with 1000 kr., and that my publisher would be sour because my new novel takes place in the year 1000—but he is extremely encouraging about the book and will send me an advance—and I have gotten the largest fellowship that they have here. You can understand that I am having a good time now.*

---

* 1800 kr.

CHAPTER IV

LOVE—"NOT PALE, TIRED, GREY-WEATHER DREAMS"

1909-1912

Sigrid was in high spirits when she arrived at Dea's house in June. They had shared their most intimate thoughts for eleven years but had met only once—and that was six years earlier. She had a travel stipend and a large advance on her third book. She was building a reputation as an author and setting out to see the world.

Dea was proud of Sigrid's accomplishments and delighted to have her as a guest, and she did everything she could to make her stay a pleasant one. The Forsbergs lived in modest comfort and had many friends. Professor Forsberg was an attractive, intelligent man and seemed devoted to his wife and child.

Sigrid was charmed by their way of life and enamored with their bright, chirpy little baby, and slowly her success, and the trip she had been looking forward to with such pleasure, lost their allure. What good were her achievements if no one loved her? Writing fascinated her and she couldn't imagine living without it, but life would be unbearable if she had to live it alone. She longed for a companion whom she could love. Her being yearned to be caressed. And there was nothing as sweet as a chubby little baby.

Her respect for Dea grew each time they met. Perhaps, she comforted herself, a life like Dea's would pall if that were all there was to it, but when the visit was over her euphoria was gone. Did she really want to wander around the world by herself? Traveling alone was not going to be easy. Several times she thought of turning back, but since she had to finish her book before she could do anything else, she decided to continue on to Kalundborg, as planned. She was tired. She needed a rest. She would sleep late, go for long walks, and work.

As soon as she was away from Dea's happy home her good humor returned, but she was more determined than ever to find someone to love and marry. Her relatives pampered her and the book flowed with few interruptions.

It was not a modern story. Still drawn to writing about ancient times, despite the curt way that her first novel had been turned down, the new book revealed her growing confidence in her own judgment.

Inspired by Icelandic sagas, *The Story of Viga-Ljot and Vigdis*[*] takes place in the year 1000. It is based on the revenge ethic which protected family honor in Norse pagan society. Written with the rhythms of a ballad, it is neither as detailed nor as profound as her later medieval books were to be, but it is thoughtful and well researched—and a joy from the first page to the last.

Around the year 800, prosperous Norsemen settled Iceland in an effort to avoid excessive taxes in Norway and Denmark. They governed themselves through town meetings, called *Things*, which set the rules for day-to-day living and arbitrated disputes. If there was a problem that affected more than one *Thing*, it could be brought to the *Althing* which met once a year. Their culture relied on strong family ties, and strict rules were established with specific punishments for each infringement of the law. Small lapses were compensated for with the payment of goods, but more serious crimes were punishable by death—the sentence to be carried out by a member of the wronged family. Failure to punish the perpetrator entailed a loss of family honor, and endless vendettas were carried from one generation to the next. The Vikings, as they were called, were excellent seamen and, from the 9th to the 11th century they raided the coasts of Ireland, Scotland, England and Normandy; robbed the monasteries, sacked the towns, and killed wantonly and indiscriminately. Some married and settled in the communities they plundered, but the majority returned home with their booty—where strict rules of behavior had to be adhered to again.

∗   ∗   ∗

The Story of Viga-Ljot and Vigdis is about a headstrong Icelander, who, on a visit to Norway, falls in love with a beautiful Norwegian girl named Vigdis.

---

[*]   Published by Knopf in English as *Gunnar's Daughter*.

She is the only child of a wealthy landowner and stands to inherit her father's estate. She loves the Icelander but fears that his impetuous behavior will get him into trouble, and she implores him to obey the rules of courtship and ask for her hand in the accepted fashion. Custom demands a long engagement with a number of preliminary ceremonies, but he is impatient and goes about it in his own way. Knowing that she loves him, he rapes her in the belief that once she has been "deflowered" her father will permit a hasty marriage. But family honor could not be trifled with. Although rape abroad was overlooked, it was an unforgivable crime at home. Vigdis loves him passionately, but she cannot allow him to betray her family's honor, and instead of running off with him as he was sure she would do, she refuses to see him again. He will be killed if he remains in the area and he has no choice but to return to Iceland without her.

Devastated by her disgrace and her loss, she will not eat or leave the house.

> *Now I am like a bird that lies on the ground fluttering its broken wings; it cannot move from the spot where it has fallen and it cannot see farther than the stream of its own blood. If I think upon what I used to be, I remember only what is now. If I recall the time when I lived here blithe and carefree, it seems that it was only that this might come upon me.*[1]

To avenge his daughter's disgrace, Vigdis' father attacks some of Viga-Ljot's kinsman. Her father is killed and Vigdis must kill her father's killer—which she does with the same knife. She goes off into the wilderness where she gives birth to a son whom she leaves to die of exposure, but a servant saves him, and when she comes to her senses, she accepts her child.

Viga-Ljot marries and raises a family in Iceland but he cannot forget Vigdis. The gods are unforgiving and he is punished for his transgressions. His wife, who knows that he longs for another, is not happy with him, and his beautiful children fall through the ice and die before his eyes. They have another child, but it is born deformed and blind. His wife and that child die too, and he has nothing left to live for. He sells his property, changes his name, invests in a boat and leaves to raid the coast of Normandy.

Ulvar, Vigdis' son by Viga-Ljot, has grown into a handsome young man. His mother has given him an excellent education, consulted him in the management of her estate, and indulged him most generously, but she will not tell him who his father is. When he asks, she says, "I wish to forget what I cannot bear to remember."[2] One day, two Icelanders visit them and Vigdis asks if they know Viga-Ljot. They tell her that when they last saw him, he had a lovely wife and children and a prosperous farm—and that all who knew him praised him for his bravery. Ulvar is fascinated by their stories of the man's bravery and says he wishes he could be just like him.

"If you were a good son you would bring me his head and lay it in my lap," his mother blurts out in a fury.[3]

Guessing, from the violence of her reaction, who the man must be, Ulvar tells her that he could never kill his own father. She is dismayed that she has revealed her secret and informs him that it is his duty to avenge her for what his father did to her, just as she avenged her father's death.

When he is of age, Ulvar leaves on a Viking voyage. His ship is lost in a storm and Viga-Ljot, who has changed his name to Uspak (Imprudent), saves him. They raid the coasts of England and France together and when Uspak discovers who the boy's mother is, he is overwhelmed. He never knew he had a son with Vigdis—and what a magnificent son he is! He reveals his identity and when Ulvar is ready to return home, he invites his father to visit them.

When Vigdis sees Viga-Ljot,

> All that had grown up with the years slipped away from her as a landslide scrapes the trees and growth from a mountainside 'til the rock is left bare, and it seemed to her that all these years she had only been waiting for the game to be played out between them.[4]

She knows that she still loves him but all she can think of is revenge. Viga-Ljot tells her that he never stopped loving her and that he still wants to marry her, and she says,

> I have never heard of a man ravished by a woman, nor can you know what it is to be powerless—feeling within oneself the growing child of a man whom I would fain have seen torn asunder by wild horses . . . I bore [him] one night on a bed of stone in the forest . . . You sailed and you rowed and you longed for me. That was a great help to me when they brought me Gunnar [her father] bleeding with his death wound and with scorn on his lips for the same that had been put on him against my will.[5]

She insists that her son avenge the wrong his father did her by bringing her his head. The boy cannot do it and his father helps him by throwing himself on his axe. Ulvar brings his mother his father's head and leaves—never to return.

*   *   *

Sigrid's publishers were enthusiastic about the book and she was able to continue her travels in good spirits.[*]

The directors of AEG, for whom she had worked for ten years but whom she had never met, had invited her to visit them in Berlin and she decided to await the proofs of her book there. They tried to entertain her, but they were elderly and lived "in an atmosphere of self-importance convinced that whatever they do is the only right thing to be done."[6]

She spent eight weeks in Berlin. Afraid to set out alone, she visited galleries and museums and explored the city until she found the courage to continue. Finally, with Florence as her goal, she headed south through Bavaria and Austria. In Denmark, she had befriended the Danish writer Nils Collett Vogt, and she wrote to him that she liked the churches in Nuremberg and found Bamberg a dream world though very pious, but she was lonely and frightened and didn't know what she was living for. Nevertheless, she was determined to keep going, and since she was already there, she wanted to see everything.

She stopped in Rothenburg, Dinkelsbül, Munich and Bozano and arrived in Florence in November.[7] Disappointed that "ruins which she had read about and imagined standing in a romantic frame of green leaves with flowers in the crevices, as you see them in old etchings . . . were in reality dirty and shabby with bits of paper, empty dented tins and rubbish lying about,"[8] she still found them beautiful. She was living in a terrible *pensione* full of stupid old ladies who irritated her and it was miserably cold.

On December 13th she wrote to Dea from Rome.

> . . . *it is only now that I realize what a wonderful city Florence really is. Through Germany I traveled as in a daze but now I feel like I am living my life again and thinking of beginning a new work. My last book is another success. It looks as if it is probably the most successful of all. I have a travel grant and I ought to pull myself together and be happy, but I am apprehensive each time I start a new book. I think it is dangerous to have luck like this, but I swear that it shall not make me less careful about every word I put down.*

---

[*]   It is the only one of her early books that is available in English.

She was staying in a *pensione* that catered to Norwegian students this time, but it was cold there, too, and so noisy that she couldn't work. "A great longing to be young, to love and be loved"[9] overcame her and she tried harder to make friends. The people she was meeting were students and artists who "had not read in books about every stone and every place until their eyes could not see the beauty in anything unless it corresponded to the pictures they had already made,"[10] and "slowly, furtively, like one who has escaped from prison,"[11] she began to join them in exploring the city and sitting around in the cafes until late into the nights.

Taking her time, she looked until she found an attic apartment at 138 Via Frattina,* "in a street that is not supposed to be so nice or so healthy, but it is a lovely room and up my chicken-steps-of-a-stairway my new friends find their way at all times of the night and day," she wrote to Dea on December 13th. That morning, sitting on her own sofa, in her nightgown, drinking tea which she had made for herself, she had enjoyed the sun and warmth and her view over the old grey roofs and terraces of Rome—terraces with palm trees and orange trees, and broken wash bowls and laundry which had been hung out to dry—and over the whole she could see the statue of Maria Immacolata in the Piazza Martiri with glimpses of Monte Pincio in the background. She had gotten into the habit of staying up late in all-night cafes, she continued, and had had all sorts of interesting experiences. One day, she came home for breakfast after having been to morning Mass and had seen the sun rise over Monte Pincio.

The night before, five or six of her friends had been in a wine cellar with her, about three o'clock in the morning, when a pale Italian girl, called Elena, who was about seven years old, came in to sell newspapers.

> With us was a woman who was about forty. She was beautiful, especially on a party night, when we have drunk a lot of this wonderful Italian wine from which one doesn't get drunk or stupid or tired only warm and happy and in a mood—you can't imagine how wonderful this Roman wine is—and she who was forty years old was beautiful and elegant and shining and spiritual . . . There was a warmth from her and a smile in her dark brown eyes. She put her arms around the little Elena and stroked the black shawl from the child's forehead and spoke to her in Italian and her voice became so strange and tender and her smile so suddenly pleading while she put some coins and candied fruit

---

*   Three years earlier, James Joyce had lived at 52 Via Frattina.

into the skirt folds of the little girl—and I felt the way I do down here
when the beggars show their crippled limbs and horrible wounds.

Sigrid described another lesbian encounter in *Jenny*, the book she was writing in Rome. Loulou Schulin makes a pass at Jenny when she is despondent and very drunk, and a male friend says "I cannot understand your putting up with her advances. Personally, I would rather do anything—eat a plateful of live worms," and Jenny tells him not to worry. She is "not going to end up that way." She didn't really like it and knew where to stop. She just felt sorry for the woman. "I don't think she is perverse by nature," her friend says, "only stupid and full of vanity. It was all put on. If it were the fashion now to be virtuous she would sit up darning children's stockings, and would be the best of housewives."[12]

The matter-of-fact handling of this scene is incredibly modern for 1911* and typical of Sigrid's straightforward way of discussing anything pertaining to sex.

Christmas was approaching. It was strange to have a Christmas without snow. Oranges hung on the trees and camellia bushes as large as the lilac trees in Norway were blooming in the churchyards.

The leisurely unstructured life in the sun warmed Sigrid's soul as it had thawed Hans Christian Andersen's and Ibsen's when they had fled the bigotry and backbiting of their countrymen—and she was coming to life just as they had.

Sigrid's knowledge was already prodigious and she was a witty, entertaining storyteller. As she and her friends pondered the meaning of existence, while wine and sexual titillations intoxicated them, she lost the stiff, self-consciousness that had stood in her way in social situations. For the first time in her life, she was appreciated for her exceptionalness and beauty. She had a delightful sense of humor and knew the cultures she described so thoroughly that she could recreate them in a lusty fashion. She had been accused of lacking a sense of humor, but that only became a part of her personality when she had little left to laugh about. In Rome, and for most of her life, she was bubbling with wit and her brilliant quips were often repeated.

In that relaxed atmosphere of pleasure, the event for which she had been yearning finally took place. She fell in love and her love was returned.

---

* *The Well of Loneliness* by Radclyffe Hall, which dealt with a lesbian relationship, didn't appear until 1928—and when it did, it was banned in England and the United States.

Anders Castus Svarstad was a Norwegian painter who had already achieved a considerable reputation in Norway and abroad. He was a dedicated artist, well informed, and unlike many of the men Undset had met at home, he was not a religious bigot. He had studied with Courtois in Paris, Tuxen in Copenhagen, and Christian Krohg in Christiania, and he had traveled extensively, including a prolonged visit with his sister in Chicago. He painted smoky cities, factories, gas tanks, and working-class homes in somber greys, blacks, dark reds and dusty greens. Not interested in experimenting with style, or painting pretty pictures for middle and upper-class homes, his work reflected the effects of industrialization on the terrain and lives of the people. Thirteen years older than Sigrid,[*] he was tall and painfully thin. He had an unpleasant voice, a persistent cough, and a caustic manner, but his mouth was wonderfully seductive and his eyes were piercingly blue—and he was an experienced lover. It would have been perfect—if he hadn't a wife and three children in Christiania.

Sigrid was twenty-seven years old and this was her first serious love affair. She was determined to have it and she was not conflicted about consummating it. She had longed for love for years. She had fantasized about how it would be. Her characters could never get enough of it, but she had never guessed how much the sensual side of lovemaking would appeal to her in reality. Sex was unbelievable! It wasn't only sex, life with a man was far more exciting than she had ever been led to believe. The father she remembered had been an invalid. After his death, her mother had deified his memory—and she had grown up without male companionship. To see Rome with the man she loved—a mature, well-informed, hard-working artist—to walk the streets arm in arm and stop to kiss under a tree—to make love on a balcony that overlooked that fabulous city—and to talk of serious things while he painted her portrait—it was more, far more, than she had ever hoped to have.

The fact that he had a wife and children at home was disturbing but it didn't stand in her way. As he described it to her, it had never been much of a marriage. They had been separated for long periods of time. He described his wife as a person who had had affairs with other men and had a life of her own. Sigrid knew her, but not well. They had been at Ragna Nielsen's school together, but since she was a year younger than Sigrid, they had not been in the same class. She remembered her as a flighty, disorganized and superficial, but beautiful, redhead. He said there was no problem. He would get a divorce as soon as they returned to Norway.

---

[*]   Born May 22, 1869.

Before she reached Rome, she had written to Vogt, she felt, "untruthful, frozen and goalless" but now,

> . . . the long spring of grey rain is over and the pale frozen buds have opened and are blooming like white almond trees . . . I will not complain now if I should experience the darkest hell. I have had my time of bliss . . . I can only hope that this happiness will continue. My friend and I shall be together always. Now he shall go home to Norway. There are things he has to put in order there.[13]

For Sigrid, this was not a holiday romance. Although she didn't know, at first, just how many women he had taken "lightheartedly" before he met her, she realized instinctively that this was different for him, as well. He had reached her innermost being sexually, and she had found the intelligent friends and companion with whom she could share her ideas and feelings. She was a strong, passionate woman and she had fallen deeply in love. Sigrid had strong principles for herself. She could never have reacted casually to an affair, but this was much more than a grand passion or a chance to save face in the community. She had no patience with the prudery and phony piety that surrounded her in Norway. Each person had the right to live his or her life as he or she saw fit, but she wanted to live *her* life responsibly—not just drift and let things happen. She was determined to let nothing interfere with her chance for happiness, and she was ready to take the consequences of her actions without complaint.

In *Jenny*, she described her situation.

> It was the first time [Jenny] had kissed a man. She was twenty-eight and she couldn't deny that she longed to love and be loved by a man—to nestle in his arms, young, healthy and good to look at as she was. Her blood was hot and she was yearning but she had eyes that saw clearly, and she had never lied to herself.[14]
>
> She dared not kiss his hot, red mouth for the sake of something intangible, intoxicating, frivolous, which would last only while they were there amid the sun and anemones—something irresponsible. She dared not put aside her old self; she felt that she could not take a flirtation lightheartedly . . . [15]

She was well aware of the strength of sexual attraction and would not criticize those who settled for only that, but she rejected mindless bed-hopping for herself.

She and Svarstad had seven glorious months together.[*] They discussed each other's work, world events, art, and what they both wanted from life. He was a passionate lover and she felt beautiful and dizzy-makingly desirable. It was truly her "time of bliss," but she was not surprised that it couldn't last forever. Svarstad's money had run out and he had teaching commitments to fulfill in Norway. They vowed that their separation would be a short one, and went to Paris together before he returned.

Travel pieces which Sigrid sent from Rome appeared in the Norwegian paper *Morgenbladet* in February, June, August and September 1910; and her glowing description of the performances of sacred scenes by six—and seven-year-old children at the Church of Ara Coeli during the Feast of Epiphany was imbued with the euphoria she was feeling at the time. *Pinse in Rome*[**] which compared the country sides of Norway and Italy was also written in such a mood.

Seeing Paris together was another intoxicating first experience, and in the article which appeared in August about her visit to the graves of Heloise and Abelard, she wrote:

> *Heloise, who was a learned and clever woman was totally obedient to Abelard, the man in her life . . . These learned and wise women knew that a man was the center of a woman's life and that if that were to be changed everything would fall apart.*

Sigrid wanted Svarstad, and before she could have him, he had to get a divorce from a wife who was neither meek nor obedient. She was always confounded by the success of women who seemed to have special appeal for men even though they were selfish and ordinary. They did nothing to pay their way yet they always seemed to get what they wanted.

Of the new marriage ceremony that was being introduced in Norway, which eliminated the words "Thy desire shall be to thy husband and he shall rule over thee," she wrote:

> *Did not these women consider that if a woman goes to the altar not wishing to hear such words, then she must take that position at the risk of destroying her home? Those words carry nature's own legal prescription for marriage: a woman shall marry only that man whom she can call her lord—and not any other.*

---

[*] They were together from the end of December 1909 until August 1910.
[**] Pinse is Whitesuntide—the seventh day after Easter.

She felt that a person, male or female, should not marry without love, and once married, each had to devote himself to the marriage with respect and devotion. Marriage without love was a form of prostitution. Everyone had a right to sexual love, and one's sex life was one's private affair, but marriage was a responsibility that no one had a right to undertake unless he or she was ready to accept it "for better or for worse." She took an even stronger position about a parent's responsibility to a child—each parent—but especially the mother.

After Svarstad returned to Norway there was little to keep her abroad and she came home too, but at home the situation was not what she had expected. Svarstad had returned to his family. He felt, he said, that he had to be home for a while before he could broach the subject of divorce. Living with her mother and sisters while he was with his wife was too painful to bear—especially since it was difficult to find places where they could meet without someone seeing them. A woman could not walk into a hotel alone without creating a scandal, and meetings necessitated lying to her family and friends. What was even harder to bear was attending social gatherings to which he came with his wife.

By now Sigrid was an established author. She was actively involved in the writers' organization and in the fight for a woman's right to vote. She was much more outgoing than she had been in the past, but she was still not "a gay, flirtatious person" and not adept at dissembling. She had expected Svarstad to start divorce proceedings at once, but he didn't seem to be in a hurry, and their relationship had to be kept secret.

She was working on *Jenny* and writing articles and short stories. Believing that one had to do everything within one's power to make life as fulfilling as possible, not only for oneself but for those who were less fortunate, as well, she used the press to express her opinions about literature, women's rights, illegitimate children, and help for their mothers. It is almost impossible to locate all of the articles she wrote during her lifetime, but well over a thousand have been traced. Two pieces appeared in *Morgenbladet* in October and December of that year: "Jeanne de France" which makes fun of what people in Christiania called French Fashions, and "Forefathers" which was about the middle-class preoccupation with status. In their Christmas issue, (1910), *Urd* published a story called "Robber on the Cross."

While reading the classics and medieval history, she was also catching up on books that had appeared during her absence. When she was in Rome, she had been impressed with a novel called *Benedicte Stendal* By Nini Roll Anker.

She wrote to its author, and when she returned to Norway, Nini Anker was one of the first people she met. They became close friends and Sigrid, who had always confided in Dea, was soon also confiding in Nini. Nini found it astounding that she was so sure that Svarstad wanted to marry her. Everyone, except Sigrid, she thought, knew that he had had extramarital relationships before. Sigrid, of course, knew about them, but she was convinced that this was different.

In her book, *My Friend Sigrid Undset* (*Min Venn Sigrid Undset*),* Nini wrote that Sigrid's figure and behavior made a deep impression upon her. She seemed completely out of the ordinary.

> *Everything about her made the imagination about her move—large eyes with the strange way of looking which seemed to see as much inside as out, but which anyway caught everything in her surroundings with the sharp looks that her books reveal. The beautiful narrow hands which once in a while moved when the conversation made an impression on her. The lazy, monotonous voice with quite a Danish accent on some words. She was also extraordinarily beautiful. Slender as a boy—something classical about her head which she hardly moved, something a little somnambulant over the careful tripping walk, but her whole being let one also feel a physical force and strength for which later in her life she would have such need.*[16]

Months passed and Svarstad was still living with his wife. It wasn't that he didn't want Sigrid, they were passionately in need of each other, but he was reluctant to confront his wife.

When Anders Svarstad was a boy, his father had signed a note for a relative who defaulted on the loan, and he had been forced to sell a major portion of their farm to satisfy the debt. Devastated, his father became ill and died, and Anders' mother was left to bring up the children in greatly reduced circumstances. By then, Anders was a young man but he was too involved in his own pursuits to offer his mother any help. He had talent for painting and could always manage to get scholarships for studying at home and abroad, and nothing was ever allowed to interfere with his work. After several bouts with tuberculosis, for which he was confined to sanatoriums, he met Ragna Moe.

---

*   Not published in English.

Ragna's mother had left her husband and an infant son in a small Norwegian town and was supporting herself and three of her daughters by giving piano lessons and running a boarding house for artists and writers in Christiania—and Anders was one of her boarders. Ragna was an uninhibited beauty with a lovely figure and little ambition, and although she was still in her early teens, she moved in with him. He was away on art scholarships for long periods of time and she went out with other men when he wasn't there.

They had three children: Ebba (b. 1903), Gunhild (b. 1905) and Trond (b. 1908)—but they didn't marry until December 1904, when Ragna was twenty-one and Anders thirty-five, and they were expecting their second child.

While Anders was in Rome with Sigrid, Ragna had been caring for their children with little money, and no help. Trond was only a year old when he left, and it is not hard to understand why he felt uncomfortable about asking her for a divorce as soon as he returned. In such a small community, it was not easy to maintain a secret relationship. Although he denied its existence, Ragna followed him and made scenes. The atmosphere became so charged that Sigrid was forced to move to the country so that he could visit her—and she often waited for him in vain. Just before Christmas, he finally arranged for a legal separation and moved to a studio, but confirmation of the suspicions which he had been denying so vehemently enraged Ragna so much that the scenes she created were enacted in public.

When Nini first visited Sigrid's home she expected that "the newly famous person, namely Sigrid, would dominate the household," but that was not so, she wrote. Sigrid's mother always took over. Nini described her as a small, slender, beautiful person, shining with intelligence, but willful. She was proud of her daughter but not beyond criticizing her.[17]

"The little angry marquise, how enticing she was," Nils Collett Vogt once said after visiting the Undsets. "I have never met a person who sparkled in the way that Mrs. Undset did and have rarely been in a home where the atmosphere was as refreshingly salty, unsentimental and exciting."[18]

In *Vaaren*, (*The Spring*),* which Sigrid wrote five years later, Mrs. Wegner (who is modeled after her mother) "was so close to her family that she could never really give herself to her husband. When she married . . . he had simply become part of her family" and when he died, "she lived her life as if all of her behavior was being surveyed and judged by her parents . . . and husband." She never complained about her poverty and loneliness and dropped all

---

* Not available in English.

of her friends "like one forgets friends one knew in the dining room of a
sanatorium."[19]

Mrs. Wegner was angry with her daughter when she refused to be
confirmed.

> When she said she was a free thinker, her mother said, 'What
> nonsense.' When she explained all that she didn't believe in, her
> mother said, 'Oh, that. I don't believe in that either. That no one
> believes, but we are not free thinkers.' By that she meant people who
> spoke in loud voices and expressed themselves badly. Life was eternal
> because her husband was as alive for her as anyone else . . . Since
> the Church had blessed her marriage, her child's baptism, and her
> husband's grave, it should also bless her daughter when she stepped
> into adulthood. That was all she really knew about religion . . .
> She believed in signs and warnings, in good and evil days, amulets,
> and prayers whose meaning she never gave a thought to, and she
> worshipped her own dead . . . [20]

Sigrid's mother was more intelligent and far more enlightened than
Mrs. Wegner, but she still could not condone her daughter's behavior with
a married man. Not only was he married, but he was considerably older and
had had several bouts with TB. She had to admit that he was a fine painter
and an interesting man, but he had never been much of a provider, and he
had three children. Was Sigrid ready to take their father from them and leave
them without any means of support?

After the legal separation they were able to see each other whenever they
liked, but a year after he left Ragna, he and Sigrid were still living apart, and
there was still no divorce.

In August, she was at a *pensione* in Bundefjorden working on her book
during a terrible heat wave.

"I live in a sort of attic chamber of lead and eat polenta pudding every
day with red sauce," she wrote to Nini,

> . . . but it's okay. I write all day, but between dinner and coffee, I
> rest by embroidering sheets. It's good for me to work so hard for a while
> and to be completely alone—because that I am—I eat every meal in
> complete lonely majesty.[21]

In 1910, shortly after Sigrid returned to Norway, Aschehoug had published a book of her poetry called *Youth.*˙ She knew that it wasn't distinguished and she never tried to publish poetry again, but it expressed her yearnings and an attitude towards life which changed little as she grew older.

In the poem *Credo* she wrote:

> *That which is my fate in life, no God can take away*
> *Of burdens that are given me, I haven't much to say*
> *Why beg and plead, lament in vain?*
> *I'll hide my tears. I won't complain . . .*
> *From the joyful, I will try to hide my sadness when I cry,*
> *And bow in worship when I face contented people in a festive place . . .* [22]

Jenny appeared in the fall of 1911˙˙ and it created a furor.

Jenny, a twenty-eight year old Norwegian girl, comes to Rome to paint. She meets a group of artists and writers whose opinions she respects. They work hard at their crafts during the days and carouse in the cafes late into the nights and she enjoys a camaraderie that she has never known before. She shares a room with Francesca, a beautiful, flirtatious young woman who is clever and talented but undisciplined about her life. They grow fond of each other and live frugally so that they can allow themselves occasional splurges. Jenny buys herself pink crystal beads, and Francesca is considering a string of corals. For Jenny, luxuries are essential. She was poor as a child and had only been allowed the strictest necessities, and now she would rather save on food and buy a silk scarf if she wants it.

Their discussions in the cafes are stimulating. Will the movement to revive folk art bring matters to such a pass "that the Norwegian national emblem will be a wooden porringer with painted roses and some carvings . . . ? Is there no better praise to bestow on an artist than that 'he has broken away?'"[23]

When Jenny first arrived she seemed "very reserved and hard, almost armor plated,"[24] but the Roman sun and enjoyable company have relaxed her, and her sense of humor and prodigious knowledge begin to emerge. Night after night she regales her friends with spellbinding tales of medieval days. She is a born storyteller and they find her fascinating.

˙ Not available in English.

˙˙ Published in English by Alfred A. Knopf in 1921.

She changes. The black dress with the white collar is replaced by a soft, silver grey one which she wears with pink crystal beads, purple stockings and bead-embroidered evening shoes, and she entertains in a Japanese kimono. She is radiant, and longs for love.

> *The joy she coveted should be fiery, consuming, but spotlessly clean. She would be loyal and true to the men to whom she gave herself, but he must know how to take her wholly, to possess her body and soul, so that not a single possibility in her would be wasted or left neglected in some corner of her soul—to decay and fester.*[25]

Jenny is drawn toward Helge Gram who has taken leave from his job as a teacher to come to Rome to write, but he, like most of the other men in their group, is attracted to Francesca. Francesca "would let one man after another kiss and fondle her and it made no difference."[26]

Helge is two years younger than Jenny, but although "he had a small weak mouth with a tired expression under his mustache,"[27] he is intelligent and attractive. As he gets to know the two women, he begins to prefer Jenny. They become engaged. She has to return to Norway. He will follow later. She longs for him to sweep her off her feet and make passionate love to her before they part, but he doesn't. She is sad, but also relieved. She tells herself that it is better that way but she can't control "the tears that streamed down her cheeks as she lay in bed. She tried to tell herself that there was no sense in crying like that, as if something were gone forever."[28]

She visits her fiancé's family in Christiania. His mother (who was partly patterned after Svarstad's wife) was once "uncommonly pretty." She had large teeth, large brown eyes, was "no lady as far as language and manners went,"[29] was spiteful, a dreadful nag, a terrible housekeeper, and a worse cook, and she liked to flirt and make her husband jealous. Their house had a long hall cluttered with boxes and cases, green plush curtains and furniture, and a carpet of many colors which was strewn with Sunday supplements and family photographs.

Helge's father, Gert Gram is an artist and his pictures hang on the walls. They are somber and technically well done, but except for a portrait of his wife when she was younger, Jenny doesn't like them very much. Gram is unhappy in his marriage. Beyond his wife's "faculty for loving, there was nothing in her. She was vane and uneducated, envious and crude. There could be no mental fellowship between them."[30]

He begins to visit Jenny without his wife's knowledge and they become lovers. That is, Jenny doesn't love him, but she is inflamed with the passion of their physical relationship and they see each other often. She doesn't mention it in her letters to Helge. Mrs. Gram is suspicious. Her husband had been unfaithful before. She follows him and makes scenes. Jenny hates the squabbles, the ugliness, and the need for secrecy, and wants to break with him—but her physical desire for him is too great.

When Helge returns, Jenny finds him immature. She never loved him and breaks their engagement. She tells him that she has been seeing his father without his mother's knowledge, but he doesn't suspect the nature of their relationship.

Jenny's affair with Gert Gram continues and just before Christmas, he leaves his wife and moves to a studio. He will get a separation from her after she is convinced that he doesn't intend to come back.

Jenny feels guilty. She enjoys making love to him, but she doesn't love him, and she knows that he doesn't understand that "she had sought shelter in his arms when he was the only one who had offered her shelter—when she was weary to death."[31] In the beginning, she had been as passionate as he, but that had been all she had wanted from him. Now, she was only feigning.

Just when she decides to stop seeing him, she discovers that she is pregnant. Her lover is delighted and promises to marry her as soon as his divorce comes through, but she will not hear of it. She doesn't love him, she says, and will not marry for propriety's sake. He gives her money to go to the country to have the baby and visits her as often as she will permit him to come, but she had developed such a distaste for him that she can't bear to have him near her. She refuses to see him and decides to bring up the baby alone.

In a deep depression, she awaits the birth of her child and is doing poorly when Gunnar, whom she had known in Rome, hears of her situation and visits her. He brings her books, takes her for walks, and writes to her after he leaves.

The baby dies and Gunnar, who has fallen in love with her, invites her to recover in Rome. Their apartments are on the same floor. He is a young, loving companion and she knows that she has found her true mate but she is afraid that her precipitous behavior with Gert Gram has made her unworthy of him. Her feeling of unworthiness is not due to her having slept with a man out of wedlock, or because the man she slept with was already married, it is due to her having allowed her physical hunger to affect her judgment—because she made love to a man whom she knew from the start that she didn't love.

"If anything irreparable happens to you, it is always your own fault," Jenny says earlier in the book, "and if you cannot train your will to master your moods and impulses and haven't control of yourself, you might as well commit suicide at once."[32]

"I wanted to live in such a way that I needed never to be ashamed of myself either as a woman or as an artist," she says to Gunnar.

> *Never to do a thing I did not think right myself. I wanted to be upright, firm and good, and never to have anyone else's sorrow on my conscience. And what was the origin of the wrong—the cause of it all? It was that I yearned for love without there being any particular man whose love I wanted.*
>
> *One day, I changed my course in an instant. I found it so severe and hard to live the life I considered the most worthy—so lonely, you see. I left the road for a bit, wanting to be young and to play, and thus came into a current that carried me away, ending in something I never for a second had thought could possibly happen to me.*[33]

Gunnar paints her portrait and she begins to hope that perhaps it isn't too late, when Helge arrives in Rome. It is three years since he saw Jenny but he has not been able to forget her, and he asks her, again, to marry him. She says it is impossible because there has been another man in her life. He believes that he lost her because he was too inexperienced to make love to her, and he grabs her and kisses her violently. She struggles and tries to fend him off, but he thinks she is resisting him as any "proper" young lady would do. Determined to display his newly acquired masculine prowess, he tries to force her. She breaks away and runs to Gunnar's apartment for help, but he isn't home. Helge catches her and rapes her.

> *She was very tired . . . She saw her own body as it lay under the cover, white, bare, beautiful—a thing that she had flung away as she had her gloves. It was not hers anymore . . .*[34]
>
> *She had wanted to change her nature, to fall in with the others who lived, although she knew she would always be a stranger among them because she was of a different kind . . .*
>
> *She had not been able to stand alone, a prisoner, so to speak, of her own nature.*[35]

She slashes her wrists and dies.

*   *   *

It is difficult in today's climate, to realize just how revolutionary that book was, in its time. Although the story was based on a real incident that had been reported in the press before Sigrid left Rome, the use she made of the material enraged even her closest friends.

"Sigrid needed a strong back to bear the reception it got," Nini wrote. "The papers were full of it. Its moral and immoral aspects were talked about all over town."[36]

The Lutheran Church was not just another church, it was the State Church of Norway. Passion and pleasure from sex, on the part of the woman, was too sinful to be taken lightly. It was a woman's duty to satisfy her husband's erotic needs so that he wouldn't become lustful, but to portray a woman enjoying sex was just not indelicate, it was evil. For a "nice girl" to have sex with a married man was bad, to have done so with the father of her former fiancé was worse, but to have continued to do so because she couldn't give up the pleasure when she knew that she would never want to marry him—was a concept that had to be stamped out at once.

Strindberg believed that a man's sexual desire was a curse. He hated women because he felt they took advantage of men since they knew that men couldn't live without them. That women could have needs of their own was no concern of his. Ibsen championed social and economic equality for women, but didn't tackle sexual equality. Tolstoy's women loved passionately but they demonstrated it when they "gave themselves" to their lovers. Of her contemporaries, D.H. Lawrence would write freely about sex, which he saw as a battle for domination between the sexes, but he had not yet published anything. Neither James Joyce nor Virginia Woolf had published either. Joyce, who used every "dirty" word he could come up with like a naughty boy trying to shock the nuns, wrote of women as thought they were born to service men, and Virginia Woolf avoided writing about sex until she wrote *Orlando* which was about lesbian love.

The basic story line of *Jenny* is not autobiographical, although Sigrid used experiences in Rome and characters that are partially based on people she knew. *Jenny* is a development in Sigrid's ongoing effort to explode the hypocrisy of prevailing attitudes towards women and sex. The females in her stories are never docile, even if they are the victims of their male dominated society. They don't abandon their roles as mothers and wives at the expense of others. She satirizes the silly, superficial, adorable dolls and the phony, idealized fabrications expected by the culture of her time. Her women have faults, weaknesses and confusions—but as her craft and understanding of people matured, her female characters grew in stature and commanded more and more of the reader's respect.

She was masterful at showing the little weaknesses and vanities in human behavior, and one has to smile at what seems like her need to protect her own image by endowing both Gert Gram and Gunnar with some of Svarstad's characteristics. If she and Svarstad didn't marry, it would appear that he was the model for Gert Gram whom Jenny wanted only for sex, and if he married her, then one could assume that he was the model for Gunnar, whom Jenny loved.

Everyone was talking about *Jenny* but few approved of it, and least of all, women. The suffragette movement was very strong in Norway and Sigrid was active in it. (The first woman had been admitted to a Norwegian university the year that she was born and a woman was elected to the Storting in 1907. Women won the right to vote in Norway in 1913, a year after *Jenny* was published.)[*]

A special meeting was called to discuss *Jenny*, and three hundred irate women gathered at the Grand Hotel in February of 1912, who, according to Nini, were outraged at what they called "the awful male eroticism" in the book.

> *Regine Normann stood up and turned her whole large body and her burning eyes toward her sisters and said that she had come to meet the elite of female intelligence and instead had met roughness of thought and a cold way of laughing about something that was a very serious matter. Things she would never have experienced if she were in a gathering of working-class women. How could they show such a lack of refinement? Women who fought for their rights were always being accused of being harlots and Sigrid's description of a woman's pleasure in sex, especially without love, would do the women's movement irreparable harm.*[37]

Although the meeting ended in an uproar, Sigrid sat quietly, with a little smile on her face, saying nothing. When the chairman asked her if she was

---

[*]   In the United States, women didn't win the right to vote until 1920. Great Britain in 1928, France in 1945, and many of the Middle Eastern countries will still not allow women to vote, despite efforts on the part of the United Nations to get all member nations to do so.

angry or disappointed,. She said, "On the contrary—I had not expected anything else."

After the meeting, Sigrid told Nini that she was surprised that they weren't swinging their pocketbooks at each other before they were finished.

Sigrid was particularly serene throughout the onslaught because she had received word from Svarstad, just before the meeting began, that his divorce had finally been granted.

"*Jenny* had it's baptism of fire," Nini wrote, "but all who were for or against knew that Norway had an author who from then on had to be reckoned amongst the great ones."[38]

*   *   *

In January, a month before the divorce became final, when she was still living with her mother and sisters, Sigrid had written to Dea to thank her for some embroidered napkins and explained that she had not gotten many such gifts because their plans still had to be kept secret. Due to Norwegian divorce laws, Svarstad would not be free to remarry in Norway for two years, and since they didn't want to wait, they planned to get married abroad and announce it after the fact.

Because Svarstad had been slow in extricating himself from his marriage, and because Sigrid felt that Dea was too conventional to accept her situation, she found it necessary, repeatedly, to convince her friend that all of the pre-marital formalities were being followed.

"My sweetheart and I have bought a few beautiful pieces of furniture when we came across them at antique stores, and I have gotten some wonderful old glasses and porcelain," she wrote, "but everything else has been put away in a storehouse for later." She had searched all over town for an old-fashioned bridal chest like the one that Dea's sister Maggi had shown her the first time Sigrid visited Malmø, but she had had to settle for "a little birch chest of drawers in the Empire style." They planned to be abroad for a few years and they didn't' know what kind of home they would have when they returned so all other purchases would have to wait. She hoped they would have a little child with them when they got back, she added. She was longing for a child with her "wonderful boy." The two years of waiting had brought her and her lover much closer together. Svarstad had gone to Stockholm the past autumn planning to stay for three months, but had returned after five weeks because he said he was longing for her. There was no one else he could speak sense with, he told her. It wasn't only her kisses he missed—she was also the only good friend he had ever had. He planned to return to Stockholm in April for an exhibition of his work, and she wanted desperately to go with him but her mother insisted it would create too much gossip. Her mother was strict and old-fashioned, and she had been forced to lie to her more during the past two years than she had done in her whole life before. Nevertheless, her mother was very fond of Svarstad and he was sweet to her in all kinds of ways. Their plans had not yet been finalized, but she would probably be in Copenhagen in April and go on to London from there, and she hoped that Svarstad would be able to get away as soon as his exhibition was over so that they could be married in Copenhagen and go on to England together. She was eager for Dea to meet him.

> *You will probably think he is terribly ugly because most people think so, but I think he is the most beautiful person on earth with his strangely irregular, lean face with a thousand changing, playing, alive expressions . . .*
>
> *I've gotten another travel stipend and also earned quite a bit from Jenny, which, to my colossal astonishment became one of the best successes of the year and has come out in a third edition. If you'd like to translate it I would be delighted. It would probably be possible to get a publisher for that one because it has not only been praised here, but it was also admired and reviewed in the Danish papers—even Tilskveren had quite a thorough-going review.*[39]

But they didn't get to Copenhagen in April. As Sigrid found out early in their relationship, nothing would ever take precedence over Svarstad's work. When he got involved in a project, everything else had to wait until he was ready to leave it. Also, it was not easy for him to wind up his affairs. He had to raise money for his ex-wife and children to live on while he would be away* and arrange for someone to forward his belongings when they knew where he would be living.

In all fairness, although it might seem that he was in no hurry to legalize their relationship, it is the opinion of her family and close friends that he loved her deeply. It was the conviction amongst "creative" men that they owed their total dedication to their art, and that "ordinary people" had to be sacrificed, if necessary, for their needs. Concern for family and societal problems could not be one of their priorities (although begetting children was not something they were interested in giving up). Sigrid could not be described

---

*   Perhaps he tried, but he left very little.

as a liability to his freedom as an artist. Her intelligence and understanding, her passionate devotion, her royalties, travel stipends and the money she earned from journalism, offered him stimulation and an opportunity to live abroad and work freely with few financial worries.

In any case, nature seems to have stepped in to speed things up. On June 12, Sigrid wrote to Dea from the Hotel Kong Fredrik in Copenhagen. She was there alone, three months pregnant, and still unmarried.

> I'm so close, I'd very much like to see you. It's a sort of wedding trip but I'm here alone. My sweetheart is coming to meet me here as soon as he can. We will be married by the Norwegian Consul in Antwerp and then travel from there to London and after that out in the world for as long as our money will last. It will probably be for at least a year. Now it is difficult to go to Åkorp because I don't know when Svarstad is coming and also I'm not quite well, throwing up a lot, and under the circumstances I would not like to be a guest anywhere. You can understand. But if you are going to Malmø some day, we could meet there. Otherwise, I'm happy. Very happy. I'm longing very much for my fiancé, but I'm sure he will not be in Christiania one minute more than he has to—perhaps you can imagine what it will mean for two people who can't live without each other, who for more than two years have had to steal and lie and be parted when we most needed to be together . . . finally to be able to live together in peace and quiet.
>
> You can see that I really can't believe that soon, soon, we shall never need to part more than a single hour if we don't want it ourselves.

Dea came to see her, but Svarstad hadn't arrived yet. He was finally there near the end of June and they arranged for the ceremony to take place in Antwerp as planned. Since they had a week to wait, they visited Sigrid's relatives in Kalundborg. Sigrid's great-aunt saw them off at the station.

"She didn't like Anders very much," Sigrid wrote to Dea, "but on the last day he got a telegram that a portrait of me was sold to a gallery in Bergen for 2000 kr. And this changed my aunt's feeling absolutely and incredibly. It was in a ladies' toilet at the station that she expressed her admiration."[*40]

---

[*] The portrait is now in the Rasmus Meyers Collection at the museum in Bergen and was reproduced on a Norwegian postage stamp ii May 1982 in honor of the 100th Anniversary of Sigrid's birth.

CHAPTER V

MARRIAGE

1912

They were married at the Norwegian consulate in Antwerp, on June 30, 1912. Sigrid was thirty and Anders forty-three.

"Anders delivered our papers at ten o'clock and at five we were married by a young person whom we politely called Mr. Vice-Consul, but who was surely very subordinate to that," she wrote to Dea on October 12th.

> *He functioned with the worthiness of an archbishop, gave a dinner for us the next day, whereupon we had to give a breakfast, and then he ran after us all the time in Antwerp. He wanted to make up to us for our lack of family and was extremely nice and about the most boring individual I never met.*
>
> *It was with great difficulty that we got rid of him but we managed a peaceful party by ourselves, and toasted with champagne, both born and unborn family members, in a beautiful restaurant in the zoological gardens. Otherwise, the honeymoon was not as successful as our other honeymoons have been. It rained continually, the hotel was terrible, and I was sick most of the time. Although we had some nice evenings in Brugge which was wonderful—all those Flemish towns are—but lots of rain and nausea took away a little of the mood. We were both relieved when we left Antwerp and our consular friend—I with roses and chocolates—all from the charming Vice-Consul.[*]*

---

[*]   This is described in detail in her novel *The Spring*.

They loved England from the minute they got there. They loved the porter, the conductor, and the driver of the horse-drawn carriage that took care of them and their belongings "like angels." London was "too wonderful in sunshine and high summer" but their *pensione* in Bloomsbury was awful and they soon moved to much nicer rooms at 64, The Grove, in Hammersmith.

Anders' room looked out on a "pretty little street with small Noah's Ark trees and one of those small English front gardens with a grass lawn as big as a dining table and a bowl of red geraniums in the center," she wrote to Nini on July 29th. "I have a room that looks out on a comparatively large backyard with two pear trees and a railroad wall—with factories in the distance. The area is nice. In the evenings people meet on the streets and there are speakers for the anarchists, socialists, anti-socialists, Salvation Army, Catholic Missions and this and that."

Hammersmith-Broadway was a busy street with music and pubs and cinemas where they could sit in the orchestra for two shillings. They saw "wild and wonderful melodramas about the slave trade, Indians, cowboys, and stagecoach robberies where at the crucial moment the hero 'prayed to God' and was able to 'shoot the enemy,'" she continued in her letter to Nini.

> *They smoke all over the place, but not the ladies. The workers in the balcony hold their girls in their arms and whistle at the villains and call out warnings to the heroines and clap loudly at each sign of the heroine's demure purity and are completely taken in by it all.*
>
> *Our landlady is a little dry-skinned Mrs. Tarner who is absent-minded, runs up and down the stairs 'aving so many things in 'er 'ead but she is always nice. We eat alone in a small room downstairs and our little hostess cannot do enough for us. When Svarstad had a cold and had to stay in for a few days, she made him hot soup that was full of pepper and cayenne and tasted like the fire and flames of hell.*

Svarstad felt noble when he drank it and he allowed Sigrid to pamper him.

The Thames was five minutes away. There were places to walk and boats to rent. Her husband painted the factories and workers' homes that he could see from their window, on huge canvas, in drab colors, in every detail, during the day—and in the evenings they went rowing. She had her own room with a "real writing table" and bookshelves, and he had his "with paint tubes and string and papers all over the floor . . . His writing table has every kind of mess on it—but since I am not forced to be there more than I choose, I think it is a very nice arrangement," she wrote to Nini on the 5th of October. She liked to be near him when she wasn't working and sometimes she read to him or they talked while he painted.

Middlesex was only twenty minutes from London where there was "farmland with paths through green fields with thornbushes, and blueberries and large oak trees and cows and old farms as beautiful as Christmas cards."[1] It wasn't touristy. They went there most Sundays stopping, by chance, at one or another railroad station, and ate at small inns "with gardens full of chrysanthemums and glorious hedges of lavender." It was just too bad that there was so much unfarmed land so close to the city that was full of hunger and need. It wasn't surprising that people became anarchists.[2]

Although her letters to Dea and Nini reported the same events, there was a difference in approach. To Dea, Sigrid wrote as a newlywed mother-to-be, and with Nini she discussed her problems and literary ideas.

It was a good time. They were in love, had no immediate money worries, and were only responsible to each other and their work. "I am very well, most of the time," she wrote to Dea on the 12th of October, and then I'm so happy that even if I'm a little ill some of the time, it doesn't change my mood in the least."

They planned to go to Rome before the baby was due. The weather would be better there and it was somehow fitting that their child should be born in the city where they met.

She was working on a collection of short stories to be called *Poor Fates*. "There is something holy in the fight for existence, even amongst the poorest among us,"[3] she wrote to Nini, and these stories were about "women who had in one way or another lost the respect of others because they were unmarried and lonely."[4] (Sigrid, who had been one of them until recently knew, only too well, how society robbed them of their dignity.)

Their rooms were cold and drafty and the only sources of heat were the gas fires in the fireplaces. One had to "sit in them to get the least bit warm." She was reading English literature and enjoying it immensely. Webster, Massinger and Marlow, "fabulous stuff . . . My reactions to the pathos and wildness and hot passions that took place in 16th century Italy are a bit disturbing to my work now. It is quite far from Christiania and small seamstresses and the way aging ladies in offices behave in life." "Old Webster" she admired totally and was on her knees to a literature that could call him "one of their minor poets." When it was too wet and cold to do very much else, it was wonderful to tuck her feet under her and curl up in pure excitement.

"For me, it is a miraculous thing that these flaming, burning passions are hundreds of years old and that they can hold one and grip one so totally and that there is something in life that never changes."[5]

She was reading the sisters Bröntes' poems and agreed with Nini that they were marvelous.

It was an exhilarating time. She was with the man she loved and he was a stimulating man. She was learning how varied reactions could be when creative people of different disciplines lived together. When they went to art galleries she looked for content, color and form, while Svarstad who felt that pictures should mirror familiar scenes in everyday life and that they should be painted realistically, was often critical of artists who strayed from the rigid standards that he approved of. At the National Portrait Gallery, she wrote to Nini, she was fascinated with a portrait of Shelley which Svarstad criticized as "swinery" as a painting, and when she stood too long in front of a portrait of Keats because she loved Keats' poems and didn't know of anything more gripping than the story of how Severn cared for his dying friend, Svarstad reproached her for spending so much time over it when it was obviously not a good painting. At the Tate, she had to confess to her husband that her dear Rosseti was, after all, not a very good painter either.[6]

It was great fun to watch the audiences at the local cinemas, but it was more stimulating to see great theater. Sigrid was unhappy with a production of Shakespeare's *The Winter's Tale* which was done with "Postimpressionist costumes and sets. There was nothing which could have fought the characters and language of the play more," she wrote to Nini.[7] They fought the intentions of Shakespeare's diction and the atmosphere of the Renaissance.

> Many times a character who is supposed to express rough or wild human feelings with a profound play on words has to fight ornamental pictures. These studies of the human being which are realistic to the navel were being performed against acanthus leaves. I think it is good to play Shakespeare on an empty stage with a curtain as a background, but when the curtain is a light Liberty silk with an art nouveau spring landscape, then I can almost thank God for Jens Wang.[*][8]

The Svarstads went to the second exhibition of Postimpressionists at the Grafton Galleries, where the rooms were filled with Cezannes, Matisses, Picassos, a Bonnard, and many other now famous paintings.

---

[*]   A popular painter.

In his autobiography, Leonard Woolf, who organized the exhibition with Roger Fry, wrote that large numbers of people came and

> *. . . nine out of ten of them either roared with laughter at the pictures or were enraged by them . . . Hardly any of them made the slightest attempt to look at, let alone understand the pictures and the same inane questions or remarks were repeated to me all day long. And every now and then some well-groomed, red-faced gentleman, oozing the undercut of the best beef and most succulent of chops, carrying his top hat and grey suede gloves would come up to my table and abuse the pictures and me with the greatest rudeness.*[9]

Unfortunately, the Svarstads reacted like the rest. "Even if I'm going to be hanged for it," Sigrid wrote to Nini, "to find anything more than incredible humbug in it all is quite impossible."[10] They were quite amused, she continued, to watch the visitors straining to try to see something good in the pictures.

They were living "in the deepest closeness in work and love" she wrote to Nini on November 17, but it was getting a bit lonely. Svarstad had started a large painting called *Factories on the Thames* and was "working like a maniac," and when his work didn't go well he got depressed.

The Norwegian writer, Peter Egge, was in London with his family and they met often. Sigrid was gayer and securer than he had ever seen her, he wrote, but sometimes the super-sureness she expressed seemed a bit forced.[11]

When other Norwegians came to London, they visited them too, and Sigrid described an evening with two couples from home in a letter to Nini.[12]

It was the first time I had the honor of being reckoned among the official, authorized Missuses, you know, ugh. It was a little disgusting. They talked of the 'lonely insufficiency of a marriage that was not a marriage' and asked if 'a relationship of that kind, under such circumstances, was worth having.'"[13]

Sigrid found it difficult to listen. All she could think of was "the despair and proud resignation of those women, their loneliness which was a burning hell on earth, and about the nights when they felt all the finest roots in themselves crushed in fire and drying away without being used . . .

> *I am actually never going to feel like a wife no matter how much people will 'Mrs.' me. I think I belong with the lonely, unmarried people who have no happiness or with the illegitimate Missuses. I feel that my present legitimate happiness, in spite of everything, is like stealing from*

fate—an anomaly that I have been able to make of my life thanks to
a better fate and a more robust constitution.[14]

Still identifying with the rejected ones, her compassion for those she had
left behind was great and she was writing stories about them. Later, as other
problems developed in her life, she would write about married women.

Before leaving Christiania, Sigrid had participated in a 70th Anniversary
tribute to Georg Brandes, and when she got to London one of her first
purchases was an English edition of his complete works.* He was one of her
favorite authors. He had introduced her to Shakespeare when she was fourteen,
and when she died, that edition, an American one, and many other volumes
of his work were still in her library.

In addition to the stories, she was also sending articles to the Norwegian press
and doing research on the Brontes and Sir Thomas Malory's *Morte D'Arthur*.

Sigrid's *Poor Fates* which appeared at the end of 1912, consisted of six
stories, three of which were later included in *Four Stories*.** Although they are
exceptional, *Selma Brøter* and *Simonsen* stand out from the rest.

*   *   *

Since Selma Brøter was the eldest daughter in her family, and unmarried,
it was taken for granted that she would care for her mother when their father
abandoned them. When her mother was dying she made Selma promise to care
for her youngest brother who had always been her mother's favorite. When her
brother was caught stealing, Selma had a dreadful time until a cousin offered
him a job and fare to Capetown so that he could escape prison.

When she was finally free to live her own life, her sister Beate, who
had always been the prettiest and the most fortunate one in the family, was
widowed and left penniless and pregnant. Selma, who had a good job and
lived alone, couldn't bear to see her sister suffer and invited her to stay until
the baby was born.

---

* The Danish Geog Morris Cohen Brandes (1842-1927) was a literary critic.
He wrote *Main Currents in Nineteenth Century Literature* in which he attacked
provincialism. An opponent of Romanticism, he helped direct Scandinavian
literature toward realism and a concern with social issues, and introduced
Feminism in Denmark. He wrote about Shakespeare, Goethe, Voltaire, and a
book called *Jesus, A Myth*.[15]

** English translation published in 1959 by Knopf.

Selma works in an office with a number of other unmarried women where everyone knows everyone else's business, and they spend much of their time talking about how awful men are.

Women like Selma "must be quite possessed by this thing that they are shut out of," the perky, attractive, more fortunate Beate says, "They must be, because they go on and on about it so. Nobody's ever tried any awfulness with them, and in their hearts they resent this, and they're inquisitive and they keep harping on it and sharing what scraps of knowledge they've picked up second hand."[16]

"Don't you think it would have been better," Beate says when they are discussing Selma, if Selma "had robbed the till or perhaps had a baby? Then the cousin in Capetown would have offered *her* the free passage out, a good job, and a fine new start in life."

"I wouldn't be too sure," the young engineer to whom Beate is secretly engaged says. "It's different when it's a woman who runs off the rails."[17]

Love affairs between employees are frowned upon in their office, and Beate and her engineer are eager to keep their relationship a secret until they have saved up enough to get married. When the engineer gets two free tickets to the theater for a night when Beate has to visit her aunts, she suggests that he take Selma. They have been seen together too much of late, and his going out with someone else will confuse the office staff about the seriousness of their relationship. Selma is overwhelmed by the invitation from the handsome engineer, and arrives at the office on the day of their date with a new blouse and freshly set hair. The engaged couple begin to include her when they wish to be together in public, and Selma believes that the engineer is courting her. She has hinted about it to the staff and is embarrassed when the lovers announce their forthcoming marriage. Since he never declared himself to her, she cannot even be angry, and she tries to save face by pretending that she knew about their engagement all along.

A pharmacist from Selma's hometown had been courting her, but because he was old, bald and potbellied, she had rejected him. Just when she decides to accept him, she discovers that he has found another woman. Selma resigns herself to helping her sister bring up her child—and as the years go by, she tells more and more stories about being accosted by men on the streets.

Although *Simonsen* is about "a little, short-necked" warehouseman "with a pouchy, fat face and watery eyes . . . red veined cheeks and a rather blue blob of a nose" who "shuffled and hopped"[18] when he walked down the street, it, like other stories in this collection, is also about the plight of an unmarried woman. Simonsen's shrewish wife has died and his only son lives in another town. He drinks a bit too much and always finds excuses for himself and he has "a certain amount of practice in keeping gloomy thoughts at bay. He has dithered through his whole life . . . cowered and expected dismissal and reprimand and nagging and unpleasantness as something inevitable."[19] He has been sacked from four jobs in eight years, and each time his son finds another one for him. For six years he has been a boarder in the home of a hardworking seamstress named Olga, who is bringing up her illegitimate son. When she becomes pregnant with his child, he promises to marry her, but he keeps postponing the wedding. They have a daughter whom he loves very much, and for the first time in his life he has a woman who takes care of him, doesn't nag him, and looks the other way when he strays. He is sacked from his job and his son, once again, comes to his rescue but the job he finds is in another town. Simonsen tells him that he doesn't want it because he intends to marry Olga, with whom he has a child. His son is afraid that sooner or later he will have to support them all and he is determined to separate them. He visit's Olga, pays her debts, and promises to send her a little money once in a while for the child. He is not mean, just practical, and because he feels sorry for his father, he gives him some money for a nice Christmas. Olga pleads with Simonsen to marry her and stay, but he is too weak to defy his son. She cries and is bitter because he is leaving her in disgrace and "will start all over again in the country with his sozzling and girls."[20] He is torn but doesn't know what to do. He buys his daughter a sled and a fabulous doll and brings Olga material for a blouse, a brooch, and some eau de cologne, but he hasn't the strength to oppose his son. Olga takes him to the station. They have nothing but small talk to say to each other, and can only keep looking at the clock. He hates to leave it all—the warmth and his child who would have no one to take her tobogganing

"For a moment the wrongness of it struck a spark inside him and smarted and burned through all that life had left of Simonsen's heart."[21] He thinks of his little daughter and whimpers.

"He wiped his eyes. There must be One Above who decided these things. That must be his consolation: that there was One who decided . . ."[22] And that is how the story ends.

*   *   *

Undset's characters are neither good nor bad. They are human. Her stories are not maudlin. They have neither sad nor happy endings. Dickens painted life as he saw it, and his perception was his genius, but his novels were serialized in periodicals before they appeared as books, and he had to please his readers with happy endings which were often too sentimental and not true to life.

Sigrid described the conflicts and contradictions of her characters with as much compassion, and her knowledge of human behavior was as profound, but since she didn't' have to cater to her readers, her characters are not required to suffer retribution or enjoy rewards. The book was an immediate success and went into a second and third printing.

Sigrid had to prepare for the arrival of her baby and she was eager to get to Rome. She would have to find a midwife and arrange for a nurse after they arrived, and she knew no one there who could help her.

"When we get to Italy I shall start to prepare food and have a house and then you might send me cookbooks as you promised," she wrote to Dea.[23] Now, she was making baby clothes and she needed some advice. She had gone for a check-up to a wonderful old doctor, who she was told, was a specialist. The doctor's office was filled with exquisite Indian and Oriental rugs and artifacts, and when Sigrid asked her how she had acquired such beautiful things, the doctor explained that she had lived in India for several years where her specialty had been the Bubonic plague.

Although it wasn't about the plague that she had consulted her, Sigrid added wryly, the doctor had answered all of her questions satisfactorily, and was even able to give her wonderful patterns for very practical baby clothes. She insisted, however, that they *had* to be made of woolens—only woolens. Sigrid could understand that woolens were necessary in London where the houses were never warm enough, but they planned to be in Italy when the baby was born, and she was afraid that wool would be torture in the hot climate. What did Dea advise?

Time passed. She didn't want to have the baby on the train, but Svarstad wouldn't leave London until he had completed the pictures he had started. Although she had decided to do no more writing until after the baby was born, she wrote one more article while she waited. In 1904, Sigrid had written an impassioned letter to *Aftenposten* about an anonymous book called *Woman Created by Man*, and it was the first time she had seen her name in print. Now, after finding "a small, gold-covered book by an anonymous author"* at a magazine stand in a London subway station, called *The Truth About Man by a Spinster*, she decided to review it for *Samtiden* together with *The Man-Made World; or, Our Androcentric Culture*, by Charlotte Perkins Gilman, which had just appeared in London.**

---

*   Borghild Krane, in her biography *Sigrid Undset* says the author was Hulda Garborg.[24]

**   Included in *A Woman's Point of View*.

The little golden book described the love experiences of a sixty-two spinsters and the author concluded, and Sigrid agreed, that the more lovers a person had, the unhappier their experiences became. Just maintaining a friendship with the same or the opposite sex took up so much time that one hadn't room for many relationships, and people who were selective in their tastes did not go to places that had too much traffic.[25]

As for the American Charlotte Perkins Gilman's *The Man-Made World*, Sigrid had the "deepest veneration" and the "greatest respect and thankfulness for those who fought for women's rights at home and abroad, whatever nonsense they at times have said . . . Women's positions inside the law are such that violence and crazy behavior is understandable and as excusable as such things can be."[26]

Since working women had not yet joined the movement in large numbers, and it was composed of middle-class and wealthy women, it was understandable that "some misunderstandings of the real problems would occur . . ."[27]

> *Some women have risen against the thousand years of tyranny of the men who pressed them down and held them as slaves for their desires, in the way that they pressed down all who were weaker than themselves and made slaves of them, and they rose against these tyrants not only for themselves but also to protect the weak and helpless children . . . but, to deduce from this as Mrs. Gilman did, that 'women's instincts as a whole are to protect everything weak and helpless' is an exaggeration.*[28]

Charlotte Gilman, like many others, wrote of a Golden Age of Matriarchy, but Sigrid had never found any proof that such a time had existed.

> *Early humans were supposed to have lived in treetops, and if they did, it must have been after they came down that defending the family from animals and hunting for food fell to him, and concern for the children and work that could be done near the place where they lived, fell to her—which may have been the arrangement that was necessary for survival. But when Mrs. Gilman philosophizes that there was a greater tendency to strife in a man, and refers to a whole group of beautiful social and intellectual faculties as being characteristics of females, which she calls Motherliness—'an instinctive devotion to children and creativity'—one has to ask whether these beautiful characteristics are really theirs.*[29]

Motherliness, in the wider sense—concern for the weak and helpless, for neglected children, for the old and sick—when it was done by women, was not necessarily done by mothers, but often by childless women, and the sacrificing love which follows motherhood, the without-end willingness to serve, has unfortunately, as a rule, been concentrated upon one's own children . . .

Mrs. Gilman spoke of motherhood as if it was in a blue abstraction high above all rooftops. Had she never really come across the mothers whose sensitivity, sacrifice, willingness to serve justice, and understanding of children was limited to their own sweet children and could not be stretched to understand the terrible children on the second floor, or the porter's children who had lice, or those who came on errands? [30]

"A nice and loving mother," once told her, Sigrid continued,

. . . that her sister-in-law had heard during the night that her children's nurse had aborted her child. She took the sinner to task for this and when the girl tried to explain, the Madame demanded that she get up immediately and pack her clothes and leave her respectable house at once. It might be that any mother with a sense of responsibility might try to get her out of the house as soon as possible, but I think she deserved a horsewhipping . . . [31]

There are good women and bad women and I have never noticed that a woman's physical fertility is in any way responsible for her human values . . . [32]

There are women who give more time and devotion to the supervision of their food larders and damask tablecloths than they do to their beloved little children.[33]*

When marriage and motherhood is the only respectable profession for a woman, she has to make sure that she will be taken care of before she gets too old, and if she cannot find someone she wants she has to take the one she can get—and can no longer hope for happiness and love. The most lonely single woman who works has at least got time to wait for true love and a kind of life which these hopeless women who made do with conceiving children in a haphazard, careless or distasteful love embrace, can never imagine . . . [34]

---

* Charlotte Perkins Gilman caused a furor in America when she gave her own daughter to others to bring up.

She disagreed with the other points raised by Gilman and finished by saying that some women would like to roll up their sleeves and dive in and "clean it all up, but they should know that, like housework, changing social conditions is an endless job."[35]

"Women fought and won the right to vote, and they ought to remember that 'that right is a duty.'"[36]

* * *

Finally, with little more than a month to go, Svarstad was ready to leave London. They stopped in Paris and Milan on the way, saw a Bellini pieta, which she would never forget, in Florence, and arrived in Rome on December 18th.

Her letters to Dea were usually cheerful—she saved her worries for Nini—but now even the ones to Dea were distraught. They were in an awful hotel. They hadn't reserved in advance and would have no place to sleep on Christmas Eve. They had dreamed of returning to their old rooms on Via Frattina but they were occupied. Fortunately, the landlady was sentimental about having them back and promised to do her best. Taking credit for their marriage, (she said they were the third couple to marry after living in those rooms, and that last year a fourth couple became engaged immediately after leaving them), she freed the rooms for them, but after three years they seemed to have lost some of their charm.

They remembered Rome as sunny and warm, but they awoke the first morning to find that snow had seeped in through the terrace door. When they were lovers, being on the top floor and having a private entrance had been a great convenience, but six flights were difficult for her now, the private entrance was no longer important, and the tiny rooms which had been paradise when all they wanted was to be together, were too cramped and cold for their present needs. On the other hand, having their own petroleum stove and water came in hand, and the landlady had promised to do their laundry and get someone to help with the baby. If the weather improved before it arrived, she would be able to put it on the terrace where it could lie in the sun all day. The view of Rome and the hills beyond was as beautiful as ever. Roses were blooming and the sunsets were still spectacular. They walked in the Borghese Gardens which hadn't lost their charm and went to Pincio to have lunch at the dairy in the middle of the meadow. She was getting too heavy to climb so high and they wouldn't try it again, but they could stroll through the narrow, winding streets and could still look for the brown eagle's nest on the top of the mountain.

"When we were last here, it had seemed impossible that we should ever have children," she wrote to Nini in December. "I am incredibly happy but our carefree time when there were just the two of us is over forever and we will never be able to call it back."[37] They had enjoyed London but she "had gotten pretty sick of mutton, mutton, mutton every day and heavy pies and puddings," she wrote to Dea.[38] It was a relief to eat salads, small fried octopi, artichokes and omelets again. "I've had few problems connected with child bearing but I will be glad when it is over . . . God knows what my mother will think. The child will have come a little fast. Well, she didn't like Anders to start with, nor the little dresser I bought, nor *Jenny*, and now everything is priceless and wonderful."[39]

Her book was doing well, but there would be none the following year. It was hard to speak to her husband about her problems. He had, after all, already had three children "who had not been received with great pleasure."[40] They would be half-brother and sisters of her child when it arrived and God only knew how it would all work out.

Svarstad was hardly overjoyed at having another child. He had rarely been home with his first set of children. When they had first planned to marry, he had visualized a peaceful life abroad with a successful writer whose stipends and royalties, combined with his, would free him from financial worries. He had not anticipated a new set of children and new responsibilities.

On the morning of the 24th of January, 1913, Sigrid gave birth to a son whom they named Anders Castus. In Italian the closest name to Anders is Andrea and Sigrid wrote to Dea that since he was registered that way, he was also named after her. She had a difficult time and spent two weeks at the home of the Italian-German midwife who supervised the birth. The woman took care of her well enough, but some of her notions, though amusing, were not reassuring.

When the baby was born, the midwife told her that he weighed five kilos (over eleven pounds) which seemed a lot for so small a child. Then she discovered that the woman had only a three kilo weight and had added an iron, an alarm clock and a water glass to the scale in order to arrive at her estimate. She had weighed him "like merchandise at a fifty øre bazaar," Sigrid joked, but when she was told that he had gained the whole weight of an iron during his first fifteen days, it was no longer funny and she bought as scale.

The girl that had been hired to help with the baby didn't' show up, the landlady decided that she couldn't do their laundry, and Sigrid ended up doing everything herself. Their rooms had three outside walls and the baby's clothes, which she washed by hand, didn't dry. The main kitchen was the only place where they would, (and where she could get hot water) but that was six flights down. It was too cold to keep him on the terrace, and their rooms were so small that Anders had no place to work.

"Such a little fellow uses six shirts, twelve diapers and various other pieces of clothing in twenty-four hours," she wrote to Nini on February 19, "I worry more about the clothes than anything, but he is beautiful and strong and the doctor says he is doing fine."

Unfortunately, he was not doing fine. He was not gaining weight. She consulted two doctors who told her that her milk was too thin, and that she ought to hire a wet nurse, but she wouldn't consider it. She had no experienced friend or relative to advise her. She bought Danish and English books on child care and cooking, and consulted a book by a Norwegian doctor which had arrived from home, yet nothing she did helped the baby gain and she began to panic. She had never learned to cook or keep house. She could prepare pork chops, beef, ham and eggs, macaroni and artichokes, and was "moved to tears when she came up with anything she could be praised for," but throughout that time, trying as it all was, she kept a little notebook in which, between chores, she jotted down her experiences and ideas for future books.

She was sure that when the weather improved her life would be easier, but when the cold spell was over it got so beastly hot that the baby grew worse. She wrote to Nils Collett Vogt that she was as unhappy as a person could be, but wouldn't change her lot with anyone in the world. In the end her anxiety produced a fever and her milk dried up. She wrote to the Norwegian author of the child care book and he advised her to bring the baby home—at once.

"We have become superstitious," she wrote to Nini. "on Easter Saturday the priests go around and bless the houses with holy water. We were very happy that they blessed us here and would both have liked if our little boy had been in the house when they came, but he was on the terrace."[41]

Svarstad helped her when he could, but the baby's illness was creating exactly the kind of domestic chaos that he had run away from, and although children are conceived by fathers as well as mothers, they were considered a woman's problem and Sigrid felt responsible for subjecting him to it again. The baby continued to lose weight and she became frantic. She begged to take him home, but her husband said he had planned to be away for a year, had set work projects for himself for that length of time, and was already far behind. Since they had no place to live in Christiania and would have to stay with her mother and sisters, he would not be able to work there either. He felt that she should take the baby home and he would join them later. She couldn't imagine being parted from him, and traveling alone in that unbearable heat with such a sick child seemed unthinkable, but when she met a Danish nurse who was going north, she decided to join her. Scared out of her wits, she took her nearly dead child, who was down to half the weight he was born with and "looked like a little skeleton covered with wrinkled skin," across Europe, in third-class compartments and saved his life.

When they got to Christiania, the doctor found that the baby had developed normally despite the weight loss. His eyes were bright and clear, he held his head firmly, and he was responding to people, colors and sounds, and under the doctor's supervision, he began to grow. Each day, while he got fresh air and sunlight, Sigrid sat by his side and made clothes for him. She was pale and had dark rings around her eyes—and she was gaining weight from the diet she had been put on to improve her milk, but her baby was thriving.

Three months later, after she had found a place to live, painted it, collected their belongings and created a cozy home, Svarstad returned.

CHAPTER VI

SKI

1913-1916

Because it was all they could afford, their first home was a summer cottage in Ski, a small town not far from Christiania. It had an enclosed veranda, timbered walls and ceilings, and was surrounded by a lovely wooded area where one could go for walks and pick wild flowers, but there was no way to heat it and water had to be carried from a well. It was twenty minutes from the station and an hour's train ride from the city, and food, mail, and newspapers had to be brought from the nearby town, but their son was developing normally, and their reunion was such a passionate one that the inconveniences didn't matter. They had a blissful summer. But life with Svarstad was not ever to be peaceful for long. He had brought a number of large paintings from Rome and was preparing for an exhibition and "since he couldn't find a single studio in the entire valley near us," Sigrid explained to Dea,[1] he rented one in town in September, and came home only on weekends. It was hard to live apart again—she missed him too painfully—but it was a temporary arrangement and she had to make the best of it. Unable to concentrate on her work, she tried to keep busy by canning rhubarb and studying cookbooks. Friends said she was wasting a valuable talent. Svarstad wasn't worth it. She said her marriage was more important to her than anything else.

As a member of the Scholarship Fund Committee of the Norwegian Authors Association she had many things to do in the city, so she hired a capable woman to care for the baby and stayed in town with her husband one night a week. The child was well cared for, but the woman couldn't do much else and most of the chores fell to Sigrid.

"I became quite a good housewife after I had two maids who didn't know much more than their madam and were unable to care for the baby properly," she wrote to Dea.[2]

> *One thing has gotten better than either Svarstad or I had dared to expect—my relationship with his children. The girls ten and eight are clever, beautiful and sweet, especially Ebba, the oldest, for whom I care a great deal—more than I thought possible for me to feel for a strange child. She is so much like her father and so warm and motherly with her little half-brother, and they like me a lot too. They are here continuously when they are not in school—even when their father is not.*

When Svarstad left Norway he had made no arrangements for the support of his family and Ragna had been forced to put the girls in a school for poor and orphaned children. Privately endowed, Eugenia Steftelse's school was better than a state-run orphanage, but the girls were so miserable there that when Sigrid got back from Rome, she arranged for them to be boarded with a family near their school. They weren't happy with that arrangement either and she tried to have them with her as much as possible. Trond, who was a difficult child—high strung, awkward and slow—lived with his mother but she sent him to Sigrid for weeks at a time.

Sigrid had waited so long to have a home of her own that she threw herself into homemaking with all of her creative energy. Every piece she bought including the pottery and china, was selected with care and she preferred to do without rather than get something that she didn't' consider exceptional. She disliked luxury and ostentation and preferred straight-backed wooden chairs to overstuffed furniture. "From the time of her first home in Ski," Nini wrote,

> *. . . everything she gathered has fallen into a harmonic whole that makes her home one of Norway's most characteristic and beautiful interiors. When she sat in her living room of timbered walls at the white tablecloth covered table and served us food and drink, with her straight back, her thick, shining braid wound around her head, and her quiet movements, there was over her a sense of peace and worthiness which reminded one of former great housewives, but I was clearly not aware of it when I later met her in the city on the way to the railroad station completely loaded down with packages of all sizes and types in both hands—not unlike a horse with too large a pack.*

'There were a few other things I should have taken with me,' she said, 'but I can't carry any more' [3]

There was no book in 1913 but she continued to write for the newspapers and she participated in a 25th Anniversary celebration in honor of her publisher, William Nygaard, of Aschehoug. Svarstad had a very successful exhibition and received several excellent reviews.

For Christmas she had a full house. Her mother and sisters, and all of Svarstad's children were there. The girls arrived early and remained for several weeks into the new year and she involved them in all the preparations. Christmas was the one time of the year when the Undsets had not had to scrimp, and Sigrid's image of happiness was a house full of holiday fare and a large family around the fireplace. She cooked, and baked and prepared presents and decorations for weeks in advance, and every traditional food and delicacy was served. After dinner, she told the children stories and sewed doll clothes with them. She and her sisters had made a puppet theater out of matchboxes when she was a child and she made one for her stepchildren with elaborate costumes and sets.

Svarstad kept his studio in town and still came home only on weekends, and when he came, he usually arrived late. She was always more animated when he was there, but by the time they had finished dinner she was often falling off her feet with fatigue. She cooked, cleaned and sewed for all of them and neither her husband nor his children were easy to please. The children were untaught and neglected. When they arrived, their hair needed washing and their clothes needed mending. Deprived of love and guidance, they had no awareness of the needs of others and it was hard to get them to get up at a reasonable hour or to eat when everyone else was eating. The girls were small-boned, graceful and attractive. They had pretty faces and nice figures, but they had poor manners and were hard to teach. Having never had anything of value themselves, they had little respect for their stepmother's treasures, but they loved to come to "Sigrid's house" and she knew it.

Starved for attention, each reacted to her differently. Ebba endeared herself by helping, and since there was always much to do she was often overworked, while Gunhild, who was younger, was more cautious and less cooperative. Grownups let you down. If you showed that you were vulnerable, sooner or later, there would be a bitter price to pay, and she was not about to let herself get used. They didn't' have an easy time of it by any means. Sigrid did a great deal for them, but although she was kind, she was a strict stepmother.

In May, Svarstad announced that he had gotten another travel stipend and was going to Paris for three months. They had been together for less than a year and the family was just beginning to adjust to a way of life. Sigrid couldn't believe that he would consider another separation but he accepted the stipend and left.

She missed him so much that she left the baby with her mother and joined him. The visit was "not successful" and she returned sooner than planned. Her letter to Dea tried to make light of it. She had longed for her husband but had hated being parted from her child. "I guess I shall always have to miss one or the other. Never did I think that it was so hard to be married." She was afraid that the baby wouldn't remember her when she got back, "but he ran towards me and called me 'Mama.' He paid little attention to me the first day, but now, since his father is back, if he or mother pets me, he gets quite furious and threatens them with his little fists and says, 'my mama, my mama.'"[4]

Sigrid's stature as a human being was such that despite the load she was carrying, she could not stop being a concerned citizen, and she voiced her opinions often. Since there was no radio or television, issues of public interest were aired in the press, and she participated in a number of newspaper debates. Her thinking was original. She could pinpoint the most humane and ethical aspects of an issue regardless of the views of the establishment or its opposition, and she developed a large following of newspaper readers. She was particularly popular with young people and, in March, she was invited to speak at the annual meeting of the National Students' Association in Trondheim.

The first woman to be so honored, she chose her topic with care. Calling it *The Fourth Commandment: Honor thy father and thy mother that they days may be long upon the land which the Lord thy God giveth thee*, she said that if parents wanted the respect of their children, they had to live in a way that their children could respect. Referring to Scott's expedition to the South Pole,˙ she said that she felt humbled and grateful for the amazing donation to humanity that explorers made when they risked their lives in frozen wastelands in search of information that could benefit mankind. Civilization began when primitive people realized that at times the needs of the tribe could be more important than those of the individual. Breeding was not culture. Culture was an inheritance from the human family—from every anonymous individual who has felt himself driven to do the most he can do.

˙ Robert Falcon Scott and four companions reached the South Pole on January 12, 1912, and discovered that Roald Amundsen had gotten there one month before them. All five died on their way home, but their diaries, which were found later, were extremely helpful to future explorers.

Although she touched on many subjects of interest to young people—women's rights, sex education in schools, and the Church's over-emphasis on "thou shalt not"—she was actually addressing their parents.

"Morality," she said, "is a human concept."

> Nature is amoral and so are all human drives. It is when the conscience takes a point of view in regard to natural forces that morality is created. Virtue and vice are natural products just like vitriol and sugar, and all moral and immoral instincts are equally natural. It is after we see the results of putting sugar or vitriol into our coffee that we prefer sugar . . . A person's natural instinct for self-preservation teaches him which of his drives is good and which is evil. The collective experience decides which is bad for our welfare and creates the concept of evil and good, and in the same way, man decides what is normal and abnormal . . . [5]
>
> The manner in which a person reacts to his sexual drive is decided from childhood . . . The boy who has never felt love and confidence from anyone . . . can never give love . . . A girl who had never felt happiness as a bodily sensation never becomes a mistress, whether she comes to belong to one man or to many. She will never become aware that her body is different from the black wooden figures in the stores . . . a place to put clothes on . . . [6]
>
> The awareness that humanity's views are steadily widening gives the new generation courage to change things. The recognition that cultured people will not be unrighteous to other's children because they want to give special rights to their own; to other fatherlands because they want to give special rights to their own land—that is culture. Every home which is made desolate, every country which is taken over, is a workshop of culture made desolate.[7]*

She received an ovation and returned home from Trondheim in high spirits—but at home nothing had changed. Svarstad's ex-wife was finding it hard to care for Trond and he was bringing his son to Sigrid more frequently—and for longer periods each time. Since they were short of funds, she pushed to get a book into print.

She could only work when the family slept and when it was finished she was close to a breakdown. The doctor insisted that she go to a health farm for a rest, but Svarstad said that he couldn't' manage at home without her,

---

* Included in *A Woman's Point of View*. Not available in English.

and if she went away he would go to the mountains to paint. Unable to go on, she left her son with her mother again and went to a health farm—as for Svarstad, he went to the mountains to paint.

Her novel, *Vaaren*, was published at the end of 1914.˙ Working all day at being a model wife and mother, and writing all night when she was "tired to the bone," was not conducive to developing a good storyline, and the book is out of focus, but it has the best portrayal of one of her gay, little, flirtatious women (called Betzy this time), some of her most spectacular descriptions of nature and some daring discussions of sex.

Climate, scents and topography always affected Sigrid deeply, and in *The Spring*, she used them to strengthen the psychological impact of some scenes in masterful ways.

The book was well received despite its flaws and once it was out of the way, and she had gotten some rest at the health farm, she was in fine spirits for Christmas. They had the usual feasts and everyone was there again. Svarstad made fewer trips to the city after the holidays and it was a peaceful time for all. The children stayed through January and the girls were so cooperative that Sigrid began to talk of finding a larger house where they could all live together.

In March, she discovered that she was pregnant again.

On January 16, 1915, an article by Knut Hamsun, called *The Child!* appeared in *Morgenblatte* which infuriated Sigrid and created an outcry throughout Norway. Hamsun wrote that he had read in the papers that a young woman had received a sentence of eight months in jail for killing her newborn child.

"It didn't say eighteen years, or eight years, just eight months . . . Norway could certainly do without such mothers," he wrote . . .

> *HANG THEM . . . Life would be richer for losing them . . . It didn't mention whether it was a boy or a girl, but the child could still have measured up to something (sic) . . . The mother is hopeless.*
>
> *We put up palaces for the blind, for the handicapped, for the aged. Children's homes are no palaces. Small children have to beg from day to day for clothes and food, and when a girl kills her child she gets eight months and is then returned to us . . .*

He complained against society's "contrary constructions." There were those who were actually fighting for illegitimate children's inheritance rights and government supported help for mothers. Fathers were being chastised for spanking

---

˙   Not available in English.

their own children, while mothers who were killing their children were receiving only eight months in jail as punishment for their crimes. *HANG THEM!*
Then he waxed poetic:

> *A small child is so beautiful to have. It plays with its little hands and sometimes it looks up. It wonders so strangely when the murderer stands over it and begins her grip . . . Are they so unprotected those mothers? Isn't it possible to find the child's irresponsible father? Hang both parents. Get rid of them because they are hopeless. The first hundred would teach respect so that the terrible sentences would be bettered.*

Letters of protest poured in. Very young farm girls often became pregnant because their employers housed them in the same rooms with the male hired help, or because they were raped when they were alone at remote *saeters* while tending their employer's herds. Most of the child murders reported in the press were committed by girls who worked as servants. The fathers of the murdered children were usually the employers or the sons of their employers, who took advantage of them because they knew that the girls could not protest or complain to the woman of the house, who would dismiss them immediately. Mr. Hamsun knew very well that the fathers of such children would not come forward and had no intention of accepting responsibilities. Murder was terrible and could not be condoned, but what were such girls to do when no one would help them? People had to show some compassion. A man got off with no punishment when he got a girl pregnant. The murders usually took place immediately after birth. Mr. Hamsun knew that birth control and abortions were illegal, and that an unmarried woman who had a child would lose her job and be ostracized by the community.
On February 10th, Hamsun answered his critics, in *Morgenblatte*.

> *A woman who wrote in made the mistake of giving me all honor because I want to protect every life for society. Ah, but that I don't want at all. I would, on the contrary exterminate, purify away, those lives which are hopeless to the advantage of those which will be valuable . . . Society soothes its soul with plans for improvements as our salvation . . . They want to sacrifice everything on earth for those who are unhappy . . . Those mothers who had the unhappiness to get up to eight months for killing their children—HANG THEM.*
> *There are old people, people who are born idiots, born blind, born crippled . . . and ordinary people in the country open their hearts to*

them. The old people have been people. It is over for them. The others have never been people and never will be . . . I dare not say a thing. I will hurt the hearts of the public . . . I stand without fear, but I'll accept buying large country estates for the old people and let them shake in the fresh air with their palsies . . . but the children . . . boys and girls of the new Norway—our greatest possibilities, our Spring . . . their murderers get eight months.

Sigrid answered him in an article in *Morgenblatte* on February 18.

We must try to imagine what it means for a woman to carry a child and try to hide it . . . how a woman feels when the child she carries will not give her a moment's peace—not even five minutes during the day—and keeps her awake during the night. She cannot easily think that small children are beautiful, that we smile when they come into another room, because she has neither the two rooms, nor one room in which to have the child. She cannot comfort herself that it is, after all, a happiness to care for her child, because if she is to provide a home and food for that child, then she can't possibly look after it herself. She must give it away. So, that is one of the things she has to think of during the day and night. Just that. How on earth will she manage to earn enough money to pay for this child? She can't make it. Welfare is not available to her. No one takes up strange children for free because children are so beautiful to look at, and perhaps she has also to think about the fact that it is the child of a man whom she hates—justly and roughly and thoroughly—she hates him.

And while she goes about her work, and she has to continue her work, usually rough and heavy work in strange houses . . . she has not many moments when she can sit down and be happy with sewing and knitting for the child.

Then she bears the child in secret in a maid's room or in a closet where she lodges, or in the barn, or in a hayloft or somewhere outside. She lies alone. It feels as if her bones are slowly being broken from minute to minute that she can't live one more second—so brutally is she in pain—and there is no one who can give her even a drink of water.

Then she bears a child—a horrible rough lump of meat. A newborn child is nothing more than that except to the one who has loved it before it came into the world—or for those who are cultivated to see its possibilities, the great hope of spring. She who has never seen any possibilities for her child, not even welfare, never has had hope for it except that it should be hidden. She kills it. It is natural. It is inhuman. She who does it, is, after all, not a human being . . .

We may never know what abilities she may have had as a mother. If there had been someone with her to pick up the child, to wash it and put it down by her breast, perhaps she would have been a bad mother, perhaps a good one . . .

As long as women have to bear children in secret there will be those who will kill them, whether they decide to do so in advance or not, whatever the law and society's order and moral complexion will be . . . That which motivates them to hide their pregnancies is responsible for the later murders . . .

(History plays strange tricks. During World War II, Knut Hamsun was an ardent supporter of Hitler. He must have used up all of his compassion for little children by then because he never spoke out against the mass murders of children in the gas chambers. The torture of children in concentration cams didn't upset him either. When the war was over, he was tried and found guilty of treason. By law, he should have been sentenced to death, but he pleaded for mercy because of his advanced age and was sent to a psychiatric hospital. In time he succeeded in getting himself transferred to one of those old-age homes he had wanted to exterminate in 1915, and there he lived until he died at the age of 93, most likely "shaking with palsy in the fresh air," like the elderly people whom he had once considered superfluous.)*

Sigrid's second child was due in October and by midsummer she could hardly drag herself around. Anders had become very dependent and she was trying to finish her version of Malory's *Morte D'Arthur* before the baby arrived. She left him with her mother again and was able to submit the manuscript two weeks later, but when she picked him up, she wrote to Nini, he wouldn't let her out of his sight, calling "Sigri, Sigri" all day long. He held her legs while she worked in the kitchen and insisted on sitting in her lap when she sewed. "He is continually declaring that he will NOT go away but will always be with his Sigri—always."[8]

In 1914 war broke out in Europe.** Sigrid had befriended her doctor's wife who had four children, with whom, she wrote to Nini, she would rather talk

---

* Still a subject for debate today, people like Hamsun burn abortion clinics and threaten or murder abortionists, but do nothing about feeding undernourished and homeless children or helping their mothers to rear them.

** Norway was neutral.

about household problems and practical children's clothes than with many of her friends who had no knowledge about art but liked to talk about it anyway. They had been eating beaten eggs with sugar while watching a 17th of May parade from a balcony, and as the children marched by singing their national anthem and carrying their flags, she and her friend clutched their babies and wondered how it was possible that one day they might have to send them out to be killed.[9]

She was glad that *King Arthur* was out of the way and hoped it would look "like a colorful picture book for grownups," but she was so tired that her nerves "felt like rotten sewing threads." Several books that season had touched on religious matters and she thanked God that she had grown up "as a complete heathen. Mama complained occasionally that she hadn't managed to educate us in religion and actually there is nothing I'm more grateful to her for than the sound unchristian air in our home."[10] She breathed more freely when Regine Normann, in her latest book, let the sun in and the small poor rooms were filled with happiness—and religion, for a moment, wasn't there.[11]

The house in Ski was impossible during the winter but she hadn't been able to find anything better that they could afford before October 29, 1915, when she gave birth to a girl. Friends advised her to go to a hospital but she said she had heard of cases where the babies were exchanged, especially if they were born at night, and she didn't want to take a chance. She had a difficult delivery, but tired and sick as she was she forced herself to her feet to prepare for Christmas. Barely able to move, she seemed to exist "only for looking after difficult stoves, crying over frozen plants, and baking cakes with blue and frozen fingers.[12] There were days when she was so tired that she dreamed of how good it would be to be old, have grown children, and not have to care about art or the condition of the realm—when she could look after flowers and sit in an armchair and crochet vests for a new generation of children that she had no direct responsibility for—but when all the guests had arrived she was out of the doldrums and everyone had a wonderful time, as usual.

The baby, whom they named Maren Charlotte and called "Mosse" and "Tulla," was small and beautiful, with large blue eyes, golden blond hair and long, slender hands and feet like Sigrid's. "The boys," she wrote to Nini, "had their father's hands." She had once hoped that she would never have a daughter because a woman's fate was so difficult, and she pitied little Mosse because "naturally she will give me more sorrows and fears than ten boys."[13]

After the first of the year she began to look for a larger house where she could have all the children and where Svarstad would have a studio and space for storing his paintings. It would have to be in Christiania so that he could come home nights. That would, no doubt, be expensive, but not much more than maintaining a separate studio, transportation to the city, board for the girls, and support for Trond. Ragna was pressing Svarstad to take him and Sigrid felt it was the right thing to do.

Everyone tried to talk her out of it. Five children would be too much for her, especially since Trond was so difficult, but she wouldn't listen.

Svarstad's history was known to all who were close to them. She would be taking on his and his former wife's responsibilities at the expense of her own children and her work—and her work was too important to be set aside so that they could be freer than ever to do as they liked—but Sigrid, with her sense of duty, felt that the children had to be cared for, and she knew better than her advisors that something had to be done to bring her husband home more often. Svarstad was loving when he was there and she had to find a way for him to be there all the time.

She could be sarcastic about women "who thought of nothing but men, men, men." She wouldn't dance if she couldn't do it superbly, and was arrogant when she felt vulnerable. It was safer to be stiff, unbending and withdrawn than to risk rejection—but she was a passionate woman and she loved Svarstad too much to risk losing him.

Many of Sigrid's female characters longed to be reached in their innermost beings sexually, but she was beginning to understand that their failure to do so was not entirely due to a lack of understanding on the part of their lovers. Some of their problem was the inhibitions created by the ways the girls were brought up. Sigrid was too self-conscious to make love with total abandon. For that, she needed more time with her husband when they were relaxed—not late, hasty lovemaking when she was tired and he had been in another world all day. If she created a home for him and the children where they could be together as a family, they would have more time together and they would reach each on a deeper level. If she wanted their marriage to last, she knew that something had to be done. He couldn't stay in town for days at a time without other relationships developing. Later, in *Kristin Lavransdatter*, she would write how hard it was for a woman to set aside the needs of a household and children when her husband was in the mood for love. If a baby was crawling near a hot stove, or waiting to be fed, or about to fall out of its cradle, it was difficult to shut it all out and make love. A man resented setting aside his work for the demands of his family, but when he was ready to relax, he expected his spouse to be as ready and eager as he was. When a wife was too busy, or the children were sick too often, it was easier for him to go to a mistress who was lonely and available than to wait for his wife to be free. She didn't believe that Svarstad had mistresses but she felt that he would, eventually, if she didn't do something to draw him closer.

She was right about their needing more quiet time together, but having lost her father when she was eleven and having been brought up by one grandfather who lived without a mate for all the years that she knew him, and another who was a religious bigot, she had never witnessed love in a marriage. Her female characters are always wildly passionate, but they either manage to "rise above it" or atone for their wantonness by turning to God. She was taught to believe that a happy marriage depended on a houseful of well-fed children gathered around a protected hearth, but the last thing Svarstad wanted was a bourgeois household filled with children. She didn't have to be flirtatious and shallow to hold his interest, but a more active sex life and no children would have been more to his liking. He couldn't have had that with anyone except a sterile woman—but it was, nevertheless, what he would have preferred. His work meant more to him than anything else and the demands of a large family were only distractions.

CHAPTER VII

SINSEN

1916-1918

In the spring of 1916, Sigrid found the apartment she had been looking for. It was in Sinsen on the outskirts of Christiania and not far from Lyder Sagens Street where she had spent such happy years as a little girl. The wonderful Winter-Hjelm family didn't live there anymore, but the area reminded her of the only carefree time in her life. There were open spaces and woods for the children to play—and the apartment, which was on the second floor of a large wooden building, was sunny and cheerful and large enough to provide for the needs of the whole family. There were enough bedrooms for all, Sigrid could see her publisher and attend meetings of the writers' association without having to give up a day to do so—and most important, her husband could work at home and be there every night.

It was an active household. Five children, two of whom were babies, were not easy to manage, but she was fortunate in finding an excellent housekeeper. Asta Westbye was young and intelligent and able to free Sigrid from many chores and she applied herself to the new arrangement with vigor.

Trond, who was eight by then, was still high-strung, clumsy and slow. He couldn't keep up with his class and Sigrid tutored him at home. The girls, who were eleven and twelve, were still disorganized and undisciplined. Their clothes, the little they had, required constant mending and they needed many new things. Their hair had become infested with lice, and their table manners had not improved much.

Sigrid would get up at seven, get her stepchildren ready for school, and serve them breakfast. Then she would feed the younger children, turn them over to Asta, and go to her workroom to write. In the afternoons, she helped the older ones with their homework and spent some time with Anders, who was "developing a wonderfully active and inquiring mind." There was laundry (which had to be washed by hand, of course) and until she was able to afford a seamstress, all of the sewing—everything had to be trimmed with embroidery or lace. She did most of the cooking and guests came frequently. She was working harder than ever, but the children were enjoying the new arrangement so much that nothing seemed too difficult.

The girls were adjusting and beginning to help, and it would have all worked out well except for a creeping anxiety that had slowly begun to permeate the household. Mosse was an exquisite looking baby and easy to care for, but something about her lethargy was worrisome. Always beautifully dressed with her blond hair attractively combed she crawled about the house like a little yellow chick, but her coordination was poor and she seemed much slower to learn than Anders had been at her age. They couldn't point to anything specific, but she wasn't responding like other children. Perhaps they were spoiling her by doing too much for her so that she had no incentive to try on her own, or maybe girls developed more slowly than boys, but concern over her was building.

Sigrid was working on a long newspaper piece about the Bröntes and "in between my attempts to define the essence of genius, I have to feed little sister,[1]" she wrote to Nini. She worked on it, as usual, when everyone else had gone to bed, and in the mornings, when the children were in school she read manuscripts of aspiring authors, kept up with current literature, and continued her never-completely-abandoned research of the Middle Ages.

On April 24, 1916, her youngest sister, Signe, married Sigge Wilhelm Pantzerhielm Thomas, a classical philologist, who was an intelligent, warm, family-oriented man and little Anders' godfather. Sigrid's mother had been living with Signe and she continued to do so for the rest of her life. A year later, on March 6, 1917, Ragnhild, who had been teaching in Stockholm, married Einar Wiberg, a Swedish postmaster, and settled in Sweden.

Svarstad was home more, and although he didn't involve himself in household problems, he was pleased that his children were happier. On the surface, Sinsen seemed to be working out well, but when Sigrid spent an occasional afternoon at Nini's house, she collapsed and assured her friend a little too often that she "would make it."

Christmas was as elaborate as ever. The children were as excited about the preparations as always, and Sigrid was as pleased about it. "Yesterday we baked Fattigmand," (deep fried diamond-shaped cookies) "with thirty eggs and cut up and salted half a pig," she wrote to Nini.[2] "Today, Asta and I made Medistermat," (minced meat), "and baked egg-white cakes from fifteen whites and baked pepper cakes and made meat rolls" (another Christmas specialty) and as she was putting Mosse to bed, she was happy to hear the children running through the house screaming with excitement, just as she and her sisters once did—trying to peek, and sick with impatience.

"Yesterday evening we drove home with eighteen packages and a Christmas tree behind, and they all came running down (that is, all four who were mobile) and little Anders jumped around in the snow like a kitten, shouting 'What a tree, Mommy! We're crazy about that tree.'"[3]

"Christmas at the Svarstad's was not only a time for feasting," Nini wrote,

> . . . she had already started her extraordinary generosity which through the years would reach record heights. Her mother and sisters, relatives and friends all received presents. Incredible as it may sound, many of us got exquisite things which she herself had sewn with those fine hands—with crocheting, or tatting, or embroidery, and everything had English seams—all done with the same careful detail that she did everything.[4]

When Sigrid took the Svarstad children, Ragna Svarstad got a job at an outdoor newspaper stand and removed herself permanently from concern over them. At first her daughters stopped by to see her, but she showed little interest in their affairs. She made no effort to maintain a relationship with them, didn't remember them on birthdays or holidays, and their visits tapered off. (Many years later, when they were adults and she was suffering from a severe form of asthma, probably contracted at the outdoor stand, they renewed contact with her.)

Feeling that the welfare of the children was their responsibility (meaning her responsibility, since Svarstad changed none of his habits), Sigrid applied herself to giving them the home and training they had never had. She made pretty dresses for the girls and directed their reading. Gunhild was still sleeping late and was slow to help, but she was warming to the new environment and was tender and loving with the little ones. Trond was the only one who still remained a problem. It had become apparent that he suffered from more than an inability to concentrate. His lack of retention was so pronounced that the school refused to keep him and recommended institutionalizing him. Sigrid tried other schools and struggled to help him but, in the end, they had to face the fact that he was severely retarded, would never develop beyond a child's level, and would have to be kept at home.

When Mosse was eighteen months old, she had a seizure which Sigrid thought was an attack of cramps. A few months later she had a worse one. Sigrid panicked. She was in a cold sweat of terror until it was over and when her daughter finally calmed down and fell asleep, she walked into the bathroom and threw up. The doctor said it could have been due to teething and might never happen again, but just in case it did, he showed her what she had to do to protect the child from injuring herself. He also suggested that if it happened again it would be wise to allow a clinic to observe her for a while.

Svarstad was concerned, but it didn't change his work schedule. "He had finished five studies in the last two weeks," Sigrid wrote to Nini.

> *I understand that he has an excuse for it,* [he was preparing for an exhibition] *but he is busy all day with that and isn't much company at night.*
>
> *Although he is thirteen years older than I, he can be lazy in a green meadow on a beautiful spring evening and he is as ageless as a young boy, and I sit and look emptily at the flowers pressed down by the weight of the children, and think of new kitchen curtains, the clothes wringer that I have to buy, what they will eat for dinner, and if I got all the socks mended.*[5]

When a male writer works at home, it is generally accepted that he must not be disturbed because that is his work and all must respect it, but a woman who writes at home can never maintain the same isolation for concentration. There has been a great change in the amount of sharing that men are willing to accept since so many women have had to supplement family incomes, but if a child cries or any other crises develop while she is working, even with household help, it is not easy for a woman to concentrate on being creative. Literature requires sustained thought and it is not easy to pick up where you were after you have been disturbed a number of times.*

Sigrid had been able to get her mother to help occasionally, especially when she had a deadline to meet, when only her children were living with them, but her mother could not bear the stepchildren. And she dressed Mosse

---

* When one goes down the list of women who have become outstanding writers, it is amazing to find how few, except for those who were very wealthy, had children.

so warmly that she perspired all day, so she could not leave the baby with her for long.

In April, Sigrid's essay *A Hundred Years from Jane Austen to Ibsen* appeared in *Tidens Tegn* and her study of the Bröntes was published in *Samtiden* in three installments.*

She found Jane Austen's characters funny, but was not generous with praise for Ibsen. The Brönte sisters who lived in poverty and had to fend for themselves were closer to Sigrid's experience and she did more with her articles about them. She was particularly fond of Emily's poetry, but Charlotte's courage and profound insights, her yearning for sexual love although "God had given her an ugly little body and a face that no-one sees," and the tragedy of her death in childbirth after having finally won a husband and love, moved Sigrid the most.

"All talent in women is lost happiness. No one chooses to give art her love," she wrote.

> *One gives it at most one's life—if that can be fitted into a place in a family. As great as they were as artists, they could also have been great as women, and such great powers in women should not have to be thrown away by life. They should not have written books—they should have educated men and women. For women, art is short and life is long . . . Women who choose a profession because they consider that greater than being a mother, shouldn't have children—and those who neglect their children for their professions, do not choose art. They choose the title, the fame—something like a pair of high heels under a little person.*

(Sigrid's gay little flirtatious woman again!)

Unfortunately, like many of her statements, this was taken literally. Obviously she didn't mean that the Bröntes should not have been writers. She meant that women like the Bröntes would have been excellent mothers, and that their books could not make up for the lack of happiness in their personal lives.

In her zeal to make a point, Sigrid often overstated her case and later in life when her opinions were moderated by experience, her behavior didn't always jibe with the theories she expressed. She joked about it with her friends, but her tone was so offensive at times that she was not often forgiven. In *Yet*

---

* Later included in *Entapper* published by Aschehoug in 1929.

Being Someone Other, the South African writer Laurens van der Post wrote about his Calvinist upbringing "where austerity was maintained to fanatical degrees," and "exacting Calvinist prescriptions" had to be followed.[6] Sigrid's tone can sometimes be traced to such early indoctrination in the society in which she was reared. She was aware of it and fought it, but she couldn't always shed it.

In June she went on a short holiday to Italy with her mother and son, but they didn't stay long because her sister Signe was expecting a baby. On July 6, 1917, Signe gave birth to twin daughters. They were named Sigrid and Charlotte, (Sigrid refers to them in *Happy Times in Norway* as Siri-Kari and Anne-Lotte). They were beautiful, roly-poly, jolly little girls and were soon included in all family gatherings. Sigrid got little rest in Italy, and after the twins were born, she took her children to Laurgard I Sel where a local girl could look after them while she worked, but it was too hot to get much done.

"I have written some rubbish and I'm a little out of humor," she wrote to Nini, "all things have to be re-written several times."[7] She was reading Thackeray's *Pendennis* and finding him to be one of her favorite authors. She wanted to do nothing but lie on her back in the garden and let her children crawl all over her and she envied the ladies who had no other interests but to "sit on the staircase and crochet." She was crocheting chemises for her stepdaughter's confirmation and trying to "lock up her poor brains for a while." Art and artists were bothersome and demanding, and looking after children seemed the nicest, most peaceful thing that one could do. "If only my ambition had been hand-embroidered window shades for all of the rooms, crocheted bedspreads for all the beds, and embroidered tablecloths and napkins."*[8]

But it wasn't art and artists that were putting her out of humor. Mosse had become a source of unbearable concern. She was not developing right. There was something dreadfully wrong with her. She watched over her for signs of improvement and with each smile or slight response she told herself that she had just been imagining things.

On December 7, 1917 she wrote to Nini that she had hung a medallion of a saint over the child's bed in the hope that it would help her get over the "attacks of cramps" that she was still having from time to time. Self-conscious about bowing to superstition in which she really didn't believe, she added that

---

*   Her need for such symbols of a well-run middle-class home was so great that she actually made many such things.

Mosse thought it was a watch. The child had a sore throat and ran a high fever (as high as 40 degrees*) and she had had several attacks one after the other.

> *I have been lying with that hot little body in my arms night and day, and it's more than hot it's burning hot. When the attacks come, she clings to me and calls 'Mama, Mama' and she cries if I leave her for a moment. Now she is sleeping. She is better now, but the doctors say it will happen again with any small infection. She'd be safer at a hospital, but I can't bear to send her away. Mosse is such a huggable thing. If she is away for many months she might forget her mother. Anders isn't lovable unless he wants something. He's outside from breakfast to night. He gets food at some point and then goes out again.*

When Mosse's fever receded the doctor suggested that Sigrid bring her to the hospital for tests. Although she was beginning to face the possibility that there was something more seriously wrong with her child than occasional infections, she was able to keep her anxiety under control, but when she was told that they wanted to observe her for a month, she fell apart. Unable to function, she took Anders to her mother and went to the health farm to await the doctor's reports. The report was far worse than her most nightmarish fears. They were not sure, they said, because so little was known about such children, but it was entirely possible that she would never develop normally. They didn't know what caused her condition, possibly brain damage, or an inherited factor—such cases seemed to repeat themselves in families—but her seizures would probably continue for the rest of her life. There was no medication that could help her, and each attack could cause further damage. What Sigrid heard was so incredible she couldn't absorb it. How could they say that she wouldn't get better? New discoveries were made every day. How did they know that nothing could be done? Norwegian doctors were not well informed. She had never accepted defeat and she surely wouldn't where her child was concerned. No one knew Mosse as well as she did. She would find a way to help her. But no matter what she told herself, she wasn't sure that she would be able to survive the horror of her misfortune. Determined to find a way, she began to study the medical literature and search for doctors. She took her to the clinic after each attack—and she also started to pray.

---

*   104° Fahrenheit.

"No one can imagine what a barbed wire enclosure I live in daily, with responsibilities for everyone," she wrote to Nini.

> *I must find a good woman to help me or everything I have worked for all these years and the whole environment will begin to look like my predecessor's house. Svarstad sees impositions on him in everything I ask for. A housekeeper, for instance. He doesn't understand or care at all about any of them . . . He can't imagine that I could wish every morning when Mosse awakes at 7 o'clock that I could call on a nanny and let her dress the child and get a cup of tea and stay in bed a little.*[9]

The exhibition for which Svarstad had been preparing was postponed, and although he still couldn't find much time for his family, even he was overwhelmed by the tragedy. Mosse was such a beautiful, good-natured baby. She didn't look like an abnormal child. She looked like Sigrid.

"I remember one April day I was there when Svarstad was away," Nini wrote,

> *. . . and Sigrid sat with her maid and children at the dining table in a large light apron and on her lap sat little Mosse wearing red pearls. Sigrid was pale and tired but saw that everyone had cigarettes and wine, and she answered all of the children's questions patiently and with affection . . . On the writing desk were heaps of papers with her clear handwriting—her first drafts always looked like finished manuscripts. On the table near the window was some half-finished crochet work and on the chair next to her, many stockings waited to be mended.*[10]

In 1917, Sigrid published *Images in a Mirror** a novel which was a continuation of her story, *The Happy Age*. That story ended when Uni gave up a promising career in the theater to marry the man she loved and raise a family. The novel starts after Uni has had three children and is expecting a fourth. Her husband is loyal to her and she adores her children, but she is not happy. He admires her for being such an efficient housekeeper and wonderful mother, but he shares few of her intellectual interests and has never understood how much she gave up—how she longs to be challenged again as an actress. He is always engrossed in his work and may not be disturbed during the night

---

* Originally called *Fru Hjelde* it was published by Aschehoug in 1917 in a book called *Splinten av Troldspeilet* and by Alfred A. Knopf Inc. in English in 1938.

if a child is sick, because he has to go to work the next morning. When she looks tired he insists on helping her. After doing a few chores, he feels proud of himself and settles down with his newspaper, while she, who has been going all day, will mend or iron, shivering with fear and apprehension every time she is due to nurse the baby because her breasts are raw and irritated and the pain is unbearable. The baby isn't gaining weight and Uni is afraid to switch it to a bottle, but in the end an aunt has to be called to stay with the children while her husband takes her to a rest home to recuperate.

At the rest home she meets a man who knew her in her acting days. He values her for what she might have been. There is a strong attraction between them and when she returns to the city, she introduces him to her husband. She begins to see him secretly in his rooms, but is not yet ready to make a complete commitment and refrains from having sex. Her husband senses what is happening and forces her to make a choice. She knows that she could never leave her husband and children, and comforts herself that no life can encompass all of one's dreams. One has to make choices. If only she could stop agonizing over lost opportunities. She stops seeing the other man and knows that her marriage and children are all she will ever have in her life.

"Happiness," she muses,

> *What I was doing at my age . . . to go and believe in happiness . . . the happiness that is like a shooting star. In the brief instant that it shines, one must think of one's heart's desire and wish; and in the brief space while caresses are new and thrilling, one is called upon to understand and determine one's life. I wonder how many there are who succeed?* [11]

*   *   *

Despite her daughter's illness and the over-active household, or perhaps because of the needs of that household, she continued to publish a book a year and *The Wise Virgins*, another collection of stories, came out in 1918.

In *Thjodolf*,˙ Helene, a young servant girl, falls in love with a boy who goes off with someone else. "What happened to her is what often happens to a girl who respects herself and thinks herself above some things; the boy

---

˙   The only one of these in English. It is included in *Four Stories* published by Alfred A. Knopf, Inc. in 1959.

found a girl who wasn't above anything at all."[12] Helene meets Julius whom she likes, and since she is afraid of losing him, she allows him to make love to her. When she discovers that she is pregnant, he marries her.

"There was something she had expected; she didn't quite know what—and it had never come,"[13] but she is ashamed to complain. He is good to her, and provides for her and his old mother who lives with them. Helene loses the baby (whom she had named Tulla) and is told that she can never have another child. For six years she scrubs, cleans and keeps house for her husband and mother-in-law, "trying to fill her empty hands," and although she dislikes her, she misses her mother-in-law when she dies.

Her husband is a seaman and is away a good part of the time and she is lonely. She decides to adopt a baby. She takes in summer boarders and does embroidery to earn enough to cover the extra expense, and gets a foster child from an unwed mother with the understanding that, if they are acceptable as parents, they will be allowed to adopt it legally.

Her struggles to care for the little boy which start on the first night when she brings him to a freezing house, the clothes she makes for him, the tenderness with which she cares for him, and the pride with which she displays him to the neighbors are described with exquisite sensitivity. Her husband loves the child and spends more time at home. One day the child's mother appears on the doorstep. Fanny is a pretty woman who "didn't look like someone who had learned to be careful after being in trouble."[14] She is pathetic and hungry and Helene feeds her and invites her to stay a few days. She begins to visit often, and one day she announces that she is getting married and wants the child back. Helene is devastated but since the legal papers have not yet been signed, there is nothing she can do about it. She gives the child, and the carefully laundered clothes which she made for him, to Fanny and asks for permission to visit him. Fanny's husband is never there when she comes and Thjodolf seems so hungry and neglected that she begins to give Fanny money with which to feed him. Her visits are almost too painful to bear, but she cannot abandon the child.

One day she comes home in a rainstorm to find Fanny and a very sick Thjodolf, totally drenched, waiting for her on the doorstep. Explaining that she can no longer care for the child, Fanny begs Helene to take him back. With all the love in her strong little body, Helene manages to get the boy back on his feet, but he develops whooping cough and dies. When Fanny comes to the funeral she seems unusually friendly with Helene's husband who has been coming home less frequently of late. Helene sees them kissing and he confesses that he has been visiting Fanny in the city and, since she is going to have his child, he is going to leave with her.

Sigrid's early stories were about spinsters. They were followed by problems of married life. When she began to face the seriousness of Mosse's illness, she started to write about tragedy.

But all was not blank and dismal. Full of energy, Sigrid prepared for the usual Christmas celebration as soon as the book was out of the way. The house was decorated with flowers and lights and there was her traditional abundance of holiday foods and wines. Her mother, Signe and her family, many writers and other friends and, of course, her husband and all of the children were there and the festivities were as memorable as always.

CHAPTER VIII

LILLEHAMMER

1919

By the time Mosses was three years old, Sigrid was beginning to accept what the doctors had been trying to tell her. Her beautiful daughter would probably never be normal. Her seizures had continued and she was deteriorating a little with each attack. The child did not have Down's Syndrome. She didn't look brain damaged. She was very pretty, in fact. She was cheerful and cuddly, liked to be dressed up, could listen to phonograph records for hours, sit at the window endlessly watching a flag wave on a flagpole, or look at the birds as they pecked at the grain that her mother put out. She had trouble balancing when she walked and lacked coordination when she tried to hold something, but she enjoyed being sung to, and rocked, liked to be taken for a ride, and loved to laugh. She understood little of what was going on, but when others laughed, she laughed too—and sometimes she laughed long after everyone else had stopped. She had to be dressed and fed, but she could point to what she wanted and say a few words. It was as if a veil was separating her from the world and her mother was determined to lift it.

An endless trek to doctors and clinics began. Each time Sigrid left her for observation she hoped that some miraculous discovery would be made. Nothing came easily for her, she had learned that a long time ago, but she wouldn't give up. She would fight and she would save her daughter. It wasn't possible that she could be asked to give so much. She believed in mercy. She had not been singled out. It was a warning against her false pride that was only meant to scare her. Mosse would outgrow it. The convulsions were due to infections, to teething. She had been running a high fever when the worst attack occurred. She was strong and she would persevere. With willpower one could do anything. One had to make sacrifices, of course, nothing came free, but she would save her child.

But no matter what she told herself, a paralyzing terror, an unbelievable horror that made it hard for her to swallow and took the taste of everything that was wholesome and good away from her, was slowly becoming a reality.

Long before she married and had children, she had written in *The Stranger,*

> *No human being believes seriously that there is a blind fate that determines his life, that nothing he can do is of any use. Nobody believes in suffering. Everyone expects from second to second in their growing pain that it must stop. Someone will stop it, because human beings who complain about a lack of mercy in their innermost hearts believe in mercy and demand it as their right.*[1]

When Hans Christian Andersen, who was unusually tall, ungainly, ugly and epileptic, but a most profound, poetic writer was faced with the greatest tragedy of his life—when the girl he loved, (who loved him too), obeyed her father instead of her heart and married a man "more suitable to her station in life"—he wrote *The Little Mermaid.* The little mermaid was willing to suffer the pain of the knife that had cut her tail in two, when she walked on the legs that the witch had created for her, in her desperate effort to win the love of the prince. She had even forfeited her voice, and risked her life, on the gamble that he would marry her and make her human. But the prince married someone else. Unable to give up her love and resign herself to being a mermaid forever, she dies, but by remaining steadfast in her love, she has attained immortality.

Andersen comforted himself that although he lost the love of his life, his art would bring him immortality.

But Sigrid couldn't comfort herself with that. No recognition of her art could compensate for the health of her child. She clung to the belief that if she remained strong, she would find a way to help her. Not everyone was willing to invest what was required to obtain one's goals, but if one was ready to give unstintingly, without keeping score, one could win in the end. She had always believed in willpower. When her first book was rejected, she hadn't been discouraged. She gave up the possibility of a social life and spent lonely nights on another book, and now she was a published author.

When she was forced to face the fact that her daughter was incurable, Sigrid's belief in willpower began to founder. Willpower could achieve many goals, but nothing could be done about the "acts of God." When her father died, she had missed him terribly but she had not bemoaned her fate. She had given up going to college and had taken a job to help support her mother and sisters. Svarstad was not an Adonis, and surely not one whom most young women might have chosen for a husband, but she loved him and wanted him, and if he had three difficult children and could not be depended on, she had to accept that, (although she couldn't help writing that freedom didn't mean accepting no responsibilities). What troubled her was that some people had fathers and doting husbands and never lifted a finger to help anyone. How, if they contributed so little, did they manage to get so much? Was it, perhaps, because they made demands and didn't jump in to do things for everyone?

In the spring of 1919, the Svarstads lost the lease on their apartment. Until the last moment, it seemed that it would be renewed, and when it wasn't, they were unprepared.

Sigrid was pregnant again. Mosse was having more frequent attacks, and Svarstad was preparing for the exhibition that had been postponed. He was painting night and day and she was the only one who was looking for a place to live. There was no time to be lost or they would all be out on the street.

She looked until she thought she would drop. Her feet hurt and her back ached, and as she looked, a new problem began to register with her. If Mosse never learned to walk without help, couldn't manage stairs or go to school, what kind of place would they need? Doctors had been trying to prepare her for this. They would have to live on the ground floor. Neighborhood children might badger Mosse. They would need a backyard and it would have to be fenced. She was going to get better, of course, but what if she didn't? Friends were urging her to institutionalize the child—but that was out of the question. She had to be with her to find a way to reach her. She panicked about the child she was carrying. What if? No . . . She wouldn't think of such a thing. "Oh dear God, protect this one," she moaned.

When Regine Normann had bored her with religion, Sigrid had poked fun at her, and when she had heard herself being pious, she had made fun of herself, but after she discovered that Mosse was incurable, she began to change. Feeling helpless, she prayed, and when her daughter had a seizure, in desperation she hung a religious medal over the child's bed.

Walking the streets, she became more and more troubled about how she would care for her daughter, and as she was forced to reject one comfortable apartment after another, her tragedy overwhelmed her. Crying hysterically she dragged herself home to find Svarstad relaxing peacefully in his study while bedlam reigned in the rest of the house. The children had been quarreling all afternoon, the housekeeper told her. They had teased Mosse after she had had a violent attack.

Why hadn't her husband stopped them? Sigrid asked.

Madam knew, the housekeeper said, that he didn't like to be disturbed. She was working in the kitchen and hadn't heard what was going on until it was too late. There was so much to do, and she couldn't be everywhere at once. She had scolded the children and taken care of Mosse, who was sleeping it off.

That did it! She had had enough. She couldn't go on. She was sick, herself. Her pregnancy was weighing heavily on her. Crying wildly, she rushed up to see her daughter. Every time she left the house, something happened. The doctor had explained that each attack could make her worse. This noisy, overactive household was too much for the poor child. Her nerves were so frayed, and her body so tired, she couldn't think. No one was lifting a finger. It was unbelievable to what an extent she had gotten her husband accustomed to being carried. They had no place to live and he was waiting for her to work it all out. Mosse needed peace and quiet. In a fury of frustration, she began to throw clothes into a suitcase. She would take her children to go to the country and when Svarstad finished preparing for his exhibition and found a place to live, she would come home.

Svarstad thought it was a good idea. She had been working too hard, he said. She needed a rest. They discussed where she should go and decided on Lillehammer. It was a ski resort and would not be expensive off-season. There were several small hotels there that would be comfortable. He took them to the train the next day.

Lillehammer was a village of 5,000 situated on the northern end of Lake Mjøsa in the valley of Gudbrandsdal. It was a two-hour train ride from Christiania and a half hour from Hamar where her father had once explored medieval ruins. Popular with artists and writers and scenically beautiful, with mountains and farmland that came right down to the water's edge, it was so quiet and peaceful that she felt calmer as soon as she had unpacked. Anders loved it and Mosse seemed more relaxed.

Weeks passed. The time had come to vacate the apartment and since Svarstad had not found anything, he put the furniture in storage, boarded the children, and moved in with friends. The baby was due in August. Sigrid had to make arrangements for her confinement, and it was hard to care for the children in a hotel room. An old, recently remodeled, timbered farmhouse that had been moved from the valley to a hill above the town was being advertised for rent. Electricity had been installed but there was no inside bath or toilet. It was sparsely furnished but all the essentials were there—a huge living room, a nice kitchen, and a small dining room on one floor, and a large bedroom and two small ones above.

It was in a beautiful spot at the end of a riding field with a lot of land with large, old birch trees and many bushes—and for some strange reason, the city limits went right through the idle of the property. It wasn't fenced in or tidied up, and since no one had ever lived there, she had no idea what problems might arise after they moved in.

"My extraordinary pig's luck is," she wrote to Nini, "that from July 1, I have a Swedish Whitecross sister who is educated as a midwife and nurse, and since she is available when I will need her, I have engaged her for six months. I can hardly believe it is me who is going to have such an easy time. Now, if I can find a maid, everything will be set up so I can have some easy days for a while."[2]

There was a hitch which made her hesitate for a few days. The artist Sverre Hjorth, who was the owner, would not rent it for fewer than fifteen months, but it was so much cheaper than a hotel or a house in the city would be, that she decided to take it and worry about disposing of the lease when the time came to face it.

Svarstad came up with the other children and loved it. The girls were not happy where they were, he said, and the people who were boarding Trond didn't want to keep him. Lillehammer was a wonderful idea. It would solve their problem for the summer, and by the time the children had to go back to school he would have found a place to live.

But Sigrid said she couldn't permit the children to stay. She had been right not to trust in her "pig's luck." The maid with whom she had corresponded for weeks decided not to come and the Swedish nurse cancelled. She was getting closer to her due date and she had no one to help her. Mosse needed care around the clock, the house needed things done to it, and she had committed herself to a collection of her articles and speeches on the question of women's rights. She had to write an introduction for it and collect and edit the material. Since Svarstad was not earning very much, they needed what she earned to live on. Mosse was calmer—and for all these reasons, she explained to her husband, the other children would have to return with him. The house was a temporary arrangement and too small to accommodate them all. She would be happy to try to manage if Svarstad were able to be there to help her, but if he didn't look, he would never find a place to live—so until the baby was born it would be better if she stayed in Lillehammer with the two youngest children and he took the others back to the city.

He was annoyed, but he took them back and promised to look harder. They came up again during the summer. The girls tried to be helpful, but the house was crowded and noisy and although they begged to stay, Sigrid insisted that they go back when their father left. In the end, she could only find a laundress for two days a week, and her mother had to come up when the baby arrived.

"If you think I was tired when you last saw me," she wrote to Nini, "now I am really tired. You can count on that. I have taken off three kilos despite my being in the sixth month and I have had to use a red wine compress at night in order to be able to sleep."[3]

Just when she was feeling the most depressed Svarstad surprised her. He had sold several large paintings and had used the money as a down payment on a house. He came to Lillehammer with Ebba to tell her about it in person. The house was in Kampen, a working-class area in the center of town where a number of artists had studios. It had a large apartment on the ground floor, with room for all of them, a huge studio above that, and an unfinished attic at the top. It was such a find that he had acted quickly so as not to lose it.

Sigrid was overjoyed. He was loving and helpful and they had a few wonderful days together, but when she asked when they would be able to move in, he said there was a bit of a problem. It seemed that when he bought the house he had failed to ascertain whether he could legally oust the tenants who were living in the apartment, and his lawyer said it might take time. Since they would all be able to live there eventually, Sigrid could keep the children in Lillehammer after the baby was born, and when the flat was available, they would all be able to move to the city.

She couldn't believe that even he could have done a thing like that. He had purchased a house that took care of only his needs! Not wanting to show how upset she was, she simply repeated what she had said before: when they could all live together, she would join him, but she would not have the other children if he were not there.

Gunhild had quarreled with the woman who was boarding them, he said, and no one wanted to keep Trond. He was sorry about the mix-up, but what was he to do with the children? It might take a long time. He had no place for them. He knew nothing about bringing up children. They needed a mother to care for them.

She was beginning to understand his thinking. It was unlike him to have bought a house without discussing it with her, but she thought he had done it because it was an emergency. With the baby due any minute, she couldn't very well have come down to see it, and he didn't want to lose it, but now it appeared he had had another purpose. When they had first set up house together, he had maintained a studio in town and had come home on weekends. They had only one child then. The others were boarding with strangers. Now he expected her to take all six children, while he would live in town and come up when, and if, he could manage it. Too upset to trust herself to speak, she said nothing. He left, and promised to return when the baby was due.

In July she wrote to Nini:

> I'm very sorry for Svarstad. Gunhild has quarreled with the woman who cares for them and now he must find another place . . . She's never satisfied. She was not happy with us and not happy any place else. I have had just as many problems with them as he had with their mother. If I don't ask for anything for myself and let them have as much as he can provide, then that should be enough, and he may one time see that they weren't very easy for me, those three years in Sinsen. I have a bad conscience about them, but I don't want to ignore my work and my children for them anymore. Now that those three years are over, I know I will not involve myself in that again,. The need to tie my offspring to that bitch's offspring is not such a good idea after all. Mosse won't let me go to the bathroom without screaming, and that is enough to worry about.

Svarstad came up and stayed for a week, Sigrid continued,

> If I could have gone with him now, a lot might be different. It is as though he and I have come out of that barbed wire enclosure bloody but peaceful and ready to be kind to each other—but with too many experiences between us that can't be discussed.[4]

Little Anders had noticed that she had taken her wedding ring off, (it had been sent to the jeweler to be made larger because she had gained weight during her pregnancy), and he asked if they were getting a divorce.

> He was afraid that he would have no place to live like the other children. Luckily, we could both reassure him, but you can imagine how it pained his father to hear him talk like that. It is so sad that if there had been just us and our kids we could have found a solution. Anders had left the three of them, including that terrible boy about whom he

*doesn't even know if he is his, and my efforts to help him with that
load have only ruined things for all of us. It has hurt me more deeply
than any person knows.*[5]

On August 27, 1919, Sigrid gave birth to a boy, whom they named Hans
Benedict. "It was fast and easy," she wrote in a shaky, penciled note to Nini.
"He looks wonderful, but so did Mosse."[6]

Svarstad was unable to get there for the birth. He promised to come after
she and the baby got home, but she wasn't sure he would be able to manage
that either. "I have a bad feeling that I am being difficult with him, but I can't
anymore . . ." she wrote to Nini.[7]

When he finally came, he was loving and helpful. She had been prepared
for quarrels, but he was in good humor, delighted with his new son and
"carried Mosse around on his shoulder wherever he went."[8] He said the girls
were getting along well. They were living in the attic of the house in Kampen,
and he had found a family to board Trond, but there was no news about the
availability of the flat.

*It was a sin for me to have tried all these years to create a middle-
class home. What he might have needed I have not been able to give
him and he has given me what I have always wanted—children.*[9]

"I am so happy that it is over," she wrote to Nini. "Happy I have a strong,
healthy little boy, and I am amazed that he was born with the ability to nurse.
The others took a long time to learn, but this one started without wondering
for a second when I put him to my breast."[10] The children were enjoying the
baby. Mosse watched him constantly and Anders was planning to teach him
all sorts of things and preparing things to give him for Christmas. Although
she was "feeling at low tide with sand in her head,"[11] and deeply worried
about her situation with Svarstad, she prepared the usual feasts for Christmas.
Svarstad brought only Ebba (because she was the most helpful), but Sigrid's
mother, Signe and her family, and many friends were there. Everyone was
in a festive mood. Sigrid's sister Ragnhild had given birth to a daughter in
November. In the future, when the cousins would get together, Ulla would
be a fine playmate for Hans.

Svarstad came up again in May and they had "a very nice time," until
he told her that he was going to Paris and Antwerp on the 20th and would
be away for at least eight months. He didn't say what he wanted to do about
their relationship, or her rental, which would be up before he returned, but

he pressed her again to take the other children, "just until he came back." He said he couldn't bear to see them so unhappy—they so much wanted to be with her.[12]

Appalled at his total disregard for her situation, she could only repeat what she had said before: If he wanted to live in Lillehammer, she would find a larger house and they could all be together, or, if he sold the house in Kampen and bought something that was large enough for all, she would move back to the city.

Friends were aghast at what he had done, and amazed that she still believed she would be joining him, but she continued to call it a temporary arrangement. She knew that "people were speculating," she wrote to Nini, "but there was no third person involved."[13] Apart from her other problems she found it necessary to "save face."

"He left without a word about the future," she wrote to Nini.[14]

After he was gone, a friend wrote to Sigrid to ask her to take Trond for the summer. She refused, but in the end she had the girls for several months.

*   *   *

As time passed, the peace and quiet of Lillehammer began to affect her. She continued to be concerned with the affairs of her stepchildren. They came every Christmas and for most of the summer, sometimes with and sometimes without their father. She continued to be involved in planning their education, and often contributed financially for their needs, but she never again tried to create one household for all.

Although it looked very much like Svarstad had arranged the Kampen situation deliberately, it is entirely possible that he had not intended it to turn out the way it did. He was sufficiently vague to have been capable of buying a house without checking on whether he could get the tenants out of the flat, and if he had gotten possession of the whole house it would have suited their needs perfectly. Perhaps it was only when he discovered that he couldn't get the flat that a new possibility presented itself. Sigrid loved Lillehammer and needed some peace and quiet for Mosse and her work, and since she believed so strongly in the welfare of his children, he couldn't see why they couldn't all live there with her. He needed to be in town, so he would stay at his studio.

His daughter, Gunhild, believes that he loved Sigrid as much as he was capable of loving anyone.[15] He doesn't seem to have wanted anyone else. All he really wanted was to work in peace. He would come up as often as he could, and since she earned more than he did, and living up there was much cheaper than in the city, she would take care of their needs there, and he would contribute as much as he could—when, and if, he could. With such an arrangement, he would be free to travel and work undisturbed and she would have what she wanted—a family.

If there had not been two very sick children, Sigrid might have settled for that, but Trond was an impossible burden, and Mosse's illness was so devastating that she couldn't cope with more. Also, her stepdaughters were too much like their mother for her to feel comfortable with them.

It was not easy to have a conversation with her husband. His reactions were slow and deliberate, and he kept his thoughts to himself. He had wit and intelligence, but he used them mostly with acidity and sarcasm. Like Sigrid, he was highly critical and could answer sharply when pressed. He didn't get along with other painters and found literary conversations boring, but he was tender and loving with her. She liked the way he dismissed pretensions and "artiness" and she respected his serious approach to his work. For her everyday problems she had learned, long ago, to confide in a woman. At first it was Dea; now it was Nini.

She kept thinking that she had made it too easy for him, and that if he understood what he could do, he would do it. He had one mentally ill child when she met him, and the possibility that Mosse's illness was inherited from his family was real.˙ She couldn't believe that with two such children he would not be willing to accept some responsibilities. But time passed and the arrangement remained the same. He lived at Kampen and traveled when he could, and she welcomed him and his children whenever he wished to come to Lillehammer.

Asta, who had worked for her in Sinsen, could not come to Lillehammer. After Hans was born, Sigrid hired Mary Andersen who was devoted to her and the children and tender with Mosse—and, as the years went by, Sigrid was able to turn more of the daily care of the children over to her. She stayed from 1919 to 1928, when she married a farmer (called Stendhal) from the area. Mary left, and Sigrid tried to train Ebba to act as her secretary and run the house with the help of two farm girls, but when that proved too much for her, Sigrid hired Mathea Morgenstuen. Thea was equally attentive to Mosse and was also an excellent housekeeper—and after Sigrid sent her to Christiania to study cooking with Mrs. Boman-Hansen, the chef of the famous Theater

---

˙ Ebba had problems later on, and Hans had a neurological awkwardness as he grew older.

Café, she became an outstanding cook. More family friend than servant, she stayed with Sigrid for the rest of Sigrid's life.

When Mary Andersen got married, Sigrid arranged to board Trond with her on her husband's farm. He was severely retarded, but he was big and strong and able to work. The Stendhals cared for him as if he were a member of their family and he remained with them for the rest of his life. (When Sigrid died, she left a sum of money for the continuation of his keep which the Stendhals set aside for him and when he died˙ the family offered the money to his sisters. Trond was blind for the last part of his life.˙˙ The Stendhals had cared for him for more than fifty years, and his sisters refused the money.)

Sigrid was a disciplinarian and demanded much from her servants but they were always devoted to her. She was a gracious hostess and loved to entertain, and because she was tireless herself, they were overworked. She liked the idea of being a model housewife and insisted that fruits be canned when they were in season and meats preserved in large quantities,˙˙˙ but she participated only sporadically in these activities.

The housekeeper, whoever it was, shared a room with Mosse because her worst attacks took place during the night, and although there were always one or two other servants, there was much to be done and they were often tired and irritable. They had to be strict with the children and their friends, in order to get the work done, and because they were hard to replace, Sigrid rarely overruled them when the children complained. Sigrid was a loving mother but when she tried to instruct them her knowledge was so prodigious that she usually told them more than they wanted to know. Nevertheless, Lillehammer served its purpose well. Once she established a routine, the children were well cared for and she could work in peace.

˙   October 4, 1980.
˙˙   Svarstad's mother was also blind towards the end of her life.
˙˙˙   In *Happy Times in Norway* she wrote that one year, when there were many cloudberries available, Thea had asked her to buy a "hundred quarts if possible," for canning.

CHAPTER IX

A WOMAN'S POINT OF VIEW
1919

During the most traumatic period of her life, Sigrid collected the articles she had written about women's rights, and *A Woman's Point of View** was published a few months after Hans was born. Beginning with a phrase from a Norwegian folk song:

> *How on earth can the green grass grow*
> *If a son cannot trust his own mother?*

It included an expanded version of her article about the Charlotte Perkins Gilman book, *The Man-Made World*, the speech she gave at the National Students' Convention, a collection of her reviews of books written by women during the war, an exchange about women's rights that she had had in the press, and instead of the introduction she had promised her publisher—a postscript. Since many of the positions she took are still being discussed today, I am quoting some of the most provocative things she had to say.

The first two articles have already been dealt with. The third, *Women and War* was a collection of Sigrid's reviews of books by women, not women's books (a designation she objected to), which had appeared up to June 1918.

Referring to women as a "camp of the quiet," (a quote from the Norwegian writer, Camilla Collett) she wrote:

---

* Not published in English.

> *Women do not speak out. For thousands of years they have been quiet while their fruitfulness, their will to work, their virtuous resignation, or their foolish fripperies have all been painfully decided for them in relation to the needs of nations . . .* [1]

"Progress," she believed, had only one goal during the last hundred years, and that was a striving towards material well-being. The few women who, "through their male family members' social positions had been able to achieve material well-being" were turning to useless work because they didn't have useful work and seemed to "long for fruitless suffering if they didn't have fruitful suffering." Any man who doubted this could try to live for a single day in a tight corset and high-heeled shoes one size smaller than his feet.[2]

There was little that women wrote during the war that was exceptional, but as always, during a war, they were taking over the work of the men to keep society going and perhaps now, they would speak out. Fighting together, men developed a spirit of camaraderie which gave them courage to fight, but that is a feeling most foreign to women. Women were isolated in their homes and needed to share more with each other.[3]

The reviews were followed by *A Confusion of Ideas*, and several articles which Sigrid had written for *Tidens Tegn* in April, 1919, as an answer to a pamphlet written by Katti Anker Møller called *Women's Birth Politics*.

Katti Anker Møller[·] was wealthy and single, and had turned over her substantial estate to unwed, pregnant women whom she cared for until their children were born. She was an ardent fighter for women's rights and wrote that men have too long had control over the bodies of women. Norway ought to adopt the Roman law that life begins after birth. A fetus was a part of the mother's body until then, and she should have the right to an abortion if she so desired. There should be no punishment from society for a birth out of wedlock. There would be fewer abortions if the government gave child support to unwed mothers.

Birth control, which was illegal but practiced by wealthy women, should be legalized and made available to all. Women who worked at home all of their lives should not have to be dependent on men but should be paid by the government for each child. Unmarried women should have the same insurance as married women, which was too little in any case, (one krone per day for the last part of a pregnancy), and should be paid for the entire pregnancy and nursing period. Since children were society's most precious possessions, a

---

[·]   1868-1945. She is not to be confused with Ingeborg Møller.

mother's production should receive a price equal to its value—and if women refused to have children, they would win whatever they wanted.*

Men, who wrote most of the books, recommended that women nurse, but they didn't mention that many women were forced to stop nursing because of a new pregnancy soon after a birth. Sex was permitted six weeks after a birth but women who had given nine months to a pregnancy, and nursed for nine months, needed more time before starting another child. The needs of the children should be as important as the sexual urges of the men. Women should never be forced to have sex. All children should be conceived with full consent of the mother, and as a protest against the position of the Church in this matter, she recommended civil marriages.

In marriage, wives are the employees of husbands, and motherhood should be seen as a profession. Any commodity had a price set by the seller and a mother should put a price on each child. That way they would control the market. When women fight for equal pay and the right to vote, they stress that they are the same as men, but their interests are not the same. If they would control childbirth, their power in society would be unlimited.[4]

*   *   *

Although Sigrid agreed with many of Katti Anker Møller's statements, she felt that some were excessive and she made cogent comments in contradiction to others.

"Science has made humanity forget about the soul," Sigrid wrote. "The ideals of materialism have happily brought the working people a long way toward bettering their conditions and getting power in society . . ." but Katti Anker Møller's statements were "quasi-scientific abracadabra."[5]

It was a "crazy misunderstanding" to say that the very bad economic situation of the family concerns women more than men. "A man who has a wife and children and a small income does not get more for his own private pleasures than some women."[6]

Katti Anker Møller was using the word "family" as though it were an industrial concern where a man engaged a woman to bear and bring up children for him. "Heaven knows from what motives, since the lady explains that bringing up, nourishing and educating children has not become nothing more than an expense . . ."[7] If a woman hired herself out to work for a man,

---

*   Norway had large tracts of uncultivated land and a small population, and the government was encouraging population growth.

bringing up his children would not be a very advantageous field for her. She would not be free to give notice and leave, and he could demand that she have the largest possible number of children for the least amount of payment. "Why he should want so many is impossible to understand—that he should pay as little as possible is easier to understand." If men were simply interested in sex, they could get it much cheaper than by "hiring a steady wife."[8]

If she was confusing payment for motherhood with mother insurance it was again a confusion of ideas. Mother insurance was insurance. "To be supported when one is unable to work, or has no work, for men or women, is not the same as being paid for getting pregnant and giving birth to a child. A forest worker is paid if he hurts himself, but he is not paid to cut his foot."[9] If she wanted to have a discussion about insurance and pensions, "which means to what degree we should insure ourselves and each other," that was a very sensible discussion, but that was not what she was talking about.[10]

Katti Anker Møller's idea that all births ought to take place in the home, could be painless, and should be supervised by women, was ridiculous. Some women might like to be examined by doctors and might enjoy lying in clinics and allowing themselves to be operated on, but not all women were equally healthy and normal and there were always special cases where a doctor, the best doctor, whether male or female, had to be called in. "Some male doctors may be unsympathetic and callous, some are in awe of motherhood, but women doctors might be jealous because they have no children."[11] Sigrid was sure that everyone would like a painless childbirth, but not everyone could achieve it. Katti Anker Møller's idea of women as birth machines and children as products brought up other questions: "Would the State pay the same for mentally defective or crippled children as for first-class healthy ones? Should children who resulted from rape be worth the same payment as a theft from a store?"[12] What she was suggesting—"that women use their naturally endowed qualities for gain—is a form of prostitution . . . That we as mothers shall be able to exist by ourselves and no longer be dependent on men, can never be achieved . . . unless the lady has a patent for virgin birth."[13]

Katti Anker Møller was not poor. She spoke as if working people had no sensitivity and lacked spiritual and human emotion. She referred to economically deprived people as "that kind of people"—and described them as coming together like animals because they were incapable of feeling the finer nuances of lovemaking—and she described the spiritual needs of "such people" spitefully.[14]

"A number of years ago," Sigrid continued, "Katti Anker Møller had arranged an exhibition which showed the horrors of a room where a very poor but child-rich mother was going to bear a child where others sleep and eat."[15] The father had his hat on, which gave the viewers the impression that he was going to or coming from a bar. "That room was truly a horror and spoke loudly of the terrible conditions in which a poor family had to try to live a private sexual life," but Sigrid found the ideal room that was on display more horrible, in some ways. It was cold and sterile—apart from being unattainable for a working class family. There were beds for children and a crib for a baby, but no place for a parent nearby. "It was said," Sigrid continued, "that the King had asked 'where is the bath thermometer?' but no one asked 'where is the mother's bed.'"[16]

Sigrid agreed that an unmarried mother should have the right to bring up a child without censure, but the

> . . . child would either be deprived of a father, the mother would have to live a celibate life, or the child would grow up with a stepfather or stepfathers, and with a few happy exceptions, we know how the words stepmother, stepfather and stepchildren have been used by all classes at all times . . . [17]

Naturally there were many physical conditions which made it criminal for some women to have many children, but it was poverty, in most cases, that wore a woman's health and nerves to pieces, and that was what created unhappiness in marriage more often than many births.

"No man has a guarantee that a child is his . . . There are women who can get a man to doubt if the sun is shining or the grass is green, and they are not less able to carry children than others. No woman can doubt that a child is hers . . ."[18]

The response to this article was explosive. She was accused of deliberately misunderstanding Katti Anker Møller and of being malicious and unfair. Women had to fight for their rights, and in order to counteract years of abuse, they had to be forceful to be heard.

Sigrid, like women through the ages, had a need to use herself as a creative human being, while trying to maintain a love relationship that was based on mutual respect and consideration, and raising and nurturing their children. She was fortunate to be able to utilize her endowments through writing, which she could do at home, but the inequities between what society demanded from a woman as compared to what was expected from a man preoccupied her constantly. She believed that the woman's movement, which consisted primarily of middle-class, urban women, was too one-sided in its demands.

Because women were treated like servants, judged to be lesser human beings, allowed no rights over their own bodies, and permitted no room for sexual gratification, they had to change their lots, but unless there could be sharing and understanding between the sexes, instead of spite and fight for domination of one over the other, little would be improved and the children would be the victims.

When Sigrid was defending herself, she was always at her worst. At that crucial time in her life, she was in no condition to react rationally and she blasted off like a *rocket* in several articles in *Tidens Tegn*, and in the *Postscript* of *A Woman's Point of View*, with a rebuttal that was not well thought out—and when she was attacked for some of her statements, she refused to change a word.

Starting off by admitting that her views weren't popular, and that she would probably be called a reactionary, she wrote that the social safeguarding of motherhood would permit the State to intrude in family life. They would be in a position to "demand births" and ask for "the beating of virgins." "Taking an adversary position between men and women would destroy the most important thing in our culture—the family."[19]

When men give women laws without asking them—it is because women haven't tried to participate and present their ideas. Women have it within their means to develop a generation of people who would have better values because the education of the children is in their hands—but they are kept in ignorance and not educated properly. She quoted Charlotte Gilman's *Man-Made World* that "A Servile womanhood is in a state of arrested development and as such forms a ground for the retention of ancient ideas"[20]—and, she believed that "women, when they achieved political positions, would be no more liberal than men."[21]

Oppression of women had to be eliminated but that didn't mean that they had to compete in a man's world on his terms. Women should not be forced to do two jobs, and if they didn't have to work, they would accomplish more by caring for their families. Many women said they only wanted strong men, and others only wanted to be in charge, but it would be better if they tried to educate men to achieve democracy in their homes. Most men had to work at jobs they didn't like. If women wanted to work outside the home, they should not have children.

Marriage should be for life. Divorce should be allowed "only in those cases where not getting it would create madness or death."[22] If a divorce was not easy to get, people would try harder to work out their problems. Frequently the same problems arose when they got a new mate. Constant uprooting created insecurities in children. A stable environment was essential for their nurturing.[23]

Having experienced the difficulties that arose when children of two marriages had to live together, she wrote that people who were divorced forced their children to live in families where they weren't wanted, with people whom they didn't like, and parents expected them to make the best of it. How could children be asked to do what their parents were not willing to do, when it was not they, but their parents who made the mistakes?

Parents who lived with a variety of mates created confusion about the nature of sexuality in their children, and those who left them with untrained, disgruntled, unsatisfied people (which described most servants, due to their lack of education and low salaries) were not responsible human beings.

There were many families where both parents *had* to work away from home in order to provide food and shelter, but some worked not for necessities but for bigger houses and more luxuries.

In her speech to the students she had discussed sex education in the schools, and said that it had to be taught by qualified teachers. Most teachers were unmarried and had little or no sexual experience and since children didn't all develop at the same rate, the classes should be composed of those who had reached the same rate of curiosity, rather than the same age. "Can you imagine that an accidentally brought together group of children from varied backgrounds at different stages of physical development can be forced to sit and listen to descriptions of a sexual life that they may not be ready to hear?"[24] That which is beautiful between two people can become unfruitful and sexually depraved when talked to death.

One had to be careful in teaching about sex because people who lived long in an atmosphere of disrespect for sex lost their respect for life and, like nurses, learned to live with sickness and couldn't remember what it was like outside a hospital. She couldn't imagine any description of sexual love as going too far, it was only the matter-of-fact discussions that were sick and depraved.[25] She didn't mean, she added, that one should beat a featherbed by describing "blue-eyed goddesses and angelic ethereal love,"[26] but jumping from one relationship to another made it harder to establish a good one, and often forced people to try to work things out in ways that "went against nature." Perhaps it was psychologically wrong to teach people that happiness meant having no difficulties.[27]

Nothing could replace sexual satisfaction except, perhaps, spiritual work. "Those people who do not have a sexual drive have no right to call chastity, or unchosen purity a virtue . . . We have seen too much forced abstinence.

Purity without love in its broadest meaning is only a lamp without light, but in our times people have too little respect for purity . . ."[28] When young men look at girls as something to hung—to whom they have no sense of duty or responsibility, it forces the girls to put a protective wall around themselves and they never learn how to relate to another person.[29]

People who were unfortunate enough to have to live alone had as much right to sex and children as those who were married, but marriage was a sacred commitment and once a couple had children, they had to try to stay together. Rape, she felt, should be punishable by death.

She then let loose with a virulent dose of xenophobia. She wrote that "it was overwhelmingly probably that Soviet principles would in one form or another prevail,"[30] but the portraits in the newspapers of leaders of the Russian Revolution (this was written in 1919) "with their Semitic and tartaric faces and their wild strange names were enough to frighten people."[31] Voicing the paranoia of many people at that time, (in the United States, the Hearst papers were full of the threat of "the Yellow Menace") she wrote that "cultured people fear that the spiritual things which more primitive natures know little about will be made into a desert by barbarous hoards . . ."[32] and that "Russia will show the world how much half-Asian it is."[33]

She described the Crusades, (which Will Durant described as "a two-hundred years' war for the soul of man and the profits of trade"[34]), as "not just escapades of jailbirds. They were, from the first, a folk movement that was trying to turn back terrible phantoms of a God who could not be painted in a human likeness and a fate which could not be bent."[35]

Later she dismissed the senseless brutality, rape, murder and the sacking of towns by the Vikings (which went on for two centuries) by saying that they were, "in large part, farm boys who made some expeditions before they settled down in peace at home on their farms and worked the soil and dairies."[36]

One cannot dismiss her bigotry as a reflection of the thinking of her times. She was a product of her culture, but many people at that time reacted differently. Surrounded by women, her sibling fixation about "cute little women" skewed some of her perspective. She didn't know how to relate to men. The Francescas, Betzys, Britens, Fannys and Hildurs, who were characters in her books were successful because they were superficial little flirts. Svarstad was behaving so irrationally that she was at a loss to know what to do about it—but she struggled harder than many to try to be a good person, and did more than most to make the world a better place.

Toward the end of her life, exposure to other cultures helped her lose some of her prejudices.

About many of her warnings, she cannot be faulted. She foresaw the danger of Nazism long before the Second World War and her fear that industrialization would dehumanize society by breaking up the family was certainly justified. She wrote that children who wandered the streets lonely and uncared for, or who were shuttled back and forth between parents, could develop few goals other than venting their anger and brutalizing the society which had treated them so badly—and that has certainly come true. Children and elderly people are now the prime victims of our society. Old people live in fear. Children wander the streets alone with their house keys hanging from their necks, and in the United States they carry guns, and use them. Robbery, rape, pornography, sexually transmitted disease, child abuse and child and teenage suicide are rampant beyond a sane person's comprehension—and instead of getting better, the situation is getting worse.

CHAPTER X

KRISTIN LAVRANSDATTER
1920-1922

Sigrid was prepared for an uproar when *A Woman's Point of View* came out, but people were beginning to know what to expect from her, and although she was criticized for putting herself on a pedestal for lecturing like a teacher, and for changing her position on a number of issues, reactions to the book were not as violent as she had anticipated. She insisted, her critics said, that women had to be patient with the shortcomings of their husbands and preserve their marriages even if it meant setting aside their own needs, but she wasn't doing so herself. Most women did more housework than she ever did and few found it stimulating. They advised her to "change her tone"—"truly great people have more humility."

She answered that she had never said that women should have no interests outside of their homes, only that they should not neglect their husbands and children for those interests. Working at a machine, licking stamps in an office, or being a streetcar conductor wasn't all that thrilling, and women who chose to work were not superior to those who chose to take their responsibilities as wives and mothers seriously. She wasn't speaking of poor or single women who had to work, she was referring to those who worked in order to get away from home. She had had her say about women's problems, she said, and would write no more about them. She was fed up with public debates.

Holed up in Lillehammer, she turned her attention to her children. In the hubbub at Sinsen she had not been able to devote much time to Anders. He was seven now, and she found him a refreshing companion. They took long walks together and she selected books for him to read. She was reading More's *Utopia*, Dickens, Chaucer and the works which her publisher was sending her.˙ Had Nini noticed, she wrote to her friend, that most of the current books were circling around religion?

> *It is as if people were looking for an apartment and were trying to decide if the old church was livable, if there would be money enough to make it livable, or should they build something more to their liking. Winter is coming and people haven't the courage to lie under the bushes anymore.*[1]

All of the children had whooping cough that winter and in a short story which she called *Spring Clouds*,˙˙ Sigrid, who was thirty-eight, wrote about a young mother whose children have just recovered from a childhood disease. She takes her son for a walk in the country and is amazed to find that spring is almost over. She had been so housebound that she hadn't noticed when it had arrived. She recalls a spring "an eternity ago" when she was 'young and lonely, standing in the sun and feeling herself as a living growth that has its development in front of her . . . l There were half-forgotten faces . . . not memories of great things . . ." and now she was standing there "like a tourist . . . It was strange that one could long like this after one's own longings." There were pleasures to be derived from children . . ." and yet, there was that tender tug—not to be young anymore."[2]

Her sun-filled house, with its peaceful view of the town and valley, was a welcome haven from carping critics and prying eyes. Time was passing and living arrangements with Svarstad had not been resolved. She regretted her precipitous behavior and wanted to make amends. She had been distraught over Mosse and was expecting another child when she left. She was calmer now and willing to accept a compromise. She would have a serious talk with him when he got back, but since nothing could be done until then, she relaxed and embarked upon a new project.

When she was younger and knew that she couldn't (nor did she want to) compete with the Francescas and Betzys who drifted and "just let things happen," she had tried to make something of herself. Her blood had been as red and hot as theirs, but she wouldn't make love indifferently because "the joy she coveted" had to be "all consuming."[3] When her schoolmates laughed at her for not answering the teachers' questions with the accepted formulations, "a quiet, implacable hatred had grown in her," and she had hidden her hurt behind a scornful, "indifferent smile."[4] Lonely, and misunderstood, unable to

---

˙ She kept the ones that interested her and sent the rest to a local hospital.

˙˙ Included in *Romaner Og Fortellinger*, Aschehoug 1921.

talk to her mother and without a father to turn to, she had done what would have pleased her father most—she had researched the distant past. Her situation was different now. She was a successful writer, a wife and a mother, but her husband's selfishness and her daughter's illness were forcing her to withdraw again, and again she turned to other times. It wasn't that she consciously avoided the present, it was just that she had learned, long ago, that the best cure for loneliness was an intellectual pursuit, and the project she chose provided her with a stimulating opportunity for fulfillment and inner renewal.

She had always been interested in history, but it wasn't history as such that she wanted to write about. She didn't care about heroes, battles, court intrigues or the power plays of rulers. "History," she once told a friend, "was not what a famous person ate for lunch before he made a famous speech that 'changed history.'"[5] What intrigued her was human behavior. She couldn't fathom why Svarstad, who was intelligent and kind—yes, kind (he was never rough or intentionally hurtful)—could love his wife and children and not be willing to do anything for them. She had always been baffled by women who gave nothing and expected everything. If fathers and mothers were not willing to inconvenience themselves for their children, and brothers could not live in peace, what hope was there that strangers would be willing to make sacrifices for each other? She had always believed that if people couldn't exploit each other for financial gain they would be kinder, but the Russian Revolution had made it clear that the violence that had to be resorted to in order to eliminate economic exploitation only begat more violence and new forms of exploitations. Could laws and education change people?

She decided to pick a transitional period of history, the beginning of the 14th century, and explore how different social and economic conditions affected behavior. That was a time when the people who farmed the land were beginning to demand the right to own it, while their feudal landlords were still maintaining private armies of knights and mercenaries to protect their holdings. She wanted to find out how each group settled its disputes, how it cared for the sick and poor, and if new laws and different living conditions influenced their concern for each other. There was little in print and she started by going through old church and cloister records. Then a leading medieval scholar, Fredrik Paasche, directed her to the *Diplomatarium Norvegicum* (a collection of letters, documents, lawsuits, testaments and inventories of the period) and she had what she had been looking for.

With few distractions and a more peaceful existence, her thoughts began to fall into place and she started the book she had been mulling over. Every night after the children were asleep, she drank black coffee, smoked cigarettes and tried to get a hold on it. It had to have a voice of its own. She had never been comfortable with poetry, but she reveled in ballads and folksongs. In *Viga-Ljot and Vigdis*, she had used the rhythms and speech patterns of the sagas. She wanted the new book to have the cadences of Old Norse and yet sound biblical.

"It glitters and glows and becomes quiet and nice when I sit and knit and think about it," she wrote to Nini, "but at night, when I take pen in hand, it threatens to elude me." Finally it started to pour out of her and she was having a hard time "containing it."[6]

> *Oh, if I only had some of X's and Y's happiness in their own beautiful children. That would be so good to have . . . a little of their sandpiper's joy . . . delight in their own fine progeny and a little confidence in critics so that I could care about their rules and enjoy their praise and worry about their criticism. I don't think there is a single one who can teach me anything. I know I need to learn an awful lot. It is, by the way, not only with my work, I have a feeling that I'm teetering quite alone in the world of streams, looking around for a fixed point from which I can unfold. I long for a church on a cliff which never has said a thing that is good because it is new or good if it is old, but on the contrary has as a sacrament the wine which is best when it is old and the bread which is best when it is new."[7]*

The lease on her house expired but since Svarstad was still abroad she renewed it for another year and went on writing. She had two farm girls to help her and she could work until two or three o'clock in the morning. She would get up for breakfast with the children, turn them over to the housekeeper after Anders left for school, and go back to bed to pore over the ledgers and journals that she had collected.

"I'm afraid I've taken an advance on the eighty or ninety years that we usually live in my family," she wrote to Nini, "but the book has taken possession of me."[8] She was addicted to it. She couldn't stay away from it.

In April, she published an article about the life of St. Halvard in *Tidens Tegn*, and she spoke about St. Olav on the steps of an old church in Maihaugen[*] during the summer.

Svarstad returned in November and she spent ten days with him in Kampen. His trip had not been successful, and he was out-of-sorts and

---

[*] A reconstruction of an ancient village. Now a museum, it was assembled by Anders Sandvig, a dentist, who had accepted old artifacts and implements from the barns and homes of local farmers as payment for his service.

unwilling to commit himself to any plans for the future. Nothing was decided and she returned home deeply disappointed, but he came up for Christmas with the children and all of the special foods and presents were there for them as usual.

Despite her inner turmoil, giving birth to Hans, tending to the needs of her sick daughter, spending time with Anders, and getting her house in order, the first volume of her masterpiece—*Kristin Lavransdatter*—appeared a year and a half after she got to Lillehammer. With hypnotic magic, that uniquely intuitive portrayal of the lives and emotions of the people of medieval Norway poured out of her with such passion that there were few corrections to be made on her finished manuscript.

The first book, *The Bridal Wreath*, starts when Kristin, the eldest daughter of Ragnfrid and Lavrans Björgulfsön, is still a little girl. Her parents are prosperous farmers and pious Christians, and since they have no sons and she will inherit Jörundgaard, (their substantial farm in Gudbrandsdalen), it is important that she make a suitable marriage. When she is fifteen, her father promises her to Simon Andressön, a young farmer whose family's land borders on his. She would have preferred Arne, her childhood playmate, but he has no land to add to the family estate and she is a dutiful daughter and will do as she is told. "She liked Simon well enough—most, though, when he talked with others and did not touch or talk to her."[9]

Bentein, the ne'er-do-well son of a local priest attacks her on a lonely road and she barely escapes being raped. Arne defends her honor and is killed, and Kristin, who feels responsible for his death, begs to be allowed to enter a cloister. Sigrid's characters are not simplistic. We learn that Arne's death is not the only reason that Kristin wants to go to a cloister. It would provide an opportunity for postponing her marriage to Simon, give her a chance to pray for better health for her sister, and most of all, help her atone for the guilt with which the local priest has been burdening her because her sister Ulvhild, who is a cripple, has been promised to the Church and she, who is healthy, was not.

"To God," he told her, "people give the daughters who are lame, purblind, ugly, or blemished, or they let Him have back the children when they deem Him to have given them more than they need. And they wonder that all who dwell in the cloisters are not holy men and maids."[10]

Lavrans is a pious man but he would never permit Kristin to become a nun. She is his only hope for an heir, and as much as he loves the Church, his need for continuing his line is greater. However, a little time in a convent might be good training for her and he agrees to a short stay.

While on an outing from the cloister, she is saved from an unpleasant encounter by a dashing young knight. Sir Erlend Nikulaussön is wealthy, handsome and related to the King. He insists on escorting her to the convent so that she will not get into trouble again, and when he lifts her onto his horse, "a sweet and happy thrill ran through her to feel how carefully he held her from him as though afraid to come near her. At home, no one ever minded how tightly they held her when they helped her on to a horse. She felt marvelously honored and uplifted."[11]

They begin to meet secretly and are strongly attracted to each other. When he kisses her the look on his face reminds her of a starving man who had kissed the bread the nuns had given him that morning. Their hunger for each other becomes so great that before she understands what is happening, they are sexually united. She is surprised at how much she needs him after that, and in her innocence she expects that they will get married immediately and never be parted, but he says there are a number of problems that have to be resolved first. She has an engagement to break and he has to free himself from a long involvement with a woman.

When he was a young man, Erlend explains, he had an affair with Eline Ormsdatter, who was married. Her elderly husband discovered their liaison and Erlend was banished from the land. Eline followed, and they had two children. After his banishment was over, he brought them to Husaby, his family estate. Eline was slothful, and since Erlend was often away on knightly errands, his properties deteriorated. She was still living at Husaby and waiting for her husband to die so that they could marry, but he had long been looking for a way to rid himself of that relationship.

Kristin is horrified, especially when he says that he can not continue to live on his estate because he can't trust himself not to fall back into sin if Eline were near. She begs him to allow her to stay with him while they resolve their problems but he says he doesn't want to live as an outcast again. He wants to marry her properly.

Although Simon is in love with Kristin, he releases her from her pledge, but her father will not permit her to marry Erlend. It is true that Erlend is an aristocrat and she is only a farmer's daughter, but he has disgraced himself with a married woman and has behaved so irresponsibly that no good Christian father would give him his innocent child. Kristin pleads with him but when time passes and it seems that he will never give his consent, the lovers decide to elope. They meet at Erlend's aunt's house, but Eline has followed them. She tries to poison Kristin, and in the struggle which ensues, she pulls a dagger. Erlend attempts to take it from her and she turns it on herself and dies. They manage to dispose of the body, but under the circumstances it is too risky to elope and Kristin has no choice but to return to her father's house.

They continue to meet secretly, and after more than three years of waiting, when unbeknownst to her father, Kristin is already pregnant, her mother finally persuades him to give his consent. He makes an elaborate wedding, but when the newlyweds are put to bed, he is shocked at his daughter's lack of modesty and guesses that the marriage has already been consummated.

Lavrans has been described as a God-fearing man who, though younger and better looking than his wife, is always gentle and loving, while Ragnfrid, who comes from a wealthier, more important family—though hard-working—is silent, "chary to show affection," and "somewhat strange and heavy of mood."[12] They lost three sons before Kristin was born, and a daughter who was crippled, and one assumes that her lack of cheer is due to those tragedies, but in a beautifully written fugue-like scene which takes place after Kristin's wedding, we discover that all is not as it appears.

Lavrans is unable to forget the sensuous look on his daughter's face and complains to his wife that he doesn't know why God has given him so many sorrows when he was always tried so faithfully to do God's will. Why did they lose their little boys and their poor crippled daughter, and why did his favorite child have to go to her bridal bed "honorless, to an untrusty and witless man?"[13]

Believing that he has guessed the secret which she has kept from him all the years of their marriage, Ragnfrid turns away in fear—but his thoughts are elsewhere. Envious of the passion he has witnessed, he says, "But 'twas that I *could* not—be as you would have had me—when we were so young. I am not such a one— . . ."

> Thoughts crowded and tossed to and fro within him. That single unveiled glance in which the hearts of bridegroom and bride had leapt together—the two young faces flushing up redly—to him it seemed a very shamelessness. It had been agony, a scorching pain to him, that this was his daughter. But the sight of those eyes would not leave him; and wildly and blindly he strove against the tearing away of the veil from something in his own heart, something that he had never owned was there, that he had guarded against his own wife when she sought for it.
>
> 'Twas that I could not, he says again stubbornly to himself. In the devil's name—he had been married off as a boy; he had not chosen for himself; she was older than he—he had not desired her; he had no

will to learn this of her—to love. He grew hot with shame even now when he thought of it—that she would have had him lover her. That she had proffered him all this that he had never prayed for.

He had been a good husband to her—so he had ever thought. He had shown her all the honor he could, given her full power in her own affairs, and asked her counsel in all things; he had been true to her—and they had had six children together. All he had asked had been that he might live with her, without her forever grasping at this thing in his heart that he could not lay bare . . . [14]

So he had turned to his children—

. . . the young ones in the nest—they had been the little warm green spot in the wilderness—the inmost, sweetest joy of his life. Those little girl-heads under his hand . . .

He remembered Kristin's little two-year-old body on his shoulder, her flaxen silky hair against his cheek, her small hands holding to his belt, while she butted her round hard child's forehead against his shoulder blades, when he rode out with her behind him on his horse.

And now she had that same glow in her eyes—and she had one what was hers. She sat there in the half-shadow against the silken pillows of the bed. In the candlelight she was all golden—golden crown and golden shift and golden hair spread over the naked golden arms. Her eyes were no longer—

Her father winced with shame.

And yet, it was as though his heart were bleeding within him, for what he himself had never won; and for his wife, there by his side, whom he had never given what should have been hers.

Weak with pity, he felt in the darkness for Ragnfrid's hand.

". . . Methought it was well with us in our life together," he said. "Methought 'twas but that you sorrowed for our children—ay, that you were born heavy of mood. Never did it come to my mind, it might be that I was no good husband to you—" [15]

Ragnfrid assures him that he was ever a good husband, but he says,

"Yet had it mayhap been better with you, if you had been wedded even as our daughter was today—" [16]

His wife cries out and haltingly confesses that she was pregnant when they were married. He never knew that, and he is aghast, but she goes on. The man refused to marry her, but he had returned a year after she was married and told her that he loved her and would have married her if she had still been free. "He said so," she muses. "God knows if he said true . . ."[17]

And Lavrans understands, for the first time, that all those years she was longing for what that man had given her that he, her husband, had never been able to.*

Husband and wife are silent for a long time. Then she asks him if he remembers the ancient lay they once heard about a man who came back from the dead and said that the "groaning from Hell's deepest ground" was the sound "of untrue women grinding mould for their husband's meat."[18]

Lavrans says nothing for a while and then answers sadly, "Mayhap mould must needs be ground, my Ragnfrid, before the meat can grow."[19] And the first volume of *Kristin Lavransdatter* ends with "And so they sat on, motionless, speaking no word more."[20]

Years later, when Tormod Skagestad dramatized *The Bridal Wreath*, Sigrid insisted that nothing be cut from that scene because she considered it the most important one in the book.[21]

The second volume of *Kristin Lavransdatter*, *The Mistress of Husaby*, appeared a year later. It deals with Kristin and Erlend's life as man and wife. Erlend is a passionate lover, gentle, and delightfully charming, but not a stimulating conversationalist. He has made no effort to conserve the wealth he inherited and Kristin finds his estate in shambles. Beautifully situated near the sea (in an area near Trondheim), it is larger and more elegant than Jörundgaard, but everything, including the morale of the servants, is in decay. She gets rid of the mould, has the necessary repairs done, and organizes it so well that his property is restored to its former affluence. Although she isn't fond of her stepchildren, she insists that they live with them. She is happy, but she hasn't forgotten that the child she carries was conceived in sin, and turning to the Church for forgiveness, she prays for her unborn child.

Erlend's younger brother, Gunnulf, is a priest. He has always envied Erlend for his charm, for being their mother's favorite, and for being the one who inherited the family estate, and although he is a fine scholar and a dedicated man of the cloth, he cannot rid himself of this envy. When Erlend

---

*   Eight years after *The Bridal Wreath* appeared, D. H. Lawrence published *Lady Chatterley's Lover*.

brings home such a beautiful and capable wife, and he discovers that she was pregnant when they were married, he has to struggle even harder to be a loving brother. He begins to devote himself to Kristin's religious instruction and although he is not her confessor, she discusses her problems with him. She has promised her confessor that she will do a special penance if her child is born healthy, and although she almost dies in childbirth, both she and the baby survive. Before she has fully recovered, Gunnulf suggests that as a penance for her sins, she walk to the Cathedral in Nidaros in bare feet, and lay down upon St. Olaf's grave "the golden garland of maidenhood which she had guarded so ill and borne so wrongfully."[22] To prepare for this pilgrimage she should stay away from her husband's bed, pray, read, meditate and fast—but "the last with due measure, for the sake of the child at her breast."[23]

When Erlend sees her in bare feet and clad in sack cloth, setting out to walk twenty miles in the cold, with their child strapped to her back, carrying the golden garland and a little bread and salt, he falls to the ground and weeps. He asks her brother why he has lain such a heavy penance upon her. Couldn't he have absolved her? Hadn't he, the child's father, done enough penance by buying thirty days of masses and vigils, a yearly mass on her death day forever, and a grave in hallowed ground? Had he not confessed their sin to Bishop Helge and made a pilgrimage to the Holy Blood at Schwerin? Could none of this help his wife?

His brother says that they each have to seek forgiveness separately, and not once but all of their lives and Erlend accuses him of being unnecessarily hard on Kristin because he is in love with her.

Gunnulf tells Kristin that her sins were not all hers, since it was Erlend who had constantly led her astray, but she denies it and insists that she wanted him as much as he wanted her. He is unable to bear her devotion to his brother and by constantly pressing her to be more pious, he sees to it that she doesn't get rid of her guilt. (Later, after Erlend has died, she lets Gunnulf know that she has always been aware of his jealousy, and that she knew that his piety was not always innocent.)

After she has done her penance, Kristin grows "dizzy and wild again" when Erlend "comes near with his smiling face and his venture-loving eyes . . . She is drunk, as it were, with him and his overflowing gladness,"[24] and it isn't long before she is pregnant again, but this time Erlend is not pleased. "Methought that once you were mine it would be like drinking Yuletide every day," he says, "but it looks as though most of the time will be long fasts."[25]

Gunnulf lectures her about willpower and physical restraint, but she says she cannot resist her husband's advances.

When they have had five sons, (two are twins), and their estate is prospering, Erlend begins to sell off land each time he's short of ready cash and she nags him for doing so. Her constant carping becomes more than he can bear and he accepts an assignment from the King to go abroad for two years. She can't believe that he is willing to be away from her for such a long time, but he goes.

Kristin is at the landing place when he returns.

> She was grown so fair that Erlend caught his breath when he saw her . . . The girlish look that had still come back to her after she had come through each childbed—the tender, frail, nunlike look under the matrons' coif—was gone. She was a young blooming wife and mother. Her cheeks were round and freshly red between the white lappets of her coif; her bosom full and firm for chins and brooches to glitter on. Her thighs were rounder and fuller under the keybelt and the gilded case that held knife and scissors. Yes, yes—she had but grown more fair—she looked not now as though they could blow her away from him to heaven so lightly as before. Even the long narrow hands were grown fuller and more white.[26]
>
> . . . now there came on Kristin a recklessness the likes of which she had never known. She grew livelier and less still in her mien when she was among strangers—for she felt herself very fair, and since she was healthful and fresh for the first time since she had been wed. and at night when Erlend and she lay in a strange be in a loft in one of the great folks' manors in the hall of a farm, they laughed and whispered and made sport of the folk they had met and jested over tidings they had heard. Erlend's tongue was more devil-may-care than ever, and folk seemed to like him better than ever before.[27]

One day, Erlend finds his daughter by Eline in bed with a married man, and he cuts off the married man's hand. In a fury, Kristin reminds him that her father forgave *them* when they did the same thing. Erlend accuses her of calling back "sins that have been confessed, done penance for, and been granted forgiveness for" not out of holiness, but only to have a weapon over him when he differs from her. He says she is "too greedy to rule," and that she "speaks to him as if he were a thrall"[28]—and in a fury, he visits a lady whom he had befriended when he was abroad. He has been involved in political intrigue, and forgets some incriminating papers in her house.* Her husband turns them over to the authorities and Erlend is arrested. Kristin knows that he doesn't love that woman, but was only there because she had driven him away by her frequent coldness and her venomous words. Full of remorse, she drops everything to help him.

Erlend is tortured and condemned to death, but Simon, who has married Kristin's youngest sister, manages to have him freed. Erlend's properties are confiscated. Stripped of all his worldly possessions, he is forced to move his family to Jörundgaard, which Kristin inherited after her father died.

The last volume, *The Cross*, describes their life after their ruin. They have seven sons by then, and Jörundgaard seems small and claustrophobic after the grandeur of Husaby. They miss the sea. Although he has lost everything, Erlend is less devastated by their downfall than Kristin—but he will not condescend to farm the land. He lazes around, goes hunting with his sons and teaches them knightly skills, while Kristin manages the farm and worries about their future.

When the children were small Erlend had paid little attention to them, but now he is their favored parent, and she fears they will end up like him. Their passion for each other has never waned, but they quarrel more frequently. Erlend cannot understand that times have changed and the days of knighthood and sea adventures are over. He believes that his sons will go into the service of noblemen, forgetting that even were such opportunities still available, his disgrace would disqualify them.

Kristin chastises him for not being a churchgoing man and he says he has seen too many priests who "came and went in his house like grey swine"[29] and they did little but wrangle. "They were hardhearted and unmerciful to their own archbishop . . . and they, who each day held in their hands the holiest of holy things and had lifted God Himself aloft in the bread and wine,"[30] were no more peace loving than anyone else. He cannot see how "storing up wrath and never forgetting"[31] was God's word. Often when she spoke so softly and sweetly as though her mouth were filled with honey, she was thinking most

---

* In 1319 Haakon V died and his grandson, Magnus, inherited the thrones of both Sweden and Norway. Since Magnus was still a child, Norway was ruled from Sweden by regents, but when he came of age and continued to rule from there, the Norwegian nobles had had enough of absentee kings. Although they were heavily taxed the King was not seeing their needs and they plotted to put his half-brother on the throne of Norway. That much is history. Sigrid took the liberty of putting her fictional Erlend in the center of such a plot.

of old wrongs—and God may judge whether her heart was full as pious as her mouth.[32]

She accuses him of relying on her father's prayers to save his sons "even as they are fed by his lands,"[33] and reminds him that their ruin was due to a meaningless dalliance—and, she adds—she knows that it had produced a child. Her last remark makes him furious. He says it was her coldness that drove him there—and leaves. She believes that he will return, but he doesn't.

Alone with his dogs and his horse, unkempt and uncared for, he lives in poverty in his aunt's abandoned house, but he has dishonored his knightly vows by working on the land like a thrall.

"What went on rankling," for Kristin, "were all the little wounds he had dealt her with his unkind heedlessness, his childish lack of patience, even with his wild and thoughtless way of loving . . ."[34] But she misses him so much that she swallows her pride and goes to him to ask him to come home—and what follows is one of the most exquisite love scenes in literature.

> *The wind from the mountains swept, cool and fresh, against her hot cheeks as she came up over the last rise. The sun shone golden upon the small grey houses, casting long shadows across the courtyard. The corn up here would soon be earing—it showed fairly upon the small plots, shimmering and swaying in the wind. On all the stone heaps and over the hillocks tall, waving willow-herb blossomed red, and in between were little haycocks. But on the farm was no living thing to be seen—not even a dog came forth to give warning . . .[35]*
>
> *An air noisome past bearing met her when she stepped in—the strong, rank smell of skins and of the stable. The first feeling that rushed over her as she stood within his house was heart-breaking remorse and pity. This dwelling seemed to her most like a bear's winter lair . . .[36]*

The windows were broken and stuffed with rags—weapons, furs and old clothes were strewn about—the filthy board was littered with leftover food, and flies buzzed high and low. Only his coat of mail, his helm and his shield had been cared for. She wonders "what must it have been for him to dwell in this house, to sleep here?"[37] (Where Eline had died.)

> *There was nothing in the bed save some sheepskins, and a pair of wadmal-covered pillows, so foul that they stank. Dust and trash showered from the bedgear when she handled it . . .*

Erlend who would don a silken shirt, velvet and fine furs on the least pretext—who chafed because she suffered his children to go clad in home-spun wadmal on workdays, and never could abide that she herself should suckle them and take a hand with her serving-women in the housework . . . Jesus, it was he himself who had brought things to this . . . [38]

She reminds herself that "she had chosen him in a frenzy of love," and that she had "chosen him anew each day"—[39]

Never could she have loved Simon . . . Yet—all that Erlend was not and that she had raged to find he was not, Simon was. But then must she herself be a pitiable woman, to murmur at her lot . . .

She . . . had raged, had stored up and brooded over every hurt . . . [40]

If he had betrayed her once and for all—and there had been an end. But he had not betrayed her—only failed her—and made her live fearful and unsure—no, never had he played her false, but never had he sustained her . . . yet she would never grow so old that he could not play upon her fondness . . . [41]

Erlend strode in, with the wood-axe in his hand and the dogs tumbling over the threshold before and after him . . . [42]

The first she saw was the wave of young, red blood that rushed over his face—the fluttering quiver about his fine, weak mouth, the great eyes deep in the shadows of the brows—

The sight of him took away her breath. She saw, indeed, the old growth of stubble upon his lower face, she saw that his unkempt hair was iron-grey—but the color came and went in his cheeks in hasty pulses, as when they were young—he was so young and comely, 'twas as though naught had availed to quell him.

He was miserably clad—his blue shirt dirty and ragged . . . Yet never, more than now, had he seemed the son of chief and nobles . . . [43]

The next morning she awoke "with his head on her shoulder."

She looked at the man's iron-grey hair. She saw her own small shrunken breasts—above and below them the high-arched curves of her ribs showed under the thin covering of flesh. A kind of terror came over her while memory after memory arose from this night . . . they two, young no longer—Disquiet and shame took hold on her when she saw the livid patches upon her work-worn mother's arms, on her shrunken bosom. Wildly she caught at the coverlid and would have covered herself—

Erlend awoke, started up on his elbow, stared into her face—his eyes were coal-black from sleep:

"Methought"—he threw himself down beside her again: a deep wild tremor went through her whole being at the rejoicing and fear in his voice. "Methought I had dreamed again—"

She pressed her open lips upon his mouth and twined her arms around his neck. Never, never had it been so blessed—

Late in the afternoon, when the sunshine was yellow already and the shadows lay long over the green courtyard, they set out down to the beck to fetch water . . . [44]

While Erlend bathed, Kristin leaned against a stone.

The fell beck thrilled and gurgled her into a doze—now and then, when the midges and gnats touched her skin, she opened her eyes a little and brushed them off. Down among the sallows around the pool she caught a glimpse of Erlend's white body—he stood with a foot upon a stone, rubbing himself with wisps of grass. She closed her eyes again and smiled, in happy weariness. She was as strengthless as ever against him—[45]

Kristin is sure that he will come home with her now, but he says he will never be a farmer and will not return to *her* house. Instead, he invites her to stay with him. It is such an irresponsible suggestion that she can't believe he means it. How can they leave their children and their farm? Their eldest son is only eighteen years old. She will not abandon the children, and has no choice but to return alone.

She gives birth to another son as a result of her visit with Erlend but the baby is weak and dies. Since her husband has been away for a long time, it is assumed that the baby must have been fathered by another man. Since she might have wanted to hide it, she is asked to prove that she didn't kill it. Erlend comes home to defend her and is wounded in a fight. She wants to call a priest, but he will not allow the priest who brought such dreadful accusations against his wife into their house. Gallant to the end, he risks his soul through all eternity to defend her honor, and dies without absolution or last rites. Kristin, though loving, is bitter to the end, but Erlend speaks only of the beauty of their love until he expires.

Years pass. One son marries a practical young woman of the "new generation" and takes over the farm, two become priests, two die and the others go out into the world. Kristin cannot get along with her daughter-in-law and knows that she must leave. It seemed as if yearnings for the past

> . . . *burst her heart in sunder—they ran hither and thither like streams of blood, seeking out ways to all places in the wide-stretched land where she had lived, to all the sons she had wandering in the world, to all her dead beneath the mould.*[46]

She sees her life as from above a high mountain, in a way that she has never seen it before and goes on another pilgrimage.

> *Never, it seemed to her, had she prayed to God for aught else than that he might grant her her own will. And she had got always what she wished—most. And now she sat here with a bruised spirit—not because she had sinned against God, but because she was miscontent that it had been granted her to follow the devices of her own heart to the journey's end.*
>
> *She had not come to God with her garland, nor with her sins and sorrows—not so long as the world still held a drop of sweetness to mix in her cup . . . but now she learned that the world is like a tavern—where he who has naught more to spend from is cast out at the door.*[47]

Her soul had

> . . . *lived as folk live on a manor through the busy summer half-year, when they move out of the great hall and bide in the storehouse loft. All day long they go to and fro past the winter hall, never thinking of going in thither, though they have but to lay their hand on a latch and push open a door. And when at last some day they have an errand thither, the house has grown strange and almost solemn, because of the air of loneliness and quiet that has come to it.*[48]

The plague breaks out in Norway and Kristin goes to a cloister to help care for the sick. She's infected and before she dies, she donates the only thing she has left, her wedding ring, for Masses for the dead.

> *The life that ring had wed her to, that she had complained against,*
> *had murmured at, had raged at and defied—none the less she had loved*
> *it so, joyed in it so, both in good days and evil, that not one day had*
> *there been when 'twould not have seemed hard to give it back to God,*
> *nor one grief that she could have forgone without regret.*[49]

When Sigrid started *The Bridal Wreath* she had been married for seven years. The passionate love scenes were described by a knowing woman, and the book was her love letter to Svarstad who, though it may be hard to believe, was her Erlend.

When she started *The Mistress of Husaby*, she still had hopes of saving her marriage and she had begun to realize that they would *both* have to bend a little, but by the time she got to *The Cross*, she knew that her marriage was over and she was ready to discuss Kristin's hubris, and the role her willfulness had played in the destruction of her marriage. No matter how hard she tried, she had not been able to conquer it. Why couldn't two people who loved each other that much bend enough to keep their marriage alive? Although they both wanted it, neither would make it possible. Would only supernatural intervention save us from ourselves?

With the oceanic force of her genius and her deep understanding of people, Sigrid presented a woman trained to set her own needs aside at the dictate of the men in her society, who struggled and succeeded, against all odds, in shaping her own life. Kristin's faults are not minimized. At no time is she idealized. She is neither on a pedestal nor a shrew. Far from perfect, she is, therefore, equal to any man. She is jealous of her husband's first love, has difficulties accepting her stepchildren, is often disappointed with her own children, is arrogant and can't forget or forgive a wrong, but she is passionate, hardworking and self-sufficient—and she is constantly trying to become a better person.

She can see Simon's virtues, but she doesn't hesitate to give herself to the erotically exciting, less responsible Erlend. When Simon asks her what she would have done if he had forced her to marry him, she says, "Methinks I had taken a knife to bed with me."[50] We know that the joy she derived from Erlend created more happiness than the security and comforts she might have had from the kind, but passionless Simon. Every sort of love and jealousy is explored. Simon's unrequited love for Kristin—Ramborg's envy of her older sister and her inability to understand why her husband, (who like Lavrans is not much of a lover) doesn't respond more to her youth and gaiety but longs for her sister who doesn't want him—Gunnulf, who is a brilliant man and a good priest but cannot rid himself of envy. All of her characters, including the clergy, have faults and questionable motivations and yet they all emerge with astounding dignity.

Nini Roll Anker wrote:

> *No one in Norway had yet received such eulogies as Sigrid received for the first volume of her masterpiece, but she was more excited about the five kilos of home-churned butter she received from a grateful country lady who loved the book, and the fact that Asta Westbye, her former housekeeper, had written that no one would ever guess that she hadn't been brought up on a farm.*[51]

Masterpieces are not easily wrought. Apart from requiring a theme of universal appeal and exceptional execution, it takes magical inspiration on the part of a great artist to create one. The *Kristin Lavransdatter* trilogy, which has all of these components, is one of the most powerful, poetic works in prose. Still in print, it has been translated into almost every known language and has mesmerized and enchanted several generations of readers. A profound study of human behavior, it is a spellbinding, meticulously researched adventure story about medieval Norway—and the adventures are both physical and psychological ones. The tapestry is as intricate and fascinating as people and societies are intricate and fascinating. The characters are dressed, live in homes, worship in churches, eat the foods, react to events as people did at the time, but their joys and passions, their humor and wit, their willfulness and weaknesses, envies and greeds, are those of people in any society—at any time—and because we recognize ourselves in them, we are immediately caught up in their story.

She points out that concepts of "right" and "wrong" may change, and events that seem mundane when they occur may have hidden and far-reaching consequences, but regardless of the governments people create, despite their capacities for altruism and brotherly love for extended periods of time when their covetousness and desire to dominate others is threatened.

Sigrid had always been popular with her readers and her editors had guarded her privacy so assiduously that she often complained that she felt she was "playing hooky" if she was allowed the slightest distraction to interrupt her work, but after the first volume of *Kristin Lavransdatter* appeared, she needed all the protection she could get. Reporters hounded her day and night, and requests for money and endorsements of "worthy causes" poured in. She avoided the visitors and reporters, but she answered the appeals from people who were in dire straits.

After *Kristin* appeared, *Jenny* was translated in English and sold as part of a "Scandinavian Package" (which included Knut Hamsun's *Growth of the Soil* and several other books) to Alfred A. Knopf in the United States. Sigrid was not happy with the translation of *Jenny* and wasn't even sure she still liked the book, but she was very pleased with Charles Archer's translation of *Kristin Lavransdatter*, and he translated most of her later books.[*]

Although *The Master of Hestviken* and some of her short stories are masterful, *Kristin Lavransdatter* was her greatest achievement. It was a best seller for the Book-of-the-Month Club for years and until recently was required reading for literature courses in most universities.

---

[*]   The three volumes of *Kristin Lavransdatter* appeared in Norway in 1920, 1921 and 1922, and in the United States in 1923, 1925 and 1927.

CHAPTER XI

HAPPY TIMES

1921-1924

After the first volume of *Kristin Lavransdatter* appeared, Sigrid was freed of financial worries. In 1921, she bought the house she had been renting. It came with a substantial piece of land much of which sloped downhill and was covered with huge boulders and thick underbrush, and included a beautiful wooded area with old birch trees and a brook. Many truckloads of rocks were hauled away before the hillside was cleared for a play area and garden, but the wooded section was left untouched.

Plants that were no longer to be found in Norway were often mentioned in the documents she was pouring over, and her interest in botany was revived. Nini had just published a book about gardening, but Sigrid's interest was more esoteric. She began to collect rare plants and her indoor and outdoor gardens became so impressive that botanists from all over the world came to see them.

Ever since the Danes ruled Norway, they have made jokes about Norwegians. They call them "Norse Norwegians from Norway" or *Bjerkebaeks* (hayseeds). In Norwegian, *bjerk* is a birch and *bekk* is brook, and since Sigrid had both birch trees and a brook on her land, she twitted her Danish relatives by naming her estate Bjerkebaek.

As soon as *Kristin Lavransdatter* was out of the way, Sigrid took Mosse to the Rikshospital for a new evaluation. She claimed that her daughter always knew when a special event was approaching. That may have been so, or she may have been reacting to tensions around her, but she managed to spill boiling water all over herself just as they were about to leave the house.

She was badly scalded and by the time Sigrid got her to Christiania and delivered her to the hospital, she was near a breakdown. The report was no more hopeful than in the past and the doctors recommended, again, that the child be institutionalized.

Sigrid knew of the excellent work that the Danish Johan Keller, and later his son Christian, had done with deaf and mute children and, in 1923, she took Mosse to Denmark for a consultation. She was impressed with their results but they said they couldn't help Mosse, who was neither deaf nor mute. She was "out of the world" and their therapy would not work for her. Since no institution felt that she could be helped, there was no point in considering any of them. Mosse stayed with her family and no child could have been treated more lovingly. Those who visited Bjerkebaek say that she was a happy child and that Sigrid's devotion to her was incredible, but the entire household had to be organized around her needs—and that could only have been done at the expense of the other children. There is no doubt that Anders and Hans suffered. They loved their sister and were gentle with her. They built endless castles for her to knock down (a game she enjoyed long after she was no longer a child) and they protected her from other children. Sigrid provided many activities for them, and their friends were always welcome, but Mosse's needs had to come before theirs, and since Sigrid spent a great deal of time at her work, their emotional problems were often overlooked. Mosse sat at the table at mealtimes, and bringing friends home was not pleasant. She drooled, had to be fed, and made it difficult to carry on a conversation. Anders withdrew and lived his life away from home, but Hans fought, what seems to have been a losing battle for attention, by trying to impress everyone, including his mother, with his exceptionalness.

Nevertheless, despite Mosse's illness and Svarstad's long absences, Bjerkebaek was a happy household. The boys were active, a way of life was established for Mosse, and Sigrid's work was going well. The walls of the house were thin. Mosse had a phonograph which was played all day long, and the "screaming record player was deafening." At first, Sigrid had a cottage built to work in, but in the summer of 1924, she bought another timbered house (part of which dated from the year 1500) and had it moved to Lillehammer. It was positioned for the best view and the three structures were connected with passageways. Modern plumbing was installed throughout, and a good kitchen and woodshed were added, but the original character of the houses was not changed. The new house was much larger than the first, and when the walls were up, the original benches attached, and the fireplace (which was as big as a mid-sized room) installed . . ." 'It is some ugly pig' to use

Hansemand's [Hans'] favorite expression," Sigrid wrote to Nini. Hans was hanging around the workmen all day learning to nail pieces of wood together and was beginning to speak like an Opplander, "'because I *am* an Opplander, Mother,' he says. He is very fond of flowers and is continually bringing flowers to all of us."[1]

Her flowers were doing very well. Out of twenty-six bourbon roses, only two didn't come up and even they were full of long, pale shoots which faded and fell off. Out of sixty salmon roses, only six died. Resvall Holmsen's yellow poppies were nice and big, and the silenes, the blue duenes and the tansy roots from Trondheim were fine too. The new house was so beautiful that Nini wouldn't believe it until she saw it for herself.

There were iron fittings from 1789, the doors were from the original house, and all of the ceilings had fruitwood beams with Kebersten Staves.* The doors had brass fittings from Lillehammer that were so magnificent that she ordered some for Nini.

A local librarian helped her catalogue and arrange her huge library, and it gave her a sense of order to have everything she might need at her fingertips. She had, long ago, begun to collect Old Norse utensils and handicrafts, and since the start of her research for *Kristin Lavransdatter*, she had been buying old church art. As she began to hang her paintings and arrange her sculpture and artifacts, her excitement grew.

"I can't wait to be at peace with only my children around me, and not have to hear and see strange people twenty-four hours a day," she wrote to her friend. "It is perhaps because my hour of freedom is so close now, that I can't bear it a single day longer."[2]

(In 1925, she put in a frost-free cellar and a room where apples could be stored and onions put to root, and while the builders were still there, she had a high wooden fence put around the property so that curious sightseers and mischievous children would not harass Mosse.

As eulogies for *Kristin Lavransdatter* poured in, hundreds of requests for money arrived. People had farms they wanted to buy, widows wanted their mortgages paid, farmers needed farm equipment and town women wanted knitting machines. She was asked to help starving children, and young couples who wanted to get married. Women ran up bills that they didn't want their husbands to know about, and men accumulated gambling debts. A small pub owner wanted her to help him buy a jukebox. She read each letter carefully and sent money to many. Alfred Knopf told me that when her lawyer, Eilif

---

* Soapstone joints used in the old wooden stave churches.

Moe, cautioned her to limit her donations to "only the most worthy," she asked whom he considered "worthy."

Sigrid had always been a gracious hostess, but as each volume of *Kristin* appeared, her generosity to her family and friends knew no bounds. Signe had three daughters: Charlotte, Sigrid and little Signe—Ragnhild had Ulla and Ingvald—Gunhild married and had Brit and Knut—and they, in addition to their spouses, Mrs. Undset, Svarstad, Ebba, Trond with the Stendhals, and many friends came to Bjerkebaek for Christmas and summer holidays and all remember those visits as some of the happiest times of their lives.*

In her enchanting memoir of her aunt,** Charlotte wrote, "If it is true that a house can have a soul, it applies more to Bjerkebaek than to any other house I have ever been in."[3]

It is difficult to describe the impression Sigrid Undset's large room and small bedroom make when one sees them for the first time," Nini wrote,

> *The strange mixture of times long ago and the life of today—of a working person's activities now, and the silences . . . of other generations. The long wall in the living room is covered with books from floor to ceiling. On top is a collection of old Norwegian tankards, old irons made of wood, wooden bowls of all kinds and all in beautiful faded colors. The many colors of the books create a most beautiful contrast to the enormous white fireplace. From the short wall facing east which also has a window, Gerhard Munthe's paintings light up. A row of small-paned windows facing south have clear white curtains and the windowsills are full of flowering plants. That is true of all the windowsills in the house, even the bathrooms. I think she said she had about 400 houseplants last year—rare and ordinary ones, tiny, little and huge, luxurious ones, climbing and hanging ones. She takes cuttings home in her hat box when she travels. Begonias from Runeberg's house in Borga, hibiscus from Denmark, beautiful old-fashioned roses from the area's farms, strangely formed cacti and growths that I never saw except in greenhouses. She looks after most of them herself. She has the most wonderful hands. Never do her large eyes shine with happiness like they do when she shows an example of a plant which caused her*

---

*   Charlotte remembered twelve Christmases at Bjerkebaek.

**   *Moster Sigrid* by Charlotte Blindheim—published by H. Aschehoug & Co., 1982. (Not available in English.)

trouble, but was now doing well, or when she hears a new migrating
bird in the garden or detects it at the bird bath. She loves birds, and
is never wrong in identifying them.

Her workroom looks like a Catholic chapel. It has one small,
square window in front of which stands the writing desk and most
of the months she has to work by the light of a lamp. In that room's
half-darkness, apart from the bookcases, there are copies of old Gothic
sculptures, pictures of saints, crucifixes and other wonderful church
arts. The typewriter and manuscripts heaped on the table tell of her
presence . . . and everything else of her fate, her dreamworld and her
sense of beauty. A long hall with a door to the garden connects the
two houses. The previous living room has become a dining room with
furniture made by one of her Danish forefathers. There is also a sofa
and a large round table covered with recent journals. She reads there
in a high-backed arm chair during the day. I believe there is rarely a
book that has come out that she doesn't know . . . and she relaxes with
detective stories.[4]

Lillehammer, which had a population of 5,000 when the skiers weren't
there, was a charming resort town, and after magazines and newspapers
had described Sigrid's house, artifacts, library, collection of old silver, hand-
embroidered linens, and exotic garden, tourists began to flock there and she
became more entrenched than ever against prying strangers—but her family
and friends were always welcome.

When she had guests, they stayed in the two smaller houses, but at other
times, the children and their friends played in the first house and the family
had their meals there. Sigrid had a small downstairs bedroom in the larger
house, Mosse shared a bedroom upstairs with whomever was caring for her
at the time, and the boys had their room.

When there were guests, everyone ate in the main house and entertainments
were held in front of the huge fireplace.[*]

In 1924 Sigrid bought a Steinway concert grand in the hope that the
children would study music, but despite her urging, none did. It was used
for musical evenings and added to the enjoyment of her guests.[**]

---

[*]   I have both interior and exterior pictures of Bjerkebaek.

[**]   In the thirties, when she was short of money for her long list of annual Christmas
       gifts to the poor, she sold the piano to enable her to send the gifts as usual—and
       when she heard that Svarstad's ex-wife was not well, she added her to the list.

Sigrid loved her new home. Her creative forces were released, and with recognition and financial security, she began to enjoy her life as she had never been able to do before. Providing comforts for so many people, while producing such an astonishing body of work required careful planning, but all of her guests remembered their visits as unique experiences.

"Rules were strictly abided by," Charlotte wrote, "no cloister could have enforced them more strictly,"[5] but everyone convalesced there and no one was ever pampered like that before or after. There were great dinners with sparkling crystal and silver on the beautifully set candle-lit table, and the smell of flowers and burning Birchwood, the sleigh rides and the dances were never forgotten. Her aunt always served plenty of homegrown vegetables and she insisted on making the dressing and tossing the salads herself. She had elegant hands with long, tapering fingers and she always prepared it in her grandfather's bowl with his old carved serving pieces. She believed that children needed plenty of exercise and fresh air and the servants needed them out of the way so that they could do their work, so she organized all sorts of outdoor activities. Her nieces become nostalgic when they describe what a treat it was to come in from the cold to platters of cookies and cakes and huge copper bowls full of fruits, nuts and dates, (a great luxury in those days.)

There were social evenings when the children would hang over the railings of the upper floor and listen to Helene Frøysland play or Einer Fagstad sing, and Sigrid never failed to come up and read *Pinocchio* or *Undine* or *A Thousand and One Nights* to them after they were in bed.

In a "thank you" note to her hostess, after a visit to Bjerkebaek in 1938, the Swedish writer Alice Lyttkens wrote:

> *When I think of those days, everything combines to make a wreath of more or less important memories around one little second. That was when I came into your large room. You stood at the door of your workroom and waited for us. A fire was burning in the fireplace . . . It was warm and cozy in that particular way that is not warmth as much as a good feeling that one can give oneself to completely, sit down in, and in which one can feel happy and cared for . . . and that warmth was you.*[6]

The nieces always got special attention. Everything she had wanted when she was a girl and would never be able to give her daughter, she lavished on them. When she went on a trip, she would return with crates full of presents and the inevitable hatbox filled with plant cuttings. She never brought "practical" gifts, only beautiful dresses, coral necklaces or "luxury" items. The moments before a box was opened were always filled with suspense—they shivered with anticipation, and never were disappointed. Sigrid had not forgotten the excitement she had shared with her sisters when the Christmas boxes arrived from their relatives.

"My aunt's hospitality, kindness and generosity to her family cannot be described in words," her niece Ulla wrote to me from South Africa.

> *To us children from a big city* [Stockholm] *every holiday at Lillehammer was a fairy-tale holiday. The winter was always so beautiful there—a snow paradise. We went skiing or were invited to sleigh-parties with our cousins. The opportunities for sports were plentiful indeed. I can especially remember my aunt with her sick daughter Mosse at her side in a sleigh. It was the greatest joy for Mosse to sit there under the warm blanket and hear the jingle bells of the horses in front of her. Her little face then shone with happiness—and if Aunt Sigrid could do anything to make her daughter happy and see a smile on her face, she did it. Oh, how she loved that sick child . . .*[7]

"For Christmas everyone always got at least one book," Charlotte told me, "and she tried to get us involved in reading by picking books that were related to our special interests. She would tempt us by reading an interesting passage from it, or by telling us something about it to pique our curiosity."

Her house meant a great deal to her and she loved clothes, hats, and antique jewelry, but her greatest pleasure came from giving. Nini was visiting her once when a huge crate of old embroideries, skirts, handkerchiefs, tablecloths and peasant dresses arrived from Hungary in lieu of royalties, and she went through the contents with delight saying, "Would you like this?" or "This will look wonderful on Mother."[8]

In time she made many friends in Lillehammer, and the closest were Eilif and Louise Moe. Eilif was her lawyer, agent, friend and advisor, and a more devoted, self-effacing friend no writer ever had. Alfred Knopf once asked him if he got ten percent of her earnings in addition to his legal fees, since he was acting in both capacities, and he looked shocked. "I would be a rich man today if I had," he said laughing, "but I wouldn't have dreamt of asking for such a thing."[9]

The Moes had three children. Tycho, who was Anders' age, Ole Henrik, who was Hans' age, and Anne Stine, who became little Signe's best friend.

Sigrid had always been interested in the theater and when Eilif Moe brought a puppet stage home from a trip to Denmark, she joined him in helping the children prepare productions of *Aladdin and His Wonderful Lamp*, *Around the World in 80 Days*, and *Captain Grant and his Family*. Their performances were so successful that they were repeated at the hospital and on birthdays and holidays, and Sigrid took time from work to write adaptations of the fairy tales *East of the Sun and West of the Moon* and *The Three Daughters of the King in the Blue Mountains* to add to their repertoire.

The adults were as excited about the productions as the children. One night, when Eilif Moe, who was preparing to take the Barrister's Examination, couldn't sleep, his wife asked him if he was worried about not passing. He was quiet for a moment, and then said, "Oh, no, it's nothing like that. I'm trying to figure out how to get the troll's head off."[10]

Lillehammer had few distractions and in order to amuse the population, there were many parades and pageants, and, when she could, Sigrid participated with her children. On one occasion the boys all wore monocles.

There was a taxi service in town that was owned by Fredrik Bøe, and Sigrid had a standing arrangement with him to take her and Mosse for a ride every afternoon. Mosse loved those rides and they rarely missed a day. When there was too much snow, they bundled her up in her fur coat and took her for a sleigh ride. When there was a parade or a fireworks display, Bøe would park where there was a good view and Mosse, wearing a costume, would sit in the car and watch. At home, she liked to sit on her mother's lap, and until she died (at the age of twenty-three), by which time she had grown into a large and heavy woman, she still sat there at times.

The boys belonged to the boy scouts. They had two large Norwegian collies called Njord and Neri, and two cats. A black and white mother cat called Sissi, and her son, whom Sigrid kept out of the kitchen whenever she could, called Sissyfoss. In *Happy Times in Norway*,[*] Sigrid wrote that Tulla (Mosse) "who didn't know better" sometimes tortured the cats, but they were always patient with her. When they couldn't bear any more, they would withdraw, but Sissyfoss always came back to sit on Tulla's lap when she had recovered.

Christmas celebrations grew more elaborate each year. A pig, a sheep, half a reindeer, blood pudding with raisins, pork sausages, headcheese, hams and every variety of Christmas cookies and cakes were made weeks in advance. In Norway, people bring flowers and plants as holiday gifts and Sigrid's house would be overflowing with rare blooms. Everyone made a special effort to bring something unusual.

---

[*]   Published in 1942 by Alfred A. Knopf.

The traditional Christmas Eve dinner consisted of rice porridge with lots of sugar, cinnamon and butter, and cold codfish with red wine. The children weren't overly fond of that menu, but candles were burning throughout the house, the Christmas tree had heaps of presents under it, everyone was dressed in their best, there were fruits and nuts and seven kinds of cookies, and they were allowed to drink some of the sweet, sticky mead. One person always got an almond in his porridge which, according to tradition, would bring the recipient good luck, but Sigrid's grandfather had wanted his children to learn to enjoy giving and had established his own tradition—the child who found the almond was allowed to distribute his or her gifts first.[11]

On New Year's Eve they played "Black Peter" and whoever lost had to have a black mustache painted on his face. Then, the guests and children would go to a dance or a party and Sigrid would stay home with Mosse.

When Mosse was eight, she could not say much more than "ding-dong," "flag," "music," and "car"—words she had learned when she was much younger[12]—but she would sit in a place of honor in a lovely new dress, with ribbons and flowers in her flowing blond hair, and for the 17th of May celebration, she wore a peasant dress like everyone else. She had a beautifully furnished room and all sorts of precious playthings including two very valuable Kathe Kollwitz dolls. She never played with them, but they stood on a shelf where she could see them and she would allow no one to touch them. She didn't like to have anything changed in her room.[13] Her brothers were loving and patient with her, when they found the time, and amused her with funny games and music. When they were busy with their own pursuits, they would put her in the garden where she could watch the birds in the birdbath.

In the spring of 1923, Sigrid's sister Ragnhild needed an operation and since there was no one with whom she could leave her children, Sigrid brought the four-year-old Ulla and the eighteen month old Ingvald to Lillehammer from Sweden and cared for them until her sister recovered in the fall. In June she wrote to Nini. "It is the will of Heaven that I shouldn't get too lazy this summer. It's a happiness that I haven't been spoiled."[14]

It turned out to be more of a chore than she had anticipated. She took the four children (Mosse stayed home with Mrs. Undset and the housekeeper) to a saeter* for a vacation and there was an invasion of lemmings. "Lemmings," Sigrid wrote in *Happy Times in Norway*,

---

* Summer cottage in the mountains.

> *. . . are dainty little animals with fine, silky, yellow-and-brown-flecked fur and white bellies. But their bodies are flat and broad, reminding one inevitably of bedbugs. And in the exact center of the face is the typical rodent's mouth with sharp, protruding teeth. They have vicious dispositions, these little animals, and stand barking and sputtering and squeaking shrilly at whomever comes upon them.*[15]

After stripping the mountainsides of everything edible, they moved to the valleys.

> *They move in hoards and travel straight ahead, stopping at nothing, and going around nothing they may encounter on their way. Automobiles run them down by the hundreds, and dogs and cats kill them right and left, but the horde forges ahead and never swerves. When they come down to a body of water they swim and masses of them drown. The dead bodies putrefy and contaminate all the brooks and rivers and wells.*[16]

Norway had one of its worst infestations that summer and she and all of the children got Lemming Fever. For six weeks they all had jaundice, diarrhea and fevers and took turns vomiting while Sigrid held them. The well at Bjerkebaek was not contaminated, but just to be safe, Mosse had been given pop and ginger ale to drink and she didn't get sick.

All of Sigrid's nieces have special memories to relate. Little Signe remembers one particular afternoon. Her aunt was in Oslo on business and took her on an outing without her twin sisters. She couldn't remember what they did first, but after whatever the entertainment was, a puppet show or something like that, and after they had refreshments, her aunt said she had a surprise for her. As Signe was always suffering from colds, Sigrid took her to a furrier and bought her the most beautiful little white fur coat and hat that she had ever seen in her life.*

Years later, after Gunhild was married and she was living in England, her son Knut "wouldn't eat willingly," she wrote to me.

> *He got all of the childhood diseases, starting with chicken pox, from his sister who was almost seven years older, and brought them home from school. He had always been a poor eater, but when he*

---

*   I have a picture of her in that outfit.

was four-and-a-half or five, he got bronchitis, and the doctor advised getting him back to Norway. I wrote to Mother [Sigrid] and at once she said he was welcome there. When her doctor looked at him he said he was a beautiful skeleton but there was nothing on it. We had been at Bjerkebaek for four or five days the summer before and Mother, like everybody else, told me that when he didn't eat, I shouldn't force him. Endless numbers of people told me what to do. Some said I should buy all new plate and cups—they all felt that they knew better than I did—but I had kept him going. He had gained a few kilos because I had arranged for him to eat at a neighbor's house where there were many children, but when he became ill, he lost all he had gained. So, when I wrote Mother, she took over.

She had advised me not to force him, but after she had him there, she wrote that allowing him not to eat, when he wouldn't, would have killed him right out. So they started to fight with him, put cream in his food, and put him to bed when he wouldn't eat. He was there from the beginning of June through July and he put on six kilos.[17]

When Sigrid helped someone, she never made a fuss about it, and when Nini asked her why she took on so much, she would say, "Oh, *that* I had to do."

The love lives of her nieces always interested her. When they started to go to parties and dances, she arranged for Thea to bring them their breakfast trays before she got hers, so that Thea could get "all the dirt."

If Sigrid wasn't writing, or reading, she was crocheting or embroidering. Sometimes she would be reading while everyone was talking around her and they would think that she didn't hear what was being said, but when they were wrong or glib, she would suddenly look up and correct them.

They all knew that she was not overly fond of Bjørnson's work, and one day Anders and Charlotte made fun of something he wrote in the belief that that would please her. She rose without saying a word, went to the bookcase, took down one of his books, and slowly and deliberately read them a very beautiful passage. Then she closed the book and said, "That is by Bjørnson."[18]

When they asked her about something, she usually sent them to look it up. "The one who is always searching may not find what he is looking for," she said, "but he will always find something worthwhile that he hadn't been looking for."[19]

She followed the courses that they were taking and suggested books for them to read. When Charlotte said she might want to be a publisher, she got

her a summer job in a bookstore in Lillehammer and when she changed her
mind and decided on archeology, she gave her all of Ingvald Undset's books,
each of which she had painstakingly located and bought back after they
were sold when they needed the money. She enjoyed visiting Charlotte on
"digs," and if the accommodations were primitive, as they usually were, she
pitched in without complaint and prepared wonderful meals for the group
with whatever they had.

Sigrid gave Isak Dinesen's *Out of Africa* to her mother once, but she herself
was not a Dinesen fan. She disliked *Seven Gothic Tales* and told her Danish
aunt Clara that it gave her a little of the same feeling that she had when she
walked on the side streets of Paris where every antique that was sold was
supposed to have belonged to Louis XVI or Marie Antoinette.[20] Isak Dinesen
was too much of a snob, made too much of art and artists, and admired
aristocrats too much to have appealed to Sigrid. She also lost huge amounts
of her family's assets and complained after each loss that they hadn't given her
enough. Although Dinesen fought for the rights of blacks in Africa, (as long
as it didn't deprive her of anything), her description of the devotion that her
black "totos" had for her, how they walked behind her carrying her parcels
and parasol, and the decadent, syphilitic, white society that she was a part
of, would surely not have appealed to Sigrid—despite Sigrid's own prejudice
against "Orientals" who, she feared, might take over the world.

Isak Dinesen devoured every word of *Kristin Lavransdatter*, and later *The
Master of Hestviken*, when her aunt sent them to her in Africa, but she found
Undset too depressing. "She has flashes of great beauty and harmony all the
same," she wrote to her aunt.

> *In the last part of Olav Audunsson* there is a description of a
> half-crazy young man and a depraved old woman and their life together
> in the woods far from other people, that is one of the most beautiful
> "idylls" I have encountered in any book. And everything she writes
> makes a great impact . . .* [21]

When Sigrid was in Christiania, she would take one or another of
her children, stepchildren or nieces to the theater, and when they were at
Bjerkebaek she tried to interest them in botany, but only her lawyer's son,
Ole Henrik developed any real enthusiasm for it. She would show him and
Hans where to find the most delicious mushrooms and how to identify plants

---

*   1st volume of *The Master of Hestviken*.

by smelling their leaves after rubbing them together. Hans adored the way she prepared mushrooms wrapped in crisp bacon and he looked for them so that she could cook them for him, but Ole Henrik preferred the finding to the eating, and usually gave his share to the Svarstads. Once, he found some when they weren't with him and gave them to another family, and Sigrid called him a traitor.

Since Svarstad wouldn't do so, Signe's husband, who was Anders' godfather, took the boys on fishing and walking trips. (Sigge seems to have had many of the characteristics of Simon in *Kristin Lavransdatter*. Mrs. Undset spent winters with Signe and her family, and summers and holidays at Lillehammer. The housekeepers made a fuss over her and served her all of her favorite foods, and as Charlotte says, "When they took care of you, at Bjerkebaek, you felt it." When her daughters were younger, Mrs. Undset exerted a strong influence over them, and when Sigrid became famous she would sometimes be competitive, but as she grew older, she settled for being the honored grandmother and the family did indeed love and honor her.

In 1923, when Sigrid was in Denmark to investigate institutions for Mosse, she had arranged for Ebba to attend a school which trained girls to become efficient housekeepers. Gunhild was studying at a business school but didn't like it and wanted to drop out, while Svarstad was visiting Sigrid's mother and sister regularly in Christiania, and complaining that he was not getting enough help from his wife in bringing up his children. He was a man and didn't know how to deal with them—and anyway, why did he have to scrounge to make ends meet when she was earning so much money?

They tried to intervene on his behalf, because "her children needed a father." Some husbands were more difficult than others, they said. One had to take the bad with the good. It was true that he would never be a provider, and that his work would always come first. He chose to live in town, while she, for Mosse's sake, had to be in Lillehammer, but he was her husband and she had to make the best of it. It wasn't an ideal arrangement, but if she refused to share her income with him she would lose him.

On April 27 (1922), Sigrid wrote to Nini that Svarstad had been to see her family and that they were urging her to help him more. "It must be fun for a man to always let women take care of things for him." Her mother and sister were doing all they could to help him with "those children that he is so angry about having to feed." If he didn't want to live with her and wasn't willing to sacrifice anything for his family, why should she? Gunhild wanted to quit school. She was spoiled enough already and shouldn't be encouraged to be lazy. She had always been uncooperative, wanting to sleep when others were up and, like her father, never wanting to do her share of what had to be done. Sigrid was always more irritated with Gunhild than Ebba, but after Ebba completed the courses in Denmark she sent Gunhild to study there.

When Ebba completed the courses she took a job as an au pair girl with a family in Copenhagen, but when Gunhild finished, she said she hated housework and refused to look for a job. Back in Christiania with nothing to do, she was drafted into keeping house for her father. Disgruntled with that too, she accepted a proposal of marriage from a bachelor relative of the family that was living in the apartment below. He was a nice-looking man and an engineer on a passenger boat, and Gunhild says she allowed her father and Sigrid to talk her into marrying him.

Gunhild was pretty, petite and flirtatious (like her mother) and was probably in some ways a model for Erlend's daughter Margaret in *Kristin Lavransdatter* of whom Sigrid wrote:

> *She* [Kristin] *could not help herself. Orm she loved like a child of her own; but 'twas not possible for her to grow to love Margaret. She had striven and striven and tried to force herself to like the child, ever since the day last winter when Ulf Haldorsson had brought her home to Husaby . . . it was a fearful thing—could she feel such misliking and wrath towards a little maid of nine years old! And well she knew that in part it was that the child was so strangely like her mother—she understood not Erlend, he showed naught but pride that his little brown-eyed daughter was so fair; never did the child seem to wake discomforting memories in her father . . . But it was not only because Margaret favored her mother that Kristin misliked her. Margaret would not endure to be taught by any; she was haughty and harsh to the service folk; untruthful was she too, and, with her father, a flatterer. She loved him not, as did Orm—it was ever to gain something that she clung to Erlend with kisses and caresses. And Erlend poured out gifts upon her and humored all the little maid's whims.*[22]

Later, in *Happy Times in Norway*, Sigrid described Gunhild's daughter Brit, when she was two years old and on a visit to Bjerkebaek for the Christmas holidays, in this way:

> *Little as she was, Brit was a finished coquette. She knew full well that Hans was miserable when she pretended she would rather have Siri-Kari and Anne-Lotte pull her around on skis. But when Hans*

sought comfort in the company of Little Signe or Ulla, she ran away
from the girls and came to him, demanding that he pay attention to
her . . . For the one thing Brit absolutely could not stand was that
anyone should not pay her full attention.[23]

It is amusing that Sigrid's hostility toward flirtatious women even applied to a two year old child, and her inability to control her jealousy—even to the third generation—says much about why she found it more difficult to relate to Gunhild than to Ebba.

CHAPTER XII

THE MASTER OF HESTVIKEN
1924-1928

When Sigrid began *Kristin Lavransdatter* her investigations into Catholicism were a part of her research, but after she was faced with the hopelessness of Mosse's illness, she began to turn to the Church for comfort. Everything she had ever believed was coming under scrutiny, and because she felt helpless she looked for miracles. Supernatural events and mysticism began to interest her. She had always believed that one could influence one's fate—that much depended on one's efforts—but willpower was of little use when one was presented with an "act of God." How much did people really know about illnesses like Mosse's?

If she had been a Lutheran she would have accepted her daughter's illness as a punishment for her sins. (In *The Burning Bush*, which she wrote later, Bjorg has a child who is "an imbecile" and she believes that its illness is God's way of chastising its parents for their sins. Bjorg " . . . saw God as a strict, extremely unamiable criminal judge who dealt her tit for tat; for each particular misdemeanor she had been guilty of, God condemned her to a misfortune.")[1] But Catholics believed that God was not cruel and vindictive. He didn't sit there watching every move one made in order to mete out punishments. One turned to God for help in bearing one's burdens and those who cared for "special" children would be especially blessed. Saints often behaved in ways that seemed mysterious or irrational—they even had seizures—but it was precisely at those moments that they saw visions not visible to ordinary people. Children like Mosse were believed to be nearer to God and were referred to as "God's chosen children." Frustrated by her inability to help her daughter, Sigrid's reading of religious literature accelerated and she began to receive instruction for conversion to Catholicism.

At first, she was apologetic about it. She would begin with, "according to my viewpoint," or, "I, for example, can have no feelings about miraculous reactions to relics, but neither can I deny that they took place."[2]—and, when she made a statement that she herself could not accept, she would say, "Well, now you see me sinking deeper and deeper into the superstitious darkness,"[3] but as time went on, she made fewer apologies and her statements became more strident and belligerent.

Nini was baffled. Sigrid had never been religious and her growing preoccupation with saints and Church dogma seemed an irrational aberration. An anti-war play by Nini was being performed in Christiania in 1921, which attacked religions for preaching brotherly love while condoning wars. In the play a woman's future daughter-in-law is raped by the soldiers of an invading army while her son is fighting that enemy elsewhere. As the woman is comforting the distraught girl, one of the rapists' compatriots is wounded in front of her door. Disregarding what his friends have just done to her family, she takes him in, stops his bleeding, and cares for him "because he is someone's son."

After Sigrid saw the play she told Nini that she didn't believe that people responded to violence so nobly. That woman would only have wanted revenge and it was wishful thinking that she would have acted as she did. Sigrid understood, only too well, the dichotomy between knowing what is right and doing what is right, and she couldn't accept such idealized behavior. There were few saints in the world, and one might even question the motives for some of *their* sacrifices.

She was seriously considering joining the Catholic Church but there were a number of obstacles in her way. Since the Church did not permit divorce and Svarstad was a divorced man when he married her, she would have to have their marriage annulled. She was angry with her husband for making a travesty of their marriage but she loved him and wanted him, and she wasn't ready for an irrevocable break. She asked him to come to see her and offered to accept any arrangement he wished as long as they could live together, but when he insisted on continuing their separate establishments, she said that in that case, their relationship could no longer be considered a marriage and she was going to have it dissolved. He would always be welcome at Bjerkebaek and she asked for nothing from him for herself or their children. She would try to help her stepchildren when it was possible, but in the future, responsibility for them and for himself would have to be his alone. She was not acting hastily, she explained, she had been receiving instruction from Monsignore Karl O. K. Kjelstrup, in Hamar, and attending services regularly at St. Torfinn's Chapel and she had decided to become a Catholic. Since he had married before, and the Church didn't recognize divorce, their marriage had not taken place as far as the Church was concerned, and she planned to file for an annulment and swear that she was not now, and would not in the future, share his bed.[*] He left in a huff.

While she waited for the annulment, she wrote an introduction to a collection of Norwegian fairy tales and started another medieval novel.

Their marriage was annulled, and on November 1, 1924 (All Saint's Day), she became a Catholic. There were fewer than three thousand Catholics in the whole of Lutheran Norway and it electrified the land. She was vilified from every pulpit, in some cases very abusively—and, in protest, Signe and her husband made a public statement that although religious training was compulsory in the schools, they would not permit their children to attend those services any longer.

Before her conversion Sigrid had gone through a period of trying to understand Catholicism rationally, but by the time she joined the Church, she was ready to suspend judgment and accept what couldn't be explained. She became a pious woman and gave enormous sums to the Church and the poor, and there is no reason to minimize the sincerity of her commitment, or the validity of her reasons for joining. She was an intelligent person and would not have taken such a serious step without due consideration. Her needs to explore every avenue of help for Mosse, and her own need for support in bearing her burden, were certainly important factors in her decision, but despite her legendary generosity, she, like all human beings, could be envious, bigoted, and insensitive when pressed, and one cannot completely dismiss the element of defiance—even face-saving—in her action.

Joining the Church was such an atypical thing for her to do that even her family was stunned, and after writing in *A Woman's Point of View* that divorce should be allowed "only in those cases where not getting it would create madness or death," her having her marriage annulled made it difficult for some of her closest associates to take her seriously, ever again.

Shortly after her conversion, Sigrid was having dinner with Nini at the Theater Café, when the journalist Nordahl Grieg came over to their table and asked if he could join them. Sigrid had been so besieged by journalists, and had been misquoted so often that she was wary of them. They interfered with her work and were always nosing about to see what Mosse looked like, but Nordahl Grieg was a friend, and wasn't there in an official capacity, and she enjoyed the evening.

---

[*]   A promise it is doubtful she kept.

The next day, a double interview appeared on the front page of his paper. She was quoted as saying that critics were people who couldn't write books themselves, that her library was insured for 60,000 kr., and that her Cranach illustrations of Luther's texts, which "was probably the most indecent book in existence," were priceless. The article went on to misquote her or to quote her out of context, and she was both hurt and angry.

She protested to the paper that they had violated her privacy and because she felt Nini had betrayed her by setting up the interview and making it appear casual meeting amongst friends. It destroyed their friendship. They worked together on writers' projects after that, and in 1935 attended a conference in Helsinki together, but the rift was a serious one. Nini was a warm, good-natured person—generous, affectionate, and gregarious—and she had so many close friends in the literary community, but Sigrid had few. Nini had been her confidant and it was an irreparable loss.

Living so far from Christiania, Sigrid had not been actively involved in the social life of the literary community, and after she became a Catholic she found herself even more isolated. She began to spend time with French Dominican clerics and nuns whom she found the most congenial of the Catholics she met. In addition to Mgr. Kjelstrup, Father Ambrosius Lutz, (who was a writer and musician), Gabriel Marie Vanneufville, and Henri Etienne Bechaux became her mentors. They came to Bjerkebaek often and she enjoyed discussing theology with them. When she came to the city, before her conversion, she usually stayed at the Bristol Hotel, but after that she stayed at the farmers' hostels (bondenheimen) or with the nuns at the St. Katarinajemmet. She continued to attend services in Hamar and there, Mother Fulgenia and Sister Rogata (a surgical nurse in the eye clinic) were her special friends.

When Sigrid came to live in Lillehammer, a debate had been raging throughout Norway about the Norwegian language. When they had been a part of Denmark, the spoken language had been Danish. Until 1811, the only available university was in Copenhagen, and most college educated Norwegians were educated in Danish. Although Norway had a printing press after 1643, most of their books were published in Danish. When Norway became a part of Sweden, their language remained the same. The country was (and still is) sparsely populated. Rural people used dialects derived from Old Norse, laced with folk expressions indigenous to their areas, and Danish often sounded like a foreign language to them. Educated Norwegians fought to keep the language "pure" with no "provincial vulgarizations," but they could not keep them all out.

In the middle of the 19th century, the Romanticists encouraged folk cultures and writers like Henrik Wergeland took the position that the dialects of the country people were more authentically Norwegian than Danish was. Peter Asbjørnsen and Jørgen Moe recorded folktales that had been orally transmitted, and although they used Danish orthography and declensions, they included many Old Norse words and phrases for which they had to create their own spelling.˙

Although there were only four million people in all of Norway, a movement was started to create a new language to be called Landsmål (peasant language) or Nynorsk (new Norwegian) to replace the official language which they called Riksmål (National language) or Bokmål (book language). Since dialects and expressions varied in different parts of the country, the backers of Nynorsk could not settle on any one form of orthography or grammar. Those who favored Riksmål said that if Nynorsk were taught in the schools, all books would have to be rewritten since they would be incomprehensible to future generations. It became a political issue. Nynorsk was taught in the schools, teachers demanded a standardized spelling and grammar; and parents, politicians and educators took sides.

Most authors, including Sigrid, were for Riksmål, but felt that some folk expressions should be included and foreign words, particularly German, should be eliminated. The debate was so heated that political enemies like Knut Hamsun (who later sympathized with the Nazis), and Arnulf Øverland (who was a left-wing radical) were both for Riksmål. Øverland felt so strongly about it that when, in 1952, the Norwegian Authors' Association agreed to be part of a language commission to study the possibility of combining the two, he left the organization and threatened to sue any publisher who tampered with an author's work. A group of writers decided to translate some of the Sagas into Riksmål as a declaration of their feelings about not changing the language and Sigrid chose the *Viga Glums*, *Kormaks* and *Bandamanna* Sagas. They were published as *Three Sagas of Icelanders* in 1923.

*   *   *

In an effort to get away from Danish names and references, the backers of Nynorsk had the names of many streets, counties and public areas renamed.

In 1925, Christiania was renamed and it became Oslo again.

˙   Unlike Danish, Norse has a feminine gender and the verb endings are different.

While the furor over her becoming a Catholic was raging, Sigrid started another medieval novel. Using the material she had gathered for her unpublished *Sven Trøst og Agnete*, which she wrote when she was twenty, *The Master of Hestviken*˙ starts in the middle of the 13ᵗʰ century, (before the period covered in *Kristin Lavransdatter*), when Christianity was just beginning to be an effective force in Norway.˙˙ At the time, feudal landowners had legal control over the lives of their subjects and many pagan customs still prevailed. Families were expected to be responsible for their kinsmen, and when a man was wronged, it was up to his family to avenge him. Feuds developed which were carried from one generation to the next. Sigrid was particularly interested in exploring how the independent, self-sufficient Norsemen, who believed in "a merciless fate," and had to battle the elements, were being persuaded by the Church to accept the belief "that they were sinful mortals who, before everything else, had need of grace and redemption."[4]

*   *   *

The story begins with the betrothal of the seven-year-old Olav to Ingunn, the daughter of his father's best friend. The two children grow up together and are devoted to each other, but when they are old enough for their marriage to take place, both sets of parents are no longer alive and there is no one to testify that they were betrothed. Olav will inherit a large estate, but it is too far away to be of much benefit to Ingunn's kinsmen and, since it would serve their interests better if she were married to someone else whose estate was closer, another match is sought for her. When the lovers hear that they may lose one another, they consummate their union sexually which, under Norse law, was considered a legal marriage (if both participated willingly) but since they acted without the permission of her relatives and deprived them of the benefits of a more profitable union, the lovers are forced to separate until Olav can reimburse them for their loss. Olav is teased for taking matters into his own hands and he kills one of Ingunn's kinsmen. He now has even greater penalties to pay and is forced to go into Foreign Service to raise the money.

˙   *The Master of Hestviken* was published as *Olav Audunssøn I Hestviken* and *Olav Audunssøn og Hans Børn* in Norwegian, in 1925 and 1927, and in four volumes called: *The Axe*, *The Snake Pit*, *In the Wilderness*, and *The Son Avenger*, by Alfred A. Knopf, Inc. in English in 1928, 1929, 1930.

˙˙   Considerably later than in the rest of Europe.

Years pass. Ingunn is thirty years old and still waiting for Olav to settle his debts and claim her, when an Icelander named Teit appears. He is handsome, dark-complexioned, tall, an excellent scribe and illuminator, and although he was trained to be a priest, he has recently become the local sheriff's clerk. He is jolly and makes her laugh, but rumor has it that he gambles, is in debt, and has been involved "in some irregularities with women."

Ingunn has had little joy in the years of waiting. She allows the Icelander to make love to her and she becomes pregnant. Teit offers to marry her, and if she were free she might have accepted him, but she is still pledged to Olav. Olav returns for a visit, but is not ready to settle his accounts and claim her. She tells him of her condition and in a blaze of jealousy and anger he rushes to town to consult the Bishop. The Church has been struggling for influence in the area, and is likely to be more lenient in settling disputes than representatives of the landowners. Olav discovers, too late, that he might have gotten better terms if he had allowed the Bishop to intervene for him in the first place, and he doesn't want to make the same mistake twice. But on the way, he realizes that the Church would not take Ingunn's adulterous behavior with the Icelander lightly, and he is at a loss about what to do. Caught between the old powers and the new, he is in a quandary when Teit comes to see him. Assuming that Olav will not want her now, he says that he and Ingunn are in love, and that he would be willing to marry her if Olav would release her. Olav is enraged and wild with jealousy. "In love," indeed. In love with *his* Ingunn? He has waited too long and worked too hard to allow this cocky upstart to destroy everything. Teit has been bragging around town and Olav believes that he has no choice but to kill him before he creates a scandal. He promises to help him, takes him on a trip, and murders him. Since Teit wronged him, he had a right to kill him, (in fact, it was his duty to do so) under the old laws, but since it is a sin to kill a man under Christian law, he takes no chances and burns all traces of his crime. Then he goes to her relatives to renegotiate. They are tired of supporting Ingunn and, under the circumstances, eager to be rid of her, and Olav is able to settle his debts advantageously. Ingunn gives birth to a son whom she names Eirik, turns him over to foster parents to rear, and leaves with Olav for his estate, which fortunately is far away.

They prosper. She gives birth to a number of children but none of them survive, and Olav decides to bring Eirik home and claim him as his son.

After Eirik has been officially acknowledged as his son and heir, Ingunn gives birth to a healthy daughter. Since Eirik has already been declared his heir, Olav's own daughter will forever be deprived of her birthright.

At every moment of crisis, Olav has taken the law into his own hands and rationalized his behavior as "being the only way." Years pass. He doesn't confess the murder of Teit, nor that Eirik is not his son, and the guilt he lives with weighs heavily upon him. Bitter about the fate that has been meted out to him, and too proud to confess his sins, he becomes a lonely, isolated man.

Eirik grows up to be tall, dark and handsome like his father; (Olav is short, stocky, blond and blue-eyed), and like his father, he is charming but irresponsible, disorganized and dishonest. He lies and lies and Olav can never discover anything that looks like a plausible reason for his doing so. He doesn't lie for gain and he seldom lies for concealment. He freely confesses his worst misdeeds.[5] In fact, he is so much like the Icelander that Olav can hardly be civil to him, but no matter how unfairly he treats him, he cannot keep the boy from loving him.

In *Kristin Lavransdatter*, Sigrid wrote that it was not

> *God punishing your sins when you must reap sorrow and humiliation because you followed your lusts and overweening pride over paths that God has forbidden His children to tread. Would you say that you had punished your children if they scalded their hands when they took up the boiling kettle you had forbidden them to touch, or if the slippery ice broke under them that you had warned them not to go upon?*[6]

It is only when one "lets go God's hand" that one is drowned.

But by the time she wrote *The Master of Hestviken*, she was putting it differently. The priest Asbjørn all-fat says to Olav:

> *It is an easy matter to be a good Christian so long as God asks no more of you than to hear sweet singing in Church, and to yield Him obedience while He caresses you with the hand of a father. But a man's faith is put to the test on the day God's will is not his.*[7]

No longer able to believe in the reliability of willpower, Sigrid was ready to put herself in the hands of the Lord.

*   *   *

The Master of Hestviken, which she considered her best work, has some breathtaking descriptions. Torhild, Cecilia, and Eldrid are magnificent women, and there are some unforgettable relationships—especially between Olav and Eirik—or Eirik and Eldrid, but the massive work is too long and often belabored. When Sigrid started *Kristin Lavransdatter* she had no idea how it would end. Purely emotional in its inspiration, it flowed like hot lava and her characters are passionate and vulnerable, and therefore prototypes for all humanity—but when she started *The Master of Hestviken*, she was a newly converted Catholic and her purpose was to proselytize and perhaps strengthen her own conviction. Although it reflects her genius in many ways, it lacks the magic of *Kristin Lavransdatter*.

CHAPTER XIII

THE NOBEL PRIZE
1928

After Sigrid moved to Lillehammer her productivity was phenomenal. She got there in the spring of 1919, only a few months before Hans was born, but *A Woman's Point of View* appeared by the end of that year, and despite the incredible amount of research required, (which she had been accumulating for years, of course), the first volume of *Kristin Lavransdatter* appeared in 1920, the second in 1921 and the last in 1922. In addition to a number of articles on religion, *Three Sagas of Icelanders* appeared in 1923, and *Saint Halvard's Life, Death and Miracles*, and the first volume of *The Master of Hestviken* were published in 1925.

Exhausted before the first half of that huge work was finished, she took a vacation as soon as it was in the hands of her publisher. Taking Anders and her mother, she went to Italy again. Italy always made her more religious and when she got back she wrote several articles for Catholic periodicals.

In 1926, her play *In The Grey Light of Dawn* (written in 1908) was published in a collection edited by Fredrik Paasche, and the second half of *The Master of Hestviken* appeared in 1927. Like *Kristin Lavransdatter*, it was translated into many languages and eulogized wherever it appeared and there was no longer any doubt about Sigrid's international reputation.

Despite the annulment of their marriage, Svarstad continued to come to Bjerkebaek and Sigrid continued to be concerned with the welfare of her stepchildren. After Ebba had completed the courses in Denmark, she had taken a job with a Catholic family, moved to London with them, and become a Catholic. On her way back from Italy, Sigrid visited her in London. Her housekeeper was getting married and she asked Ebba if she would like to be her secretary and manage the servants at Bjerkebaek. She would not be required to cook or do housework, but she would have to sleep in Mosse's room in order to be with her if she had a seizure during the night. Ebba said she would like to try it and came to Lillehammer.

They were attending to correspondence on a day in November, when Signe called to say that a friend at *Aftenposten* had just heard that Sigrid was going to get the Nobel Prize. Sigrid said she heard that Olav Dunn was going to get it and she believed that he deserved it. Since she had been considered for it the year before and no prize had been awarded, she had to assume that she was permanently out of the running—but her hopes were revived, and she was not completely unprepared when the woman who was in charge of the local telegraph office appeared personally at her door. Telegrams usually scared her, but this one might be *IT*. Her hand shook as she opened it and read:

> The Swedish Academy has today, the 13th of November, 1928, given
> the Nobel Prize for Literature for the year 1928 to Sigrid Undset.

The Nobel Prize! It was hard to absorb it. Life could be beautiful after all.

She reached for the telephone to tell her sister, but before she could complete the call a young woman appeared at the door to ask for an interview. Although she desperately wanted some time alone to digest the incredible news, Sigrid invited her in. There would be many reporters now, and she knew she would have to receive them all.

The journalist asked how she felt, whether receiving the Nobel Prize made her happy, and if it were true that she liked gardening. It is amazing how often reporters ask obvious questions— like asking a person who has just lost a child in an accident, "How do you feel?" Reporters like that usually assign a favorite subject to each person of note and bore their readers to death by dwelling on it—as do the English journalists who, too often, ask the Queen about her horses. Gardening seems to have been the subject assigned to Sigrid.)

Neighbors, friends and relatives arrived. Flowers and telegrams were pouring in from all over the world, but the articles in the press had little to say about her work and much to say about her garden. The next day, an article in *Aftenposten* by the Norwegian author, Barbra Ring, covered a bit more. She described Sigrid as standing tall and proud in front of her house with her children playing around her "like a young and fruitful mother Earth." "Her large, deep, iron-grey eyes that no picture can describe are beautiful—sometimes veiled as if seeing into time or strong and searching." Ring praised her for having a point of view of her own even when many were against her. She couldn't be bought or influenced with pretty words. Her house was full of old and precious things but they were in use and not on display like a museum, and despite her great erudition, she was a first-class mother, housewife, cook and hostess. She had "the intuition of a genius and a secure, cold brain." And "an image that had not been completely worked out never satisfied her." Those who knew her well didn't know whom to put higher, the post genius, or the good, wise, proud human being that she was.

The awards ceremony was to take place in Stockholm on December 10th, and there would be dinners and receptions to attend. She was ecstatic to be getting the prize but panicked at having to face it alone. She asked Signe to accompany her but her sister couldn't leave her family. Then, Eilif Moe, her friend, attorney and agent, agreed to go with her.

As soon as she was sure that she wouldn't have to go alone, she rushed to Oslo to buy some clothes. She got some dresses, a black caracul fur coat with a feathered cloche and several other hats, but she couldn't settle on a suitable outfit for the presentation. A friend suggested she splurge and have one made at Molstad's, the best couturier in Oslo, and took her there.

Sigrid had gained a considerable amount of weight and her friend wasn't exactly a sylph. Wearing shapeless dresses of nondescript colors and unknown vintages, the two women entered the posh shop and were seated in the center of the showroom on a large, low "pouf." Slim, elegantly groomed models in exquisite gowns paraded before them, and they were having a wonderful time until they caught a glimpse of themselves in a huge mirror. The scene was so ludicrous that they began to giggle. At first they tried to stifle their laughter, but when they became hysterical, the modeling had to stop. It took a while for them to calm down enough for Sigrid to be able to order a fine, soft, golden velvet dress with a square neckline (that would show her antique topaz necklace to advantage). It was to have long sleeves and a shawl of silk lace dyed to match, and she bought shoes, a handbag and stockings to be dyed the same color.

With that important chore out of the way, she could begin to enjoy the festivities, and there were many.

Interviews, parties, and all kinds of celebrations were being arranged in her honor. The newspapers were full of pictures and stories about her. At

forty-six, she was the second youngest author to receive the literary prize.[*]
She was the third woman,[**] and the third Norwegian.[***]

She was compared to Scott, Tolstoy and Dostoyevsky.

She had "created a Nordic Iliad and thrown light over the society which was the background for her culture."

"A greatness of that kind must have its roots in a great and wholly conceived nature."

The Students' Associations made her a life member.

Since it was the 35th anniversary of the Norwegian Authors' Association and her publisher's 25th anniversary, they jointly sponsored a dinner in her honor. A huge horseshoe-shaped table decorated with blue and red streamers and many flowers was set up in the center of the Rococo Room of the Grand Hotel, with a smaller table inside the U to accommodate the 173 guests who attended. The president of the Storting, her publisher, leading artists and writers, officials of foreign governments and her family and friends were there.

When Sigrid entered on the arm of Ronald Fangen, the Chairman of the Norwegian Author's Association, she received a tremendous ovation. Seated at the center of the U under a model of a Norwegian farmhouse, and flanked by honored guests, she was crowned with a laurel wreath and given a "3X3 Shout of Hurrah." Dignitaries spoke. The proceedings were broadcast by radio all over the world.

"The edifice of her work was not rococo," the Chairman of the Author's Association said. "It was not a Roman cathedral, nor a temple for airy sprites, but a temple for people."

Nini Roll Anker amused the group when she said, "a farmer sobered up temporarily once when he saw Sigrid Undset and shouted, 'I want that girl—I want *her* and no other,' and now fame is following his example."

It was a magnificent tribute from her peers.

The next morning, Sigrid placed her laurel wreath on the alter of the Blessed Virgin at the Church of St. Dominic in Oslo. At the dinner the night before, her mother had announced that she too would soon become a Catholic.

Sigrid and Eilif Moe arrived in Stockholm on the 10th. It was 7 o'clock in the morning but the secretary of the Swedish Author's Association, journalists,

---

[*]   Rudyard Kipling was forty-two.

[**]   Selma Lageröf was the first.

[***]   Bjørnson and Hamsun had already received theirs—Ibsen never got one.

writers, and Sigrid's sister and her family were waiting at the station to greet her. There was a press conference at the Hotel Imperial as soon as she was checked in. The ceremony was scheduled for that afternoon, and an official banquet was to follow. The next day there would be a Press luncheon and a private dinner (for seventy) with the King and the royal family at the Palace. The day after that, the Concordia Catholica was giving a banquet in her honor—and the day after that, she was scheduled to attend a memorial for the Norwegian explorer of the South Pole, Roald Amundsen, who had recently died.

When she was asked, at the press conference, how she felt about the upcoming elections in Norway, she said there was "no political party that she could support without reservations," but she believed in author's rights; "Author's rights are rights—not gifts. They should be paid for radio performances."

She had little time to dress, but she had never felt more festive nor looked more radiant than when she stepped into the horse-drawn carriage that was to take her to the awards ceremony. Christmas shoppers filled the streets. Cars rushed by. A huge Christmas tree with 1000 lights welcomed her in front of the great concert hall. The King, the Crown Prince and all of the royal family, representatives of governments, science, and literature (including Selma Lagerlöf, and other past prize winners) were seated on the stage. It was indeed like a dream.

Of those who were to receive prizes, only Heinrich Wieland from Germany,* Adolf Windaus,** also from Germany and Sigrid Undset were present. Henry Bergson from France was to receive the literature prize for 1927, but he could not attend because he was ill.

Sigrid was seated in the center of the stage, just behind the dais, under a huge bust of Alfred Nobel. Hidden from the audience, an orchestra played. The proceedings began with Söderman's *Overture to the Virgin of Orleans*, and as each award was presented, music from that country was played. (Debussy for France, Wagner for Germany and Grieg for Norway.) After the awards in other categories, Per Hallström, the Chairman of the Nobel Committee, spoke about Henry Bergson's achievements and a representative of the French government accepted his prize. Then, he turned to Sigrid. Looking "gorgeous as the Queen of the Spirit which she is in her beautiful golden velvet and lace dress," the newspapers reported, surrounded by men in tails and women

* Chemistry prize for 1927.
** Chemistry prize for 1928.

in glamorous attire, she listened with a smile on her face to the reasons for selecting her for the greatest of all literary prizes.

"In her early novels and short stories, all remarkable works," Per Hallström began,

> *Sigrid Undset painted the world of young women who lived in Christiania at that time. They were a restless generation, quick to make the most important decisions in order to satisfy their aspirations for happiness without concern for the logical consequences of their sentimental and impulsive natures and passions for truth. That generation paid very dearly for their concept of reality. They had to learn many lessons before they achieved inner peace and some of them succumbed in the struggle.*
>
> *The women of that generation were strangely isolated in a disconcerting world; far from finding support from a regulated, securely established society, they consciously renounced the heritage of their pasts. They were hostile to the established order of society which they considered a useless bondage, and relied on themselves to create a new society which conformed to their convictions, sincere no doubt in their intentions, but easily misguided.*
>
> *The author depicted the lives of these young women with vivid imagination and drew them with sympathy but with unmerciful honesty; she traced the tragedy of their lives without looking to embellish or amplify and presented the evolution of their destinies with an implacable logic which carried an implicit condemnation of her heroines and the world in which they lived.* [emphasis added]

Sigrid couldn't believe she was hearing right. He was praising her for what he had hoped she would write and not for what she had written.

"The picture is knowing," he continued,

> *and to the degree that one tries to understand such people, it is moving, but not as fascinating as her wonderfully fresh and shining descriptions of nature . . . in that area her art has already reached its grandeur and that grandeur is found in all of her work when she abandoned the splintered and to a certain extent ruthless beings who had occupied her in contemporary times and turned toward the times of the far gone past.*

By now, the smile on Sigrid's face had faded and she had begun to resemble the "official" portrait of herself which, she said, made her look "like a caricature of Beethoven." What had she expected? Understanding from the "pillars of society?" All of her life there had been this mad disparity between her expectations and what she got from life. Never had she been lonelier than at that moment when she was receiving "mankind's highest award."

(One can't help wondering if it was at that moment that she recalled the incident with which she later began her autobiographical novel, *The Longest Years.*

She was very little—not two years old. She had been playing in sun-warmed sand "with a kind of orgiastic joy," and had burrowed a pit for herself "like a hen taking a dust bath,"[1] when one of her aunts arrived and thrust a doll into her arms. It had a smooth, hard, china head with an ugly, garishly-painted face, and "it was dressed in some kind of stiff, mustard-colored stuff"[2] that was trimmed with stiff lace and ribbons that pricked her and was unpleasant to the touch. She didn't like that object that they expected her to hold. She tried to put it in her mouth, but "it was too big and hard and smooth and cold,"[3] and was so nasty to the taste that she tossed it away. Her aunt reprimanded her for being so unkind to the doll and gave it back to her, and once again the doll, with its stiff and scratchy dress, was pressed against her bare arm. She remembered crushing its legs together until she heard a faint crackling sound as she laughed with delight . . . "Thick steamboats' cups," Sigrid had added wryly, "and china medicine spoons still reminded her of how horrid that doll's head had been to bite at."[4])

"With her historical novels," Per Hallström was saying,

> *she found the terrain that suited her nature and imagination. Those characters that she conjured out of the past have a greater wholeness and are forged with greater firmness than her contemporary characters. They were not confined to sterile isolation, but lived in the great solidarity of the family and the security of passing generations. Molded on a grand scale, this is quite a different model of society than the formless modern one . . .*
>
> *These people from the middle ages had, in their way, a more varied soul life than the present generation, but Sigrid Undset focuses exclusively, almost with a kind of monomania, on their pursuit of happiness through their erotic lives, with even the search for truth concentrated there . . .*

Eroticism! Was that what was bothering him?

> The erotic life of the sexes, Sigrid Undset's central psychological
> interest, is handled no differently in her historical novels than it was in
> her modern stories and criticism against this is quite understandable.

"In the documents which we have of the Middle Ages," he droned on,

> we do not see anything about the women's question and hardly
> any such depictions of the personal soul life.*
> The historian who demands proof has a right to point out that
> this is missing, but the historian does not have the only word. The
> author's point of view is equally valuable if it has a strong and intuitive
> knowledge behind it. The archeologist must presuppose that there were
> tools other than the ones that they discovered. Those that were found
> were surely a matter of accident, and an author can presuppose that
> human nature has changed little even where the past is silent . . .
> Sigrid Undset has given them words and voice and it seems at times
> that the voice is too modern and the feelings are too sensitive, since at
> that time life was not lived with poetry. The heaviness and hardness
> of the atmosphere must have made the people harder . . . but despite
> this change, if it can be called a change, the writing has the power to
> grip.
> Her writing is powerful, vigorous, and not seldom heavy. It flows
> like a torrent and continually receives new rivulets from the sides, and
> since it elaborates on each of these, it makes it strenuous for the memory
> of the reader. This is partly due to the nature of the subject . . . the
> heaviness is also due to the author's intense and immediate imagination
> which creates every detail of every trait, scene, and dialog and will
> never take the distance required for perspective, so that the flood has a
> tendency to plunge us into a kind of powerless torpor . . . but still, the
> flow of the water has the continuous freshness of nature . . . When the
> flood reaches the sea, when Kristin Lavransdatter has fought her life
> to the end, then one has nothing to complain about. The long road,
> which was her fate, gathers its overwhelming greatness and depth. To
> those scenes there are not many equals in all of literature . . .

---

* According to Sigrid, this was untrue since there were many references to eroticism
  in the ballads and in the *Diplomatarium Norvegicum*.

He was winding up. It was almost over. After a few words about *The Master of Hestviken* he finished with,

> *It is then in her full force that Sigrid Undset receives the Nobel Prize for Literature.*[*]

"Then," the newspapers reported, "Sigrid Undset rose proud as an Icelandic Viking woman" and took a few steps toward the King who had risen and was coming toward her to make the presentation.

She received the gold medal, a check for 156,000 kroner, and the following citation:

> *Undset, Sigrid (Norwegian) born 1882: Principally with regard to her powerful pictures of northern life in the medieval times. In modern Norwegian epic literature the first novel, in particular, stands out by virtue of its construction which is both firm and full of character, its psychological insights and its full expert historical knowledge.*

She bowed to the King and thanked him for honoring her. At the banquet which followed, she sat at the right of the Crown Prince, and with the exception of the King, the entire royal family was present. She thanked the Nobel Committee, brought greetings from Norway, and said that although Sweden's and Norway's mountains and rivers ran together, and they had much in common, each country stood by itself.

It should have been the greatest day of her life, she had achieved the highest recognition for her work, but once again she had been shortchanged.

Ragnhild and her family and Eilif Moe, who were in a box near the stage during the presentation (Dea was also invited, but was unable to attend), were waiting for her at the hotel when she returned from the dinner, and everyone was subdued. They were standing on the terrace of her room looking out over Stockholm, when Eilif, knowing how depressed she was asked, "Isn't that a magnificent sight?"

She didn't answer for a moment. Then, she said, "I never *have* liked big cities."[6]

---

[*] Olaf Lagerkrantz, in his biography of August Strindberg, say that Per Hallström wrote in *Svenska Dagbladet* that suggesting the Nobel Prize for Strindberg was scandalous. "It would mean honoring a libelous pamphleteer."[5]

*   *   *

The next day, the papers carried the story that Sigrid Undset was going to give away all of the prize money.

Fifteen thousand kroner were going to the Norwegian Authors' Association and the rest was to be divided between a fund for the support of families who elected to bring up their retarded children at home, and scholarships for those who wanted their children to attend Catholic schools but couldn't afford the tuition.

The announcement created an outcry. For days the press was full of it. They insisted that Nobel had not intended the money to be used as a means of destroying the State Church. He had meant to fee authors from financial worries and not for them to give his money away. But the protest tapered off when it was pointed out that he had only stipulated that the author should have an idealistic approach to life. There were no instructions as to how the money could be spent.

At a reception, a member of the royal family is said to have asked Sigrid if she was a socialist, and the story goes that she answered, "No, Madam, I am a distributionist."

While her aunt was in Stockholm, Ulla informed me, she took her and her brother to see a Chaplin film and enjoyed it as much as they did, but what Ulla could never forget was seeing her "seated on the stage in the middle of all the male winners. She was wearing a golden velvet dress which just covered her knees (the fashion in those days) and beautiful golden court shoes. But, her legs were the most elegant of all. Sigrid Undset's body was that of a rather big and stately woman, but her legs were long and slender and perfectly shaped."

Sigrid was met in Lillehammer by a torchlight parade and with a son seated on each side of her, she was taken to Bjerkebaek in a sleigh drawn by two horses.

After she got home, she sent a specially-bound edition of *Kristin Lavransdatter* to Eilif Moe with the inscription:

> *Lillehammer, December 1928. Eilif Moe, In memory of when we got the Nobel Prize. Sigrid Undset.*[7]

In a letter to Nils Collett Vogt, on December 21, she wrote that she felt more than ever that she wanted to withdraw from the world. It had just shown her its most beautiful face and although she was grateful, she felt the honor had little to do with her. Vogt had once told her to be ambitious, she wrote, but she had gotten little from ambition.

CHAPTER XIV

THE THIRTIES
1929-1940

The Nobel Prize changed Sigrid's life. She could no longer remain a private person. She traveled more and became more active in the affairs of the literary community. In 1929, she published a collection of essays called *Meetings and Partings* and that year and the next, a two-volume novel called *The Winding Road* which consisted of *The Wild Orchid* and *The Burning Bush*.

In reviewing her medieval novels, *The New York Times* had written, "Her supreme achievement is in the appealing humanity and fallibility of her characters," and that was precisely what made them great, but *The Winding Road*, which deals with the conversion of Paul Selmer to Catholicism, has none of these virtues. It is single dimensional and contrived. Using the family of a divorced couple, a liberal, a Lutheran, a cliché of "the working girl," a politician, a feminist, a boardinghouse proprietress, and a flirtatious, empty-headed, middle-class woman as symbols, the story consists of a series of blocks set up to be knocked down. Paul is a foolish, insensitive, boring prig. His conversion is unmotivated, and the book did not help her cause.

In a speech at the tenth anniversary celebration of the Gallery of Living Catholic Authors in New York on May 24, 1942, Sigrid said,

> *"The conversion of a hardened sinner is such a tremendous miracle, what with God being Almighty, and the sinner yet having his free will, that I think very few writers of fiction are able to deal adequately with such a wonderful topic. I would say, let us leave it to*

*the theologians—and don't expect all of them either to write well or
clearly about it.*[1]

It is too bad that she didn't follow her own advice.

When *Kristin Lavransdatter* and *The Master of Hestviken* appeared, they
were criticized for dwelling too much upon religion, but since Catholicism
was the only Christian religion in the 13th and 14th centuries, it was the degree
to which she dwelt on it that was criticized. But *The Winding Road* was an
attack on Lutheranism and it was not welcomed in Lutheran Norway.

"If one were willing to admit that the Bible is an inspired book," she
wrote in *The Wild Orchid*, "then it was no use picking out of it what agreed
more or less with one's own taste or opinions of probability and baking one's
own religious cake of that,"[2] but when she was asked what she thought of the
selling of indulgence, she said she was for a "church on the cliff," and not for
all the bad Catholics who were distorting the true meaning of Christianity.

When Sigrid became a Catholic, she presented the original manuscript
of *Kristin Lavransdatter* to the Pope, and in 1929, Pope Pius XI conferred
the Medal Pro Ecclesia Et Pontifice upon her, but although she was so highly
honored, the Catholic press was not unanimous in its praise of her work.
What they objected to most was the sensuality of her love scenes and the
importance she placed on sex.

On April 7, 1923, the first volume of *Kristin Lavransdatter* was reviewed
in the Catholic periodical *America* as "a melancholic tale, not exactly immoral,
but crudely plain, with its extremely realistic pictures of a primitive religious
people who find that the wages of sin is death."

And in April of 1929, after the first two volumes of *The Master of Hestviken*
were published in the United States, an article called *An Iconoclast Ventures on
a Criticism of Sigrid Undset*, by Mary E. McGill, appeared in *The Sign*.

> *It is not unusual for a brilliant mind to tilt dangerously to the
> edge of abnormal . . . There are things no artist should expose in detail,
> particularly should a Catholic not present. Her morbidity suggests a
> pathological condition . . . Perhaps her tendency to limn intimate
> relations would best be overcome by meditation on the value of an
> immortal soul's retention of its purity . . . Certain parts of Madame
> Undset's romances should be deleted before they are translated.*
>
> *Passing along the highway or through the busy streets of a great
> city, one sees much dirt, dust and debris of all kinds. The sight makes
> slight impression. Btu if someone were to throw the filth in another's*

face, the contact would physically soil. The throwing of graphic
sentences describing love when it degenerates to lust, into the mind of
the reader works similarly. Madame Undset commits this unseemly
act repeatedly . . .

Madame Undset seems sex obsessed. She is likely to lead the
undiscerning reader to believe that certain transgressions are so natural
that there is not a supernatural means of overcoming them. And such
is precisely the attitude of the world at the present time . . .

No soul is made pure by contemplation of the impure. Doctors,
nurses and social welfare workers are agreed that when the beast
of passion controls human desire that consideration of physical
consequences of sin, even eternal punishment, does not stay pursuit . . .
This being true, why should we tolerate an author's smearing of pages,
particularly a Catholic author . . . when our Catholic leaders endorse
her books for consumption by the mature, the strong-stomached and
the intellectual elite.

So many intellectuals have fallen from grace. The Index is
clogged with them! And perhaps hell is likewise lighted by their
brilliance . . . [3]

Amongst the letters that followed this article was one from Harry A.
McPolin in which he wrote, "Years have passed since a lovable Irish priest,
Canon Sheehan, wrote, 'the cry of every Catholic heart must ever be—perish
art, science and literature, rather than issue one word that could originate an
unholy thought or bring to the cheek an unholy flame . . . '"[4]

But the bulk of the Catholic community praised her work and considered
her a Catholic writer to be proud of. Theodore Maynard defended her in
The Catholic World.

The oversensitive who shudder because of the frankly depicted
scenes of childbirth and seduction should be warned that such things
are there, and in profusion; they should also be told that to leave Sigrid
Undset unread on that account is to miss the greatest Catholic fiction
ever produced.[5]

Each of the Scandinavian countries had separate Authors' Associations
although their goals were similar, (royalties for radio performances and from
libraries, amongst other things), and in 1919 they met in Copenhagen to
plan some joint actions. There was another meeting in Stockholm in 1924,

and in 1930 it was Oslo's turn. Sigrid was named Woman of the Week and pictures of her were on the front pages of all of the newspapers. She attended dinners, breakfasts, and theater performances which were organized for the entertainment of the visitors, and since that year was also the 25th anniversary of Norway's independence, and the 900th anniversary of the fall of St. Olav, she participated in ceremonies commemorating both.

She often took her children to Laurgard I Sel for vacations, and in 1931, they went to Gotland and Iceland. "Summer in Gotland"* was a lyric evocation of the area and its history, and a vehicle for further theological discussion.

There is no doubt that the medieval novels were her greatest achievements, but her short stories and some of her modern novels deserved more attention than they received. Her penetrating perceptions endowed ordinary people, especially women, whose daily sacrifices and acts of heroism often go unnoticed, with a dignity that is rare in literature.

*   *   *

In 1932, *Ida Elisabeth*** the most interesting of these novels appeared. With her passionate empathy in full force, Sigrid begins it as Ida Elisabeth is bringing her little boy home from the hospital on the overnight steamer from Bergen. It is a bitterly cold night. Alone with her fears for her child who has just had a mastoid operation and is still very sick, she spends the night trying to make him comfortable in a crowded stateroom which they are sharing with two boisterous young women. When he has finally fallen asleep, she reviews her situation.

She didn't love her husband, Frithjof, when she married him. He played the violin when they were at school and she had taken "his apish liveliness" to be a sign of talent. At times "there was apt to be something about him that reminded you of a dog torn between the desire to snatch a bite and fear of the whip," but at other times, "she herself had gone altogether crazy—she had romped with him and egged him on, cuddled him and pushed him away,"[6] and before she knew what had happened they had become lovers. When her parents found out about it there was a terrible row. "If one's dog is maimed," her father had shouted, "one shoots him—any man does who has a heart—but nobody is man enough to do that to his child."[7]

---

*   Included in Men, Women and Places.
** Published by Knopf in 1933.

After her disgrace, she tried hard to make something of herself, but when Frithjof returned four years later and asked her to marry him, her need for approval from her family was so strong that she did. Her husband was brought up to believe that he was a genius no matter how poorly he performed, and he had never been expected to see a task through to the end. Her in-laws used their belief in sharing as an excuse for arranging for others to share what they had with them, but they thought of themselves as decent, good-natured people. Only concerned with their own needs, they assumed that everyone was as interested in their happiness as they were themselves. No job was quite good enough for Frithjof. Ida Elisabeth supported them both by doing dressmaking and eventually opened a small drygoods store. Frithjof did a little gardening, was proud when he brought some fish home for dinner, and was constantly buying things on installment which they couldn't afford and she had to return—and he entertained himself, like many men in Sigrid's stories, by going to the local hotel to drink and socialize with the traveling salesmen.

> *There was something that roused a secret repugnance in her, by the very manner in which he loved her; he seemed to think a lot of himself for being such a devil of a fellow, frightfully passionate and all of that—and at the same time he gave her the idea of being always afraid someone might come in and pull him up for it.*[8]

His parents called her "dear Lisken," praised her for being such a giving person, and manipulated her into carrying them too.

> *Her mother-in-law's handwriting was large and round with thick down-strokes and many flourishes around the letters. Ida Elisabeth never saw it on the outside of a letter without a little dark foreboding that here was something coming that she would just as soon be without.*[9]

She is shamed into accepting her lazy sister-in-law, Else, "to help her in the store" when she knows she will only be another dependent. "Dear Lisken" sews for all of them "because she sews so beautifully." She resents them and their parasitic ways in the name of love, but each time she is faced with another of their crises, her compassion undermines her determination and she is again inveigled into helping them—but she knows she is being used.

Because he can't bear to see her so exploited, the local doctor gets Frithjof a job in Bergen. He seems to be doing well and Ida Elisabeth is making plans to sell the store and join him when he appears unexpectedly and says that he has come home to stay. She thinks he has been fired, but a letter "with a disgusting smell of scent"[10] arrives and she discovers that he has been having an affair and has promised to get a divorce and marry the other woman. She is pregnant as a result of his Christmas visit, but hasn't the time to tell him, and now she won't. She confronts him with the letter and tells him he can have the divorce. He says he came home because he didn't want a divorce. He only got involved with that woman because he was lonely. He hadn't expected it to go so far. She was being unreasonable. He had made a mistake. He is sure that when he has explained it all to her, she will understand and forgive him, but she is adamant. She says:

> If one has taken the devil on one's back, one has to carry him over the stream, but if the devil himself does one the kindness to jump down, you don't suppose anyone is going to be so foolish as actually to squat down and beg him to be so good as to get on again.[11]

It was as though she had been stringing beads. Every time she got some on the string, "he and those other people came and tore it out of her hands." The beads would fall to the floor and roll away into holes and corners and each time she picked them up again there were fewer of them.[12] She had to get away before it was too late. His family would soon be descending on her "to help her come to her senses," and she couldn't trust herself to remain firm.

She leaves, manages to get a divorce and opens a store in another town. All goes well for a number of years. She begins to take care of herself, and is happy with her two sons, (one was born after she left), but she knows that they aren't exceptional children. In fact, they are not bright or attractive at all. She meets Tryggve who is a good man, intelligent and a successful lawyer. They fall in love and decide to marry. He is kind to her children but it is obvious that he is not fond of them. She knows that they could use some discipline and that a man would be good for them, but it is not with love that he punishes them. The children are miserable and jealous of her love for him. His sister's children are brilliant and talented and she sees how much less attractive hers are. She believes that

> no child has the right to demand that a mother who has been left alone shall pass the rest of her life in celibacy. What they have the right to demand is that the new man who steps in shall deal fairly by them . . .[13]
> But she was longing, longing, longing. She who know what it is to have a man, but had never had a man whom she loved . . .[14]

They spend a weekend in Oslo together and

> *she made the acquaintance of an entirely different kind of joy in life. Precisely, made its acquaintance, for it was something quite new that she had met with, intensely different from the old joy which used to well up as it were from the depths within herself, draw nourishment from her own forces and from what she herself had to win for it . . .*
>
> *This was so unlike the old feeling—as the sundrenched summer air when it bakes the sides of the valley, warming earth and stones and penetrating to every leaf and blade of grass, is unlike the lonely little fire within a man's body which he himself must feed as long as he lives and which goes out when he dies. Probably she had never seriously believed that there is such a thing as happiness that merely flows from one person to another—they need do nothing, it is enough that they are together . . . happiness in love—Ida Elisabeth laughed quietly at the thought.*[15]

They are invited to a formal party and at the hairdresser's she meets one of her ex-sisters-in-law who tells her that Else has an illegitimate baby and is in desperate need of a job. She dreads getting involved with that family again, but she gets her job as a housekeeper in the town in which she lives. Then a letter from her former mother-in-law arrives addressed to "My dear good trusty Lisken." Thanking her in her usual flowery language for all she has done for her daughter, she explains that Frithjof, who never remarried, has unfortunately contracted tuberculosis. He was on his way, at that very moment, to her town where they hoped she and Else would be able to get him into the well-known sanatorium located there.

They were sending him there because he had "so longed to see his dear children again." Neither he nor any member of his family had shown the slightest interest in "his dear children" after she left, but he was already on the way, he was very sick, and she couldn't refuse to help him.

Tryggve doesn't think her children should be allowed to visit their father and they quarrel. She has become embroiled in the problems of her ex-husband's family without considering how it might affect her love.

He finds it hard to understand why she is allowing herself to be victimized again, and begins to reprimand the children for being just like their father. She knows that they are difficult children, but they are hers and she loves them. If she marries Tryggve, will she be buying her happiness at their expense?

Up to this point, *Ida Elisabeth* is an extremely sensitive portrait of a simple, brave, compassionate woman whose society expects her to service others without considering it necessary to fulfill any of her own needs. Every parent who contemplates a second marriage questions how the children will fare in the new arrangement, and knowing that Ida Elisabeth's children were "not exceptional," one can understand that she would want to be sure that Tryggve would be good to them, but that is not the end of the story. As if another writer has stepped in to finish her book, Sigrid seems to forget that "no one would be foolish enough to actually squat down and beg the devil to be so good as to get on her back again," and suspending her own logic in order to accept the dogma of her Church, she has Ida Elisabeth break with Tryggve and decide that her marriage to Frithjof should never have been dissolved. She knows that Frithjof will not change. If he lives he will take advantage of her as he always has, but she says "God has mysterious ways." No one can understand the meaning of another person's life. There is "something . . . a kind of magnetic pole of souls . . . which draws me away from the path on which my thirst for happiness would urge me, because it is now too late to follow it—which tells me that what I have signed in my cups I shall have to pay when sober."[16]

Torn between her conviction that one must fight against oppression, and her desire to put herself in God's hands, Sigrid painted herself into a corner that she couldn't get out of. If, as she has said, the continuation of civilization depends on each person's efforts to improve it, how will passive acceptance of one's fate achieve justice? That unresolved dilemma did not help her work, and although there were still glimpses of greatness in the books that followed, her need to justify the position of the Church caused her didactic tone to become strident; and the quality of her writing diminished.

After *Ida Elisabeth*, she wrote *Christmas and Twelfth Night*, and in 1933, a collection of essays called *Stages in the Road.*˙

*　　*　　*

A growing hostility amongst her peers and mixed reviews of her books were not easy to live with. Depressed and out of step with everyone around her, she was in no mood for a public celebration of her 50th birthday. She went abroad, explaining that she had been suffering from rheumatic pains, and since Bjerkebaek needed painting, it could be done while she was away.

In 1934, her autobiographical novel, *The Longest Years*˙˙ was published. It is a charming picture of her childhood and was highly praised, but her

---

˙   Published by Knopf in 1934.
˙˙   Published by Knopf in 1935.

idealized portrait of Mrs. Winter-Hjelm (Fru Wilster in the book), the perfect self-sacrificing mother, must have caused some snickering amongst her intimates.

Accolades for her medieval novels were still pouring in. New translations came out each ear and little girls all over the world were still being named Kristin. In 1935, the Turkish government issued a postage stamp with Svarstad's portrait of her on it, and she was elected Chairman of the Norwegian Authors' Association, a post she held until the Nazis invaded Norway in 1940. She was an excellent chairman, and despite her personal bias, exceptionally fair. She was on a committee that reviewed the work of young writers seeking membership in the organization, and was on a board that recommended promising writers for stipends from the Storting.

Another novel with a surprise ending, *The Faithful Wife* came out in 1936.˙ This time the story is about a career woman who, like Paul Selmer in *The Winding Road*, comes from a left-wing family. Nathalie manages a large design studio called House and Home, and is attractive, talented and able, while her husband, Sigurd, comes from a family of conservative farmers and is an engineer. They have little in common, go on business trips separately, take holidays with or without each other, sleep in separate rooms—and have no children.

Sigurd has an affair with a very young farm girl who becomes pregnant, but although he divorces Nathalie, the girl who will not marry him because she is a Catholic and won't marry a divorced man. She also refuses to have an abortion, because of her religion, and dies in childbirth. Sigurd takes his child to bring up, and becomes a Catholic. Nathalie has had an affair with a childhood friend but he also dies. She adopts the son of one of her co-workers and she and her ex-husband decide to remarry and bring up the two children together. That is contrived enough, but that isn't all.

It seems that Nathalie now understands that she was responsible for the break-up of their marriage. Although it was "right" for her to have gone back to work at the beginning, when her husband was having economic difficulties and needed her help, she had destroyed his confidence in himself by continuing to work "after she didn't have to," because they both knew that she was brighter and more successful than he was. When they remarry, her husband does not want her to work, except where she can help him a little with his modest new business. She decides to move to the small town where he has settled, stay home, care for him, and raise the two children.

˙   Published by Knopf in 1937.

*   *   *

Her devotion to the Church was forcing Sigrid to take some positions that seem hard to understand—but on some issues she still stood fast. In November, 1938, she and Nini were witnesses for Aksel Sandemose who sued the critic C. J. Hambro for slander when he called a Sandemose book pornographic.[17] Sigrid testified that "the critic had not understood a single word of the book." It was a "naked and true book" and "some words should not be taken out of context." As far as morals went, she thought that most preachy teenage books were more immoral by far.[18]

As time passed, Sigrid's "happy days" began to fade. Anders, who had always been a loner and was never much of an intellectual, decided against going to college. He chose to become an auto mechanic, went to England* as an apprentice at the Austin Motor Company and attended a technical college in Birmingham[19]. Gunhild and her family had been living in England since 1931 and both Anders and Hans were very fond of her. Sigrid was not pleased with Anders' choice of profession but she knew it was a realistic one. Hans, who was taller and more handsome than his older brother, and probably brighter, made elaborate plans but rarely carried them out. He had Sigrid's phenomenal memory, was interested in history, read a great deal, and said he wanted to be a writer, but he spent little time at writing and his style was strangely forced and archaic. Capitalizing on what he called "the fame of his parents," he developed an egocentric and affected manner and worked too hard at "being brilliant."

In *Happy Days in Norway*, Sigrid wrote that when Hans was a boy, he could not differentiate between what he imagined and what actually happened. Eirik, in *The Master of Hestviken*, and little Tryggve in *Ida Elisabeth* have the same problem.

> *Tryggve had a disposition to take refuge in boasting. And he lied like anything. Perhaps he was still too young to distinguish between what really happened, what he imagined might happen, and what he wished to happen.*[20]

Hans was twelve or thirteen when she wrote that.

As Hans grew older, he developed illusions of grandeur and would introduce himself at a party as "the son of two geniuses."[21] In a letter to a friend,

---

he once wrote that his dream was to have "an equestrian statue of himself erected in some important village square," although he didn't mention what he planned to do to merit such an honor.[22] When there was talk of a movie of *Kristin Lavransdatter*, he told friends that he would be playing Erlend. His half-sister Ebba, who died in 1984, and was institutionalized for the last years of her life, imagined that she spoke to Joan of Arc.[23]

When Sigrid became a Catholic, Anders was twelve and Hans was five. Anders went to church with her but was never baptized. Hans was. When he was ten, she sent him to St. Sunniva, a school run by St. Joseph's sisters in Oslo, but he had such a hard time adjusting to being away from home that he only stayed for one year. The sculptor Kjeld Rasmussen, who was a roommate of his, told me that he couldn't dress himself, didn't know how to care for his belongings, and couldn't tell his right shoe from his left—often putting them the wrong way around. Ole Henrik, who grew up with him in Lillehammer, says that when they went skiing, he worried that Hans might go over a cliff before he would be able to figure out another way around.

Sigrid once said that he would need a nursemaid to dress him until he was sixty, and when she was laughingly asked why only until sixty, she said, "Well, at least until then."'[24]

Unlike Anders, Hans attended classes at universities over a period of years, but never got a degree. The directions her children were taking were especially disappointing to Sigrid, because her sister's children chose academic careers and were far more involved in intellectual pursuits. Sigrid visited Anders when he was in England and spent time with Gunhild. Gunhild was a married woman and mother by then, and they were able to relate to each other as they had never done in the past. They went to Edinburgh together, stayed in a hotel, visited museums and restaurants, and enjoyed themselves thoroughly.

In 1938, *Men, Women and Places*'' appeared in Norway. It included essays about the Danish writer Marie Bregendahl, the 15th century English mystic Marery Kempe, Oliver Cromwell, Leo Weismantel, Glastonbury, "Summer in Gotland," and an essay about D. H. Lawrence,.

Calling Lawrence "a visionary and a poet of genius," she wrote that "he wanted to be a prophet, a savior of the world and a Messiah."[25]

His was an incredibly hallucinatory art, which produces on the reader the effect of direct sensations of taste, vision and feeling . . .

' Hans died in 1978 when he was fifty-nine years old.
'' Published by Alfred A. Knopf in English, 1939.

> *No matter what he wrote—novels, short stories, poetry, essays, letters,*
> *travels—in his hands the subjects became new and his own property in*
> *a curious way. Like ore that has been heated in the furnace and comes*
> *out gleaming with unsuspected colors, bright and dark, the English*
> *language is fused in his burning brain and leaves his forge re-smelted,*
> *with new and wonderful values.*[26]

Because of his father's weakness and his mother's dominance over him,
he "romanticized manliness" and

> *described the sexual relation as a war to the death between*
> *man and woman . . . Woman is a fury who rages against man for*
> *reducing her to subjection and who despises him when he fails to do*
> *so . . .*[27]
>
> *The widespread fear of the results of mechanization of existence—a*
> *slow death from loss of heat—finds voice with Lawrence in poems and*
> *description which burst like spouting blood from a severed artery in*
> *intensely animated pictures of struggling life . . . Collectivism cannot*
> *in itself be the remedy for any distress, if separate individuals are*
> *ciphers—for naught plus naught will never equal anything but naught,*
> *however many million ciphers we may add.*[28]
>
> *Much of what is happening in Europe today [1938] and more*
> *that will doubtless happen in the future are the brutal reactions of mass*
> *humanity to the problems which the exceptional man, the genius D. H.*
> *Lawrence perceived and faced, and fought against in his own way.*[29]

On January 12, 1939, Mosse died. She was twenty-three, had been
immobile for the last years of her life, and her death was not unexpected.
Both of her brothers and her aunt Signe came to Lillehammer for the funeral.
Dressed all in white, "like an angel," her cousin Charlotte reported, "they
laid her out in the fireplace room and sat with her all night."[30] It was the end
of a way of life for Sigrid. Mosse's needs had dictated her every move for so
long that it was not easy to adjust to being free. There was sorrow but also
release. "I miss her very much," Sigrid said later, "but I am happy to know
she will never have to be left to strangers. I was never at ease when I was away
from home."[31]

Shortly after Mosse died, Mrs. Undset had a stroke, and on August 23,
at the age of eighty-four, she also died.

Although they liked her autobiographical novel, the family had not been pleased with her portrait of her mother. They felt that she was wittier and more intelligent than portrayed, but Sigrid like the rest, had loved her dearly and would miss her very much. Sigrid claimed that she was brought up without religion. Her mother became a Catholic later in life, but she had imbued her children with large doses of Protestant ethic and Lutheran morality long before she took that step.

Anders came home again for his grandmother's funeral and this time he stayed. He had fallen in love with a girl who lived across the lake from Bjerkebaek and they were planning to marry. Sigrid was very fond of her and was delighted with his choice.

It was a year of deaths. In addition to her mother and daughter, Regine Normann, Sigrid's Danish Moster, and Olav Dunn died. She spoke at their funerals and mourned each of them deeply, but she was still able to finish the first volume of a new novel which she called *Madame Dorothea*.

*   *   *

Patterned after Dorthea Bisgaard Worsøe, the mother of Sigrid's Danish great-grandfather Dean Vilhelm Adolf Worsøe, the book is about 18th century Norway, when Catholicism had been all but ousted from the country and the "Age of Reason" had begun.

Dorthea is married off to a sickly old clergyman when she is sixteen years old, but she is able to marry the man she loves when her elderly husband dies. They live happily together for sixteen years and have seven children. He is the overseer of a glass factory (as Sigrid's great-grandfather had been).[32] The manufacture of glass was a new industry in Norway, and German and English glassblowers were imported to teach the Norwegian workmen the craft. Many of the foreign workers were Catholics and, since there were no longer any Catholic priests in Norway, one was imported at their request. One day, Dorthea's husband disappears. Search parties go out to try to find him but although the mountains are combed for weeks, no body is ever discovered. There are no clues. Had he been involved in something that she knew nothing about? That seemed impossible. They had been so close that she surely would have noticed something. He had no enemies. Then what could have happened to him? Dorthea has a hard time raising her children and can't stop searching for an answer and when no rational explanation is forthcoming, she turns to the priest.

During the 18th century, the works of Isaac Newton, Descartes, Spinoza, John Locke, Moses Mendelssohn, et. al., had provoked an interest in a more scientific approach to religion. Blind faith was being rejected and rational explanations were sought. Sigrid used Dorthea's dilemma as a basis for discussing Catholicism and the Enlightenment.

The best part of the novel, however, is not Sigrid's discourse on religion, but her description of Madame Dorthea's four-time married mother. One of Sigrid's few comic characters, the larger-than-life, exuberant, robust, massive, life-loving woman with her "fairly dirty, tiny little dimpled fat hands covered with rings," her "extraordinary eyes that were like great globes rolling round within the puffy old eyelids" and her sagging cheeks around the pouting little mouth with the "corners drawn down in ill-humor or derision"[33]—is also one of Sigrid's most original characters. She was a favorite ancestress for the whole family and Sigrid's nieces chuckle when they mention her.

There is an unforgettable scene when a housekeeper dies after a number of home-executed abortions. She has been forced to have them because her employer, who enjoys sleeping with her, doesn't want her to have children. He doesn't wish to marry her, but he doesn't want the neighbors to talk.

*   *   *

On August 23, 1939, the German-Soviet Pact was signed, and in November, Russia invaded Finland. Concern over Hitler had been mounting and the invasion of Finland was so close to home that Sigrid began to regret that she had written so much for Catholic publications and had neglected using her position for political influence abroad.[34]

In 1927, a German journalist, Juliana von Stockhausen, had interviewed Sigrid at Bjerkebaek and the woman's fawning, affected, overly flowery way of describing how much the Germans loved her work made Sigrid cringe. Se kept quiet until the lady referred to their "mutual Germanic culture" and then she exploded. Norwegian culture was NOT related to German culture, she said, and to underline how she felt about German culture, she told the lady that she had just given her son *All Quiet on the Western Front* by Erich Maria Remarque.[35]

Juliana von Stockhausen was shocked and asked how she could permit her son to read a book that put down the Fatherland and its brave army. "Many of the young men who fought in that war are still alive," she said, "and if it hadn't been for them, France and its army of colored soldiers [sic] would have forced themselves into the heart of Germany and destroyed everything that Germany stood for." There is no record of what Sigrid answered, but on other occasions she said that Nazism had "simply let loose the evil that was intrinsic to German nature."

In 1918, in a review of books about the First World War, Sigrid had written:

> *It seems unimaginable that Germans will willingly give up their militarism . . . Perhaps the German people need their militarism as the lobster needs its claws and shell. They have hard outside panzer shells surrounding a soft, boneless body. What a great Germany has is the hard discipline of the Prussian administration. Its determination is a shell which gives strength and locomotive power to a nation whose innermost structure is soft and spineless . . . It is not envy, nor even fear . . . which moved those who feared the advance of Germany. It is an instinctive reaction of humanity which has its firmness in its back and has a soft and feeling skin toward the world to fight the lobsters and their terrible claws . . .*
>
> *One sometimes finds meaning in small things . . . German stamps show Germany with horns on her head and two armored plates on her chest . . . Even the source of her mother's milk is iron clad.*[36]

As Chairman of the Author's Association, she corresponded with writers all over the world and many of them were German. In 1935, she wrote to Nini that she was sure that her letters were being opened. A refugee committee had been set up to help German writers, and she was working for that committee. A Thomas Mann Fund was established to solicit funds from European publishers to help German writers get out of Germany, and for the publication of banned books, and there is a letter in the files of Aschehoug, dated June 1937, in which Sigrid authorized her publisher to send money to the fund from her royalties and asked them to contribute as well.

In 1935, a collection of articles by Protestant and Catholic clergy against the persecution of Jews by the Nazis had been published entitled *The Dangers*

---

* Sigrid claims to have researched the origin of the helmet and horns which is often shown in pictures as worn by Vikings, and wrote that it was a Teutonic headdress that had never been worn by Norse people.

of Christianity from Race Hatred and The Persecution of the Jews. Sigrid had an article in it called *Progress, Race, Religion* and the Nazis had reacted to it at once. She had a large readership in Germany and the *Westdeutscher Beobachter* announced that "Her works shall no longer be found in German papers, German libraries and German bookshops." On May 15, 1937, *Fronten*, a Nazi paper published in Oslo, followed suit:

> *What Sigrid Undset publishes is not merely foreign and offensive to us—it is hostile. Sigrid Undset is certainly Nordic by birth, but her attitude of mind is most un-Nordic . . . People have been quick to lose the capacity to react against anything at all—and forces outside the State are given free scope.*

Of these "forces outside the State," the Catholic Church was listed as "one of the most corrupting."

She was put on the list of Hitler's "hostile forces outside of the State."

Reprinted later by *Vita Nova* in Lucerne.

CHAPTER XV

WAR

1940

Six years after Hitler took power, German armies were in Moravia, Bohemia, Lithuania and Poland—and millions of Jews, "dissidents" and Catholics were being arrested and tortured. After the German-Soviet Pact, Poland was divided between them, and the Russians annexed parts of Finland. Italy had signed a pact with Hitler after invading Abyssinia* and seizing Albania, and was threatening Greece. Franco had defeated the army of the elected Spanish Republic. The Japanese were in China.

No one could imagine what would happen to little Norway. As always, they had declared themselves neutral. Relying on the League of Nations and their 125 years of neutrality, they had been reducing their military budgets each year; their equipment was antiquated and they had an army of fewer than 7,000 trained soldiers. The Germans were using Norwegian waters to transport war supplies and the British were protesting, but the Norwegian government was doing nothing about it. In February, the British sank a German boat which was carrying 300 British prisoners-of-war and freed them in Norwegian waters, and there was a strong protest from both Norway and Germany, but when the Germans bombed Norwegian merchant vessels and machine-gunned the sailors as they got into lifeboats, the government did nothing about it.

On Saturday, April 7, 1940, Sigrid spoke at a meeting of the Norwegian Students' Association in Oslo. Dorothy Day, of the American Catholic Workers' Party, was the guest of honor. Anders, who was working in town

---

* The former name of Ethiopia.

and drilling with the reserves, and Hans, who was attending classes at the university, met her at Signe's house the next day for dinner. The conversation kept coming back to Hitler. What would he do next?

There was a benefit concert for Finnish Relief that evening, which Sigrid and Signe planned to attend, and Sigrid was going to donate her gold Nobel Prize medal. When Russia invaded Finland, children were evacuated from the most severely bombed parts of the country and brought for safety to Norwegian homes, and Sigrid had taken three children to Bjerkebaek. She took three because they were from the same family and very young. When she brought them home, Eira, who was two, Toimi, three, and Elmi, four, were so frightened that she had to keep them in her bed with her and cuddle them until they could fall asleep.[1]

The next morning they awoke bright and talkative, but no one could understand them. Sigrid's niece, Charlotte, who had come up to help, reports, "It was a happy day when we discovered that the Finnish word for 'chamber-pot' was *piiti*."[2] Fortunately, children learn quickly and it wasn't many days before they were able to make themselves understood.

Because of the children, Sigrid had an unexpected visit from Svarstad. He arrived, explaining that he had recently sold some pictures and wanted to make a donation to Finnish Relief. He spent a few days with her, left some money, and was so loving and warm that some of Sigrid's pent-up yearning for him was reawakened. He had never pretended to be other than he was, and "she would never grow so old that he could not play upon her fondness."[3]

At the benefit for Finland, Sigrid donated her medal and was annoyed when a woman who for years had "battled heroically to attain a position in Norwegian literary circles with a colossal energy and a diminutive talent," entered the hall "with some German-looking persons." She had been the only one in the literary community, Sigrid later wrote in *Return to the Future*, "who with Knut Hamsun unwinkingly sided with Nazi Germany."[4]

After the concert, Sigrid was reading in bed at the hotel where she was staying, when she heard sirens. She waited for them to stop, but when they didn't she put on her shoes and stockings, threw her fur coat over her nightgown and, since there was no elevator service, walked down to the lobby. Other guests had done the same. No one knew what was happening, but the hotel had an air raid shelter, and they were advised to go there. They were led

---

* It was the last time they saw each other.

to a dark, cold room in the basement where they smoked cigarettes and made feeble attempts at conversation, and when an "all clear" sounded, they went back to bed. Another alarm sounded shortly after Sigrid fell asleep, and this time she got dressed before coming down. The management was serving food and drinks when she got to the lobby, and she stayed there for the rest of the night, still not knowing what was going on. Was their merchant fleet being attacked again? Toward morning, German planes began to cruise over the city. There were sounds of shooting, but people were going to work as usual, and when they were queried, they didn't' know any more than anyone else. Since others were going about their business, Sigrid went to eight-o'clock Mass, but when she discovered that the children of the Catholic school had been evacuated during the night, she rushed to see Anders at work. He hadn't come in, so she hurried to his rooms. He wasn't there either. Her anxiety building, she returned to the hotel and found Hans waiting for her. Concerned about the children at home, she was eager to get to them, but she didn't want to leave without speaking to Anders.

They didn't know if the trains were running but decided to go to the station and try to hitch a ride if they weren't. People were saying that the King had left the city and the Storting would be meeting in Hamar. Just when they decided to leave without seeing Anders, he arrived with a knapsack and rifle. Everyone was still guessing about what was going on when a radio program was interrupted and an announcer with a strong German accent said, "Norwegians and Germans are all of the same race. If Norway is ever in trouble, Germany will be there to come to their aid."[5] There was nothing left to guess about. The Germans were obviously invading Norway.

Anders had to report to his unit at once, but would try to get to Lillehammer or send word as soon as he could, and with nothing more to wait for, Sigrid and Hans hurried to the station. There they ran into Ole Henrik, who was also carrying a knapsack and rifle, and they boarded the train together.[6] It was an hour late and packed with refugees who were eager to get as far away from the invading army as possible, but there was no panic. A bomb almost hit the train as it was pulling from the station, but no one was hurt. Each time they passed a military base, young men got off—and each time that happened, Sigrid had something to say:

"We are harvesting what we have sown."

"I thank God that Mosse is dead."

"I thank God that Mama is dead. She saw enough in her lifetime, she didn't have to live to see what's coming," and, she suddenly added, twitting Ole Henrik, "I thank God that your sister is no longer engaged to a German."[*][7]

When they got home, the children were huddled with one of the maids in the dark. There was no electricity and they were obviously remembering painful experiences they had almost forgotten. Thea and Böe had driven to Oslo to look for Sigrid. They returned during the night, after having unloaded a number of people whom they had picked up on the way back. Anders arrived much later "hungry and thirsty and very silent,"[8] and said he was worried because some of the men in his battalion were talking like collaborators. He left early the next morning and called during the day to ask Hans to bring him his uniform and some of his things. Hans came back late, took a sleeping bag and some boots, and announced that since he and Ole Henrik were too young for the army, they had volunteered for the medical corps.

"Don't worry, Mother," he said on his way out, "the medical corps isn't dangerous."[9]

Unable to sit there doing nothing, Sigrid volunteered to help at the Lillehammer Commandant's office and was put to work censoring mail. Evacuees from Oslo and Trondheim were stopping at Bjerkebaek daily—needing food and money. A German priest was sent to stay there whose crime was

> . . . that when the Jewish children were persecuted in the schools of the little Bavarian town where he was the director of the Catholic school system, he had given orders that they should be admitted to Catholic schools on the same conditions as other children, only to be excused from religious instruction. And he had accompanied a wealthy Jew to his grave—a Jew who in years of want had helped needy people and institutions on a large scale, without asking whether they were Jewish, Protestant or Catholic. And at the grave he had made a speech in commemoration of the dead man, in Hebrew.[10]

For these crimes he had been declared an "Enemy of the State" and had to leave his country.

"Day in and day out the sun shone from a cloudless, serene blue heaven," Sigrid wrote in *Return to the Future*.

---

[*] Ole Henrik's sister had fallen in love with a German soldier before the war and Sigrid had sided with her parents in objecting to their marriage.

In my garden the snow was melting, and the Finnish youngsters messed around in the water and mud to their hearts' content; they were as wet as drowned kittens each time we had to go out and call them in because air alarms sounded. Lillehammer had no air defense, so the German planes flew unbothered over the town many times a day. But for the present they made no attempt to harm us . . .

And still—in spite of the planes, in spite of the motor trucks full of soldiers which drove through the streets all day long, in spite of sentries with poised bayonets in front of all public buildings, in spite of the motorcycles with orderlies which roared through the streets—in the heavenly spring weather, it was so difficult to understand that this was really war.[11]

On April 9, the Germans had taken control of some of the radio stations, but no one believed what they said. The Norwegians were still operating the stations, but there were so many confusing announcements that when a Broadcast was heard, people would ask, "Is it true or is it German?"[12]

During the first weeks, the Nazis didn't want to anger the population so they could stave off resistance while they were getting into strategic positions, but once in position, the hostilities began. On April 15, British troops arrived but they landed too far to the North to be able to stop the German advance. Sigrid was told to get ready to move at a moment's notice but she couldn't imagine leaving while her sons were in danger. The Germans were fighting all along the roads leading to Lillehammer and since she was one of the most important anti-Nazis on Hitler's lists, she was in danger of being shot or taken hostage. The children were moved to a farm further north, and two weeks later they had to be moved again.* The German priest was helped to get to Sweden, and on April 21, Sigrid was notified that a government car would pick her up in a few hours. At first, she refused to leave, but when it was explained that her sons might be tortured in an effort to get her to cooperate with the enemy, she rushed to get ready. It was a Saturday and she had no money in the house. The banks were closed. She hadn't intended to leave and she was totally unprepared. Thea lent her 100 crowns and offered to help her pack, but she had no time to think of clothes—there was a more urgent matter to be taken care of. She had many letters from German authors which were in a

---

* Eventually the committee that brought them got them back to Finland. Sigrid remained in touch with their parents, Mr. and Mrs. Koivulas, and sent them packages all through the war.

huge chest (together with manuscripts and research materials) which had to
be destroyed. With no time to sort them, she made a fire in the fireplace and
threw all—manuscripts, research and letters—into the flames. Leaving Thea
to watch over the blaze, she put on her fur coat, threw some underclothes and
drugs into a bag, and got into the car that was already waiting.

Waving to Thea and Ingeborg Møller who had come to say goodbye, she
shouted, "The day will come!" as the car drove off.

She was taken to a farmhouse where Fredrik Paasche and his wife, their
eight—and ten-year old children, their housekeeper, and Dr. Anders Wyller
and his family were waiting for her. In an attic, above an outhouse, with their
manuscripts lying on a washing machine, the three authors made recordings
on platters, (there were no tapes then), which would be flown to England
and broadcast from there to Norway.

"Dear countrymen," Sigrid said on one of those platters,

> *Our peaceful attitude has for centuries been a virtue of necessity . . .*
> *Let us remember our great tireless strength and will to sacrifice when*
> *it had to do with saving the victims of the last war. With sorrow and*
> *bitter pride we greet our soldiers who today fight for our country's*
> *honor and freedom. We are a people who love life and protect life. We*
> *can't bear phrases about blood and iron, about blood and race, about*
> *armed fists . . . We have perhaps given the world the impression that we*
> *are tame and peaceful animals, but when men (who we, with shame*
> *and anger, are forced to call Norwegians) believe that they can sell*
> *the Norwegian lion as a watchdog for a dictator, they are shamefully*
> *wrong.*[13]

Each time the Germans advanced, the group, with their equipment,
moved north and they continued their recordings. Once, while they were
being bombed, they lay for two hours in a snowdrift, while a young soldier
was stretched out next to Sigrid regaling her with stories about a Christmas
party he had once attended at her house.[14] Finally, the fighting started with
a vengeance. The countryside was being strafed with incendiary bombs and
their group was moved again. The sun was strong, the land was beautiful,
and the dangers seemed so unreal that it was hard for children to be kept
indoors. They wanted to see what was going on and couldn't understand that
they could get hurt.

For summers, young German hikers vacationed in Norway. They came
with no more than their knapsacks and cameras. They complained about

conditions in their country and explained that they were not permitted to take more than ten marks abroad for travel, and the Norwegians allowed them to sleep in their barns, gave them lifts in their cars, food and clothing, and sometimes money. They loved the countryside, they said, and took hundreds of pictures.[15]

When a group of German paratroopers were captured, Sigrid was told that a farm woman had recognized a boy who had stayed at her house the summer before.[16] He too had taken pictures. Now he had come to kill them.

"No one can complain and ask for pity better than a German when he hasn't the power to act like a superman," Sigrid wrote later in *Return to the Future*.[17] When they attacked they howled and yelled insanely. The Norwegians found chocolate bars laced with cocaine which the Germans were given before an attack, and their "abominable bellowing" made them so loathsome that they didn't seem human.[18]

Since the Germans had planned the invasion meticulously, and the Norwegians and English were poorly equipped, they were forced to keep retreating. Sigrid and her group were moved by stages until they reached Bud on the North Sea. There they were put on a trawler with a number of soldiers and refugees. The Germans were all around, and the seas were mined. They had to travel at night and hide in coves during the days. She had heard nothing from her sons, of course, and when members of the medical corps told her that one of their group had been killed but they didn't know which one, she grew wild with anxiety. (She learned later that since Hans and Ole Henrik knew the terrain around Lillehammer so well, they had been sent on a reconnaissance mission for the army and hadn't been with the medical corps at the time.)[19]

They had still not found a safe place to settle when they had almost reached the northernmost tip of Norway and Sigrid, the Paasche family and Dr. Wyller, (who was too ill to walk and had to be carried on a stretcher) and his family decided that the only thing to do was to try to get to Sweden. If they could get off the boat, they would retrace their steps and try to cross the border where Sweden was the shortest distance from Norway. The borders were patrolled, but there were miles of woodland and it wasn't possible to patrol every inch.

The trawler found a place to land, they managed to get to Mo with short rides from townspeople, but when they were four mountainous miles from Sweden, they were told that the rest of their journey could only be made on skis. Sigrid was fifty-eight years old, overweight, hadn't been on skis since she was a girl, and she was wearing boots, silk stockings and a fur coat. They were trying to decide what to do when six young men, who were on assignment in the area, volunteered to pull Dr. Wyller and Sigrid across on a sled, but by the time they reached a mountain farm near the boarder, the escapees were so frozen and hungry they begged to stop for the night. The family offered to put them up and show them where to cross in the morning, but the young men had to get back the next day and they needed the sled. They could take them across only if they kept going, and Sigrid and the sick man were pulled over the mountain with the ailing man's teenage daughter and son skiing alongside.

In Sweden, the roads were cleared and Sigrid could walk. After two freezing miles, they reached an army post, but it was so crowded that they weren't allowed to enter. At five o'clock in the morning, they arrived at a hut which wasn't locked. A man was asleep under a red quilt, and it was almost as cold inside as out, but it was better than walking another step. While they were trying to make a fire the man awoke. He made a fire and fed them, and the last thing Sigrid remembered as she stretched out on the floor, was seeing him cover their sick companion with his red quilt.[20]

The next day, the volunteers returned to Norway with their sled, and Sigrid's group waited for the rest to catch up with them. Finally, they reached a town with a telephone and their troubles were over. Sweden was fully mobilized but neutral. They were not free to come to Norway's defense but many were eager to help refugees, and the group encountered no difficulties on the rest of the trip to Stockholm. At the end, they rode on a crowded bus that was full of children and old women who had been evacuated to Norway from Finland and were now being sent back. The driver had announced that Finns could ride for nothing but Norwegians had to pay, and a telephone worker volunteered to pay "for the old woman," (meaning Sigrid) and take her on his lap. She was able to pay for herself, she said, but when she was ready to get off he offered her a Swedish five-kroner bill "for coffee and a little food on the way." She thanked him and explained that it wasn't so bad for her because she had friends in Sweden, and he gave the money to a woman who was trying to reach her sister in Lapland.[21]

Sigrid had run out of handkerchiefs, but when she tied to buy some, the only ones available had black borders. She said she wasn't superstitious and bought one—and then worried about what she had done all the rest of the way.[22]

She telephoned her sister as soon as she reached a phone and Ragnhild and Alice Lyttkens were waiting for her at the bus station in Stockholm. They seemed uncharacteristically subdued, but she was so exhausted that she decided she was reacting to her own fatigue. All she wanted was a bath and some sleep. Since Alice's son was in the army, they suggested that she would be more comfortable if she stayed there where she could have his room, and she agreed.

After breakfast the next morning,* Alice sat down next to her and told her that her son Anders had been killed on April 27th at the Segelstad bridge in Guasdal—not far from Lillehammer—and that he had already been buried.[23]

Turning deathly pale, she grasped Alice's hand with an iron grip, and like a wounded animal, began to whimper. Trembling and still making those ghastly sounds, she sat there for quite a while. Then she went to her room and stayed there for the rest of that day and the next. They brought her food and begged her to open the door, but she said she wanted nothing—only to be left alone. After that, she got dressed and went to her sister's house.

Her nephew Ingvald was having a party that day, and his sister described what happened in a letter to me on July 1, 1983.

> *May is the month of matriculation in Sweden and the day is always celebrated with big, happy, noisy parties, mostly taking place at the home of the matriculant. So also in our home. Masses of young people storm into the rooms. They sing, drink and eat, and congratulate the matriculant in a very lively way, to say the least. Naturally, relatives are also present. My aunt, who had recently escaped from Norway, had been in Stockholm only a few days and had just received a message that her beloved oldest son Anders had fallen and lost his life in the fight against the Germans. He had died three weeks before, but the message had just reached her. Nevertheless, she had come to wish my brother good luck and happiness for the future. She was in the room with the happy crowd for only a moment. Then she withdrew to my father's room, and when my parents and I went into her, we encountered her in deepest sorrow . . . The noise from all the people in the adjoining rooms was terrific—the contrast unforgettable. Unspeakable sorrow was marked on Aunt Sigrid's face but she would shed no tears on my brother's happy day. The great, stoic woman sat there alone with the greatest pain a mother could experience in her life—yet—proud of her son who gave his life for his dear country she said that that was her greatest consolation.*

---

* May 11, 1940.

The next day, she started to pull strings to get Hans out of Norway. Southern Norway had surrendered at the beginning of the invasion, but as long as the British were there, the North had continued to fight. After sixty days of trying to hold back the Germans, the British withdrew, and Norway had become an occupied country—and in an occupied country Hans was in danger of being taken hostage as a way of getting to her.

The news from the rest of the world was appalling. The Germans had not only invaded Norway, Denmark, Holland and Belgium, but France was expected to fall. She read all of the papers, looking grimmer each day, but she only mentioned Anders once when she sighed and murmured, "Thank God, Anders doesn't have to experience this."[24] She had royalties in Sweden and could have remained there, but all she cared about was the defeat of the Nazis and she knew that she would not be able to do anything in Sweden. She was popular in the United States. She had been offered lecture tours there, and believed that by speaking to Americans she might be able to convince them to enter the war. Britain was fighting with little help and could surely not hold out much longer.

After Mosse died she had turned down a tour for Colston Leigh because her mother was ill. Now, she wrote that she would be willing to accept it if it could still be arranged. With the intercession of important Swedish officials, Hans was given a passport, but he was asked to come for his exit permit in person. The Germans frequently acted as if they wanted to cooperate with the population, and then found "irregularities" as an excuse for detaining people. Friends warned him that it could be a trap and recommended that he get out fast. "He dressed as if he were going for a walk in town," she wrote in *Return to the Future*,

> the Germans were suspicious of sport clothes. Then he took the train to an out-of-the-way station in one of the forest provinces near the Swedish border, boarded one of the buses there, and rode until he passed a path in the woods which looked promising.[25]

Several young people who were also planning to cross got off with him. The Germans were afraid to patrol too far from their posts because the Norwegians were picking off single Nazis wherever they could. Their fear of going out alone was so great that they often defecated on the floors of the farmhouses where they stayed, rather than risk going to an outhouse, and Hans was told that it was safer to stick to uninhabited areas until he found a place to cross. When a German was killed, they retaliated immediately. A boy of eleven had been shot in front of his mother and sister a few days before because a German had been shot near their farm and the child was "the only man" in the house.[26] Sometimes when attacking, they drove women and children in front of them in order to keep the Norwegians from shooting, and Sigrid wrote that some of the women were so enraged that they shouted, "Shoot, shoot—don't mind us."[27]

Waiting for Hans was unbearable. She felt that she couldn't think until he got there. She was so eager to get away that in a letter to Henrik Wilhelm von Loon she wrote that she was going to America and might stay there forever.[28]

She had not been in touch with Dea for a number of years, but on May 27th, she wrote to tell her that Anders had been killed. Colston Leigh agreed to sponsor her tour, but waiting for Hans seemed endless. Alice was researching a book, and in an effort to distract her, she took her to the library each day, and Sigrid spent the time reading what Danish authors of the Middle Ages had written about the Germans.[29] For years, Sigrid had been devoted to the work of Carl von Linne, the Swedish botanist who founded the binomial system of nomenclature,* she had even started a biography of him, and since his estate at Hammarby in Uppsala was open to the public, Alice also took her there.[30]

Sigrid had always cared about what she wore. As a young girl she had insisted on unflattering, matronly clothes, thoroughly convinced that her taste was superior to that of her mother and sisters, but her preoccupation with "buying a wardrobe for America" while she waited for Hans frightened her relatives and friends. It is true that she came with nothing and needed everything, but it was sufficiently excessive to be eerie. She even got a permanent wave.

Finally, at the end of May, Hans arrived and they were ready to leave. Getting to the United States was not going to be easy, but she managed to book space on the SS President Cleveland which would sail from Kobe, Japan, to San Francisco. In order to get there, they would have to cross the Soviet Union and Siberia, and it was during the time of the Nazi-Soviet Pact.

From Hans, she discovered how Anders had died. He had been responsible for three machine guns. They had so few that they were forced to keep moving them, and he was killed while trying to reposition them. His comrades had carried his body with them when they had to flee, and it was eventually brought to Lillehammer. Signe hitchhiked to Lillehammer to arrange his

---

* Scientific classification of plants, animals and minerals.

funeral, and faithful Thea walked all the way to Kapp pa Toten to break the terrible news to Anders' fiancée, Gunvor Hjerkinn. It was a long distance to the other side of the lake, and it was a warm, wet day, and her feet were blistered by the time she got back. Hans had also rushed to Gunvor when he got the news, and he took her to Lillehammer on his bicycle for the funeral.[31]

Having Hans calmed her. Keeping only the barest essentials, she gave all the clothes she had purchased to Alice's housekeeper, (who was her size), before she left.

On July 12th, the papers announced that Sweden had granted Germany permission to send their troops across Swedish soil in order to get to Norway, and Sigrid was relieved that she would not have to live there under those conditions.

They flew to Moscow on July 13th, arrived during a sweltering heat wave, spent nine nightmarish days and nights in a filthy, poorly-run train which had no running water, no working toilets, and received no fresh food during the entire journey, but they arrived in Vladivostok in time to make connections for Kobe. From there, their living conditions improved. The boat to Kobe was spotlessly clean and after the sailing had been delayed several times, they were finally able to board the SS President Cleveland and sail for the United States.

CHAPTER XVI

AMERICA

1940-1945

They arrived in San Francisco on August 27, 1940—a day before Hans' 21st birthday—spent a few days at the Fairmont Hotel, and took a train to New York. Ever since she was told that Anders was killed, she had been unable to think of anything except getting Hans out of Norway and getting to America. It was a grueling journey, and Sigrid felt as if she had been living underwater, but soon she would be able to surface and breathe. Then she would face what had happened to her.

Looking out of the train window, she was amazed at the beauty and vastness of the country, but she could enjoy none of it. She had prepared none of her lectures and she wasn't sure she had the strength to do what would soon be required of her. She knew English quite well, but she hadn't spoken it for a long time and she found herself reaching for every word—and when she remembered the word, her sing-song inflection made it hard for her to be understood. When she had first contemplated a lecture tour, she had planned to brush up on her English and prepare her talks in advance, and at that time she had planned to donate her fees to Finnish Relief, but now many of her royalties were frozen because of the war and she needed the money. If she couldn't be understood and the tour was to be cancelled, they would have nothing to live on. They were met at the station and taken to the Hotel Algonquin. She was looking forward to a bath and rest, but she just had time to wash her face and change her dress before she was whisked to the Colston Leigh offices for a press conference. Bewildered by all of the bustle and to-do, she was horrified to learn, when they stepped into the elevator of the skyscraper, that they were going to one of the top floors. Scared out of her wits, but not wanting to create any problems, she sat down on the floor in a corner of the elevator, closed her eyes, and put herself in the hands of the Lord, to the great amusement of her escort and the operator.

Not knowing what to expect next, she was relieved to see Alfred Knopf's gentle, smiling face waiting to greet her when the elevator door opened and she stepped out. Alfred and Blanche Knopf were not just her publishers, they were her friends. They had visited her in Norway and were the closest thing to a family she had in America, and his presence was so reassuring that she handled the press well—but she was nervous and spoke in a low monotone and few could understand her. She had aged so visibly and looked so frightened and apprehensive, (" . . . one needs distance to see the deficit she was in at this time," Alice Lyttkens had written[1]), that when the reporters began to badger her about her personal life which, Knopf knew, she had always refused to talk about, he tried to intervene. She was very tired, he said. She had just arrived after a long and harrowing journey. He was sure she would tell the press all about it after she had collected herself . . .

But before he could say another word, he was ushered into a back hall by a member of the Colston Leigh staff and asked, not too politely, to stay out of it. Couldn't he see what a problem she was going to be? He was not to interfere. They needed all the advance publicity they could get.[2]

She managed to complete the press conference, but when it was over, and she was told that she was booked for more than forty lectures at universities, women's clubs, Scandinavian centers and Catholic institutions—that they were to start at once—and that they would all take place within the next few months—she had all she could do to keep from howling out loud. It was too much. She would never make it. She had used up all her reserves just to get there. She needed time to collect herself. She had to have a few weeks to prepare her lectures and brush up on her English. At the suggestion of the Knopfs, Hans had applied to Harvard before they left Sweden and she was overjoyed when she was informed that he had been accepted, but he would have to leave for Cambridge by September 10th and she needed time to get him ready. It was all happening too fast—but after she had a good night's sleep she accomplished it all.

Carol Brandt, (who handled Sigrid's tour for Colston Leigh), told me that "she furnished a suite of rooms for Hans at great expense, with new furniture, and couldn't get to Brooks Brothers fast enough to get him the most expensive clothes in America." When she explained that the wardrobe they had selected was more suitable for a foreign diplomat than a student at Harvard, and that even the wealthiest students bought second-hand furniture and sold it to those who came after them, Sigrid said *they* were free to do as they liked. (Hans was obviously not going to wear made-over clothes or carry his grandfather's old green schoolbag at Harvard!)

When Hans had been attended to, she ordered several made-to-order outfits at Bergdorf Goodman, and Mrs. Brandt didn't approve of that either. "We all have sons," she told me, "but I don't know when I've seen a mother so infatuated with her son . . . Nothing seemed to matter to her at that moment except that son and her clothes."

"Having just lost two children," I said, "it is not hard to understand that she wanted to pamper Hans, and his being at Harvard was particularly important to her. As for buying clothes at Bergdorf's, she was a large woman, hard to fit, and a "name" speaker. I'm sure she was getting high fees—and more important than the rest, the defeat of Hitler was all that mattered to her and she wanted to make a good impression on her audience so that she could convince them of the importance of winning the war."

Mrs. Brandt thought for a while and said that perhaps I was right. She didn't know, at that time, that Sigrid had lost two children before she came to America.[3]

Once Hans was off to Harvard, Sigrid began to look for a place to live. She would be shuttling back and forth between her lectures, which were scattered all over the country, with a few days at a time in New York. The Algonquin had been selected for her because it was centrally located and popular with writers, but she wasn't interested in a social life—she needed a home.

There was a Norwegian community in Brooklyn with a church which she could attend. St. Ansgar's Scandinavian Catholic League met in that neighborhood, and Lossa Olsen Bursson, who had gone to Ragna Nielsen's school with Sigrid, ran a center for Scandinavian seamen nearby—so she settled on an inexpensive apartment in the annex of the Hotel Margaret* in that area. It was a peaceful, family neighborhood, not as frightening or impersonal as Manhattan, and near the waterfront where she could sit on a bench and watch the boats in the harbor. She had two shabbily furnished rooms and a kitchen, but there was a view of the city, plenty of light, and "the sound of boats and the smell of the sea when the tide came in,"[4] and as soon as she began to accumulate plants she was comfortable. After she moved in, Jørgine Boomer, of the Waldorf Astoria, who was a fan of hers, heard that she had been looking for a place to live and offered her a luxurious suite at

---

* 97 Columbus Heights. The hotel has since been demolished.

the Waldorf for the price she was paying in Brooklyn, but she said she would feel strange in such posh surroundings and stayed where she was.

Her first speaking engagement was at the Brooklyn Academy of Music and it took place a few days after her arrival in New York. It was a huge auditorium and she was very nervous. To protect herself, she wrote out her speech and read it in such a low, droning, sing-song that she sounded like a metronome and almost put her audience to sleep. "When Colston Leigh heard her," according to Carol Brandt, "he acted as if someone had just put a grand piano in his lap."[5] He had booked her all over the country and he didn't know what to do. He had no one of her stature with whom to replace her on such short notice. His staff was too much in awe of her to help, but she quickly agreed to work with a speech trainer. She improved after that, but it wasn't until she was properly motivated that her lectures became intelligible.

The American reporter, Leland Stowe, who was in Oslo on the day of the invasion, had released a story, picked up by wire services all over the world, that the Scandinavian countries had put up no resistance to Hitler and that the Norwegians had fallen on their knees to welcome the German invaders. That was all that was needed to light a fire under Sigrid. Concentrating on making it clear that not all Norwegians were "Quislings,"˙ that most of her countrymen were resisting the Nazis valiantly, and paying dearly for it, she annunciated more clearly and made herself understood, but she still had an uphill fight. His statements had turned many Americans against Scandinavia and it was only when Norway's resistance was revealed to the world by President Roosevelt, when he presented them with a U-Boat and said, "Look to Norway," that public opinion began to change.

Using "Scandinavians at War" as her topic, she tried to get audiences to understand how vulnerable all countries, including the United States, would be if Hitler wasn't defeated. The America First Committee, she pointed out, which was composed of people like Charles Lindberg and Henry Ford, (who both admired Hitler), was eager to keep the United States from going to Britain's defense, not because it was interested in the welfare of Americans, but because it wished to help the Nazis.

˙ Vidkun Quisling (1887-1945) was the leader of the Nazi party in Norway who paved the way for the occupation, and was in charge of the Norwegian government for the Germans during the occupied years. In May of 1945 he was arrested, tried for treason, and shot. His name is now synonymous to "traitor."

She didn't always talk of war. She chose her topics in relation to her audiences. She spoke about literature, medieval history, cooking, gardening or saints—but her purpose was always the same. She preferred university audiences to women's groups because she didn't have to attend teas and luncheons with them, but she did what was expected of her.

She made several trips to the coast and back, spoke in Boston, Baltimore, Washington, Los Angeles, San Francisco, St. Louis, Chicago, Detroit, Windsor (Canada), Tulsa, Dallas, North Carolina and Florida—but most of her lectures were in the Midwest where there was the greatest concentration of people of Scandinavian descent—and there she had problems. Most Scandinavian Americans, like the German Americans, were Lutheran—and they attended the same churches as the Germans. Sweden, though neutral, was cooperating with Hitler, and many of them wanted America to stay out of the war. They tried to discredit Sigrid in any way they could, and her conversion to Catholicism didn't help her.

Although many of her lectures were sponsored by Catholic institutions, some Catholics were not favorably disposed towards her either. After all, she was not born a Catholic—she was only a convert—and her descriptions of sex, especially a woman's pleasure in sex, were positively sinful. Nevertheless, she was a Nobel Prize winner, she had a large following of readers who adored her books, and her lectures were well attended.

Fending off constant attacks was not pleasant, and shuttling back and forth across the country, because her tour was not planned geographically, was tiring. She enjoyed the beauty of the country, but she traveled alone and she was painfully lonely. The Knopfs did what they could to make it easier for her. If she was in New York on a weekend, she spent the weekend at their home in Purchase. She was grateful for the sensitive way they looked after her, but their lifestyle was so different from hers that the efforts she was required to make only added to the strain she was under. Carol Brandt claimed that Sigrid expected to be waited on, but that she was always so appreciative that it was hard to refuse her, but Alfred Knopf denied that vehemently. She made fewer demands than any of his other authors, he said, except perhaps for Willa Cather (whom he seemed to have been especially fond of).

> *Sigrid never expected to be waited on and didn't impose her problems on others. Hans, on the other had, who came up on holidays and during the summer vacation, expected to be served and had to be prompted like a small child about the simplest courtesies.*[6]

Knopf was also Thomas Mann's publisher.

> *One of Mann's sons used to drop by the office and help himself to*
> *books, and when he was asked who had offered them to him, he said,*
> *"I don't think that is too much for you to do for Thomas Mann's son."*
> *Hans had a similar attitude about what was due him because of his*
> *mother's fame.*[7]

Many writers wanted to meet Sigrid, and the Knopfs invited them when she was going to be there. If the dinner conversation was stimulating, especially if they were discussing an author she liked, she could be fascinating and might take over to such a degree that no one else could get a word in, but if she took a dislike to a guest, or found the conversation boring, she would go to her room in the middle of a meal and stay there for the rest of the evening. The Knopfs were aware of how tired she was, and they forgave her, but it made it awkward for them with their other guests.[8]

Sigrid felt strongly about her convictions, and sometimes she created difficulties for her sponsors by her lack of tact. In Chicago, a woman of Norwegian descent called on her at the Hotel Stevens. Arriving at her door with an armful of *blaveis,*˙ she explained that she had always adored Sigrid's books and knew that these flowers were her favorites. Her husband was a wholesale florist, she continued, and since the American variety was paler than the Norwegian, he had sent a special plane to Canada to get some that were the exact color that Sigrid preferred. Sigrid was dumbfounded. People were fighting for their lives with little more than their bare hands and such extravagance was inconceivable. The news from home that day had been horrendous, and she was feeling guilty enough for being safe while all those were near and dear to her were suffering so tragically. Unable to handle the situation gracefully, she took the flowers in quivering hands, said "thank you," closed the door without inviting her in—and burst into tears.[9] Her visitor was understandably offended and the tour sponsors found it hard to placate her.

At a press conference that followed a lecture at the Sacred Heart Academy in Detroit, she called Father Charles E. Coughlin, who was haranguing his audiences on his radio broadcasts with anti-Semitic and anti-union statements, "a scoundrel." Many people agreed with her, but her saying so didn't please some of her Catholic sponsors.[10]

˙ Blue anemones.

*   *   *

She was delighted that Hans was at Harvard, but she missed him so much that she arranged to speak in Boston as often as possible. "I long wildly for Christmas to get you to New York and see you and speak to you," she wrote to him.[11] Determined to make the holiday as cheerful as possible, she decorated a small tree, built a crèche, hung greens all over the apartment, and prepared as many of his favorite dishes as she could manage in her small kitchen.

On their trip across Russia, a handsome Norwegian fur merchant (who was just about the age that Anders was when he died) had shared a train compartment with them. Later, in *Return to the Future*, Sigrid described how he was almost arrested for breaking a train window in order to get some fresh air. They became good friends on that trip, and when he arrived in New York, they saw each other several times. She invited him to attend a film preview with her, and he took her to dinner. Campbell Norsgaard,* who was not identified in the book because he was involved in war work at that time, speaks of her with tremendous respect and affection. He told me the following story.

Sigrid had introduced him to an attractive Norwegian girl from California, who was staying with her in Brooklyn and acting as her secretary. Sigrid knew that he liked her and she invited him to join them for dinner while Hans was in town. At the last moment, Sigrid couldn't be there and she asked her secretary to look after the two young men. After she left, according to Mr. Norsgaard, "the young lady had a mysterious fainting spell." A strange smell emanated from her and he thought she had poisoned herself, but when he ran to call a doctor, Hans "got quite hysterical" in his insistence that it wasn't necessary. Not allowing him to come near, Hans cared for her himself, and after some time, when she was calmer and had gone to bed, Mr. Norsgaard left. The young woman returned to California shortly after and he never saw her again. He had always wondered, he added, what had been wrong with her and why Hans had behaved so strangely.

When I said that it sounded like she might have had a seizure, and if that was so, Hans would have known how to care for her because his sister had been prone to epileptic attacks, he was stunned. He said that explanation had never occurred to him and that he had never known Sigrid had a daughter.

---

* He became an outstanding nature photographer after the war. *The Most Intimate Life of the Monarch Butterfly*, (a movie distributed by the *National Geographic* magazine) is his, as well as many other beautiful nature films.

When I asked him how she had reacted to Anders' death during the weeks they had traveled to the United States together, he said that none of them had known at the time that she had just lost a son.[12]

After her lecture in Detroit, Sigrid went to Windsor to receive a Culture Award from Assumption College,* and while she was there she became ill. Although she had written to a friend that the weather in Chicago was "subtropical compared to Norway," the rest of the country had not been that warm, and she had been troubled with colds, sinus attacks, earaches, bladder infections and bronchitis during much of the tour. By the time she got to Windsor she had developed a kidney infection. The doctor ordered her to bed, and the last few lectures had to be cancelled.

In April, she participated in a conference of the World Citizen's Association at Lake Forest, Illinois, where she met Edvard Hambro and his family. He was the critic against whom she and Nini had testified, but the war had erased their differences and after the conference was over she visited them in Princeton on several occasions. She also forgave Nordahl Grieg for printing the unauthorized interview of her when she became a Catholic, and they too saw each other occasionally.[13]

Hans stayed at Harvard for two semesters, after which he enlisted in the Free Norwegian Army. Sigrid was proud of him for wanting to fight for his country, but he was all she had left, and one can imagine how she felt. Her manner became stiffer and her appearance more forbidding, but she didn't try to stop him. He went to Toronto for basic training at the end of the summer, and from there he was sent to Scotland to be trained as a firefighter. He was then assigned to a desk job at Kingston House, in London, where he remained until the war was over. Sigrid didn't see him again until four years later when they met in Norway.

Hans' cousins, half-sisters, and friends were very fond of him. He was a loving, family-oriented person who enjoyed dispensing largesse, but he expected to be treated like a man of importance. On separate occasions, members of his family told me that they believed he would have been happiest if he had been born a prince. He was interested in becoming an author and although Gunhild says "he had a brain like a tape recorder,"[14] his style had been described as convoluted and pompous.

In 1944, when Arne Skouen arrived in New York to head the Royal Norwegian Information Service, he had come from London, and he had known Hans there. Hans, he wrote in his book *Sigrid Undset Skriver Hjem*

---

* March, 1941.

(*Sigrid Undset Writes Home*), was regarded "as an eccentric gentleman who referred to his mother in the third person." When Skouen had mentioned that he was going to America, Hans had given him a letter to deliver to her and told him "it was probably the most important letter he would be delivering in the United States."[15] Hans "may have been the least military young man who ever lived through a war," Mr. Skouen wrote,

> *He was an original talent who couldn't function in a uniform, but that bothered him little because he wore a different kind of uniform. His hero was Anthony Eden, whom he copied to the smallest detail . . . He had an exceptional ear for language and had mastered Eden's English faultlessly, and his speech, like the way he spoke Norwegian, was embellished with officialese . . . which did not go well in that circle. But he wasn't comic because his style was so thoroughly worked out.*[16]

He liked to bet the horses and could be found at the racetrack often, he added.

Writing had always been Sigrid's way of life, her salvation and her crutch. Because she had spent so much time alone, and because socializing was difficult for her, she had learned to live much of her life through her writing, and she wrote constantly during the five years that she spent in the United States. Apart from the books which were published, she wrote stories, articles, and book reviews in English and Norwegian for periodicals published in the United States, Canada and England. She wrote for *The Atlantic Monthly*, *Mademoiselle*, *Life Magazine*, *The New York Times*, *The London Times Literary Supplement*, *The Herald Tribune*, *The Saturday Review of Literature*, *America*, *The Dalhousie Review of Halifax*, *The American-Scandinavian Review*, *The St. Ansgar's Bulletin*, Norwegian papers in Grand Forks, Minneapolis and Milwaukee, *The Thomist*, *The Free World*, *The Quarterly Bulletin of the Polish Institute of Arts and Sciences in America*, *The Audubon Magazine*, *The Catholic Digest*—and *The Norseman*, *Common Ground*, *The Sign*, and *The Tablet* of London—and she was included in a number of collections and anthologies. Her story, *Thou Shalt Not Steal* was in *The Ten Commandments—Hitler's War Against the Moral Code** which was translated into many languages, and a story called *Little Pernille* was included in *Youth Replies: I Can—Stories of the Resistance*.**

---

*   Simon and Schuster, 1943.
** May Lamberston Becker, 1945

But no matter how hard she worked, she felt guilty for being safe. She knew that she would probably have been imprisoned or killed if she had remained in Norway, but that didn't help. The only way she could justify not suffering was to do all she could to help win the war.

Her articles were about Norwegian and American herbs, flowers, birds, Democracy and the Nordic People, Norwegian cooking (with recipes), animal stories, children's literature, War and Literature, Books that Last Forever, the Germans and Science, medieval and Norwegian history, and Catholicism. She lived on what she earned from her lectures and articles, but she did many jobs for which she wasn't paid. She appeared regularly on the Royal Norwegian Information Service radio programs on WNYC, and did many broadcasts for the BBC and the Office of War Information—and she threw herself into each assignment like a soldier. When she finished a broadcast, she liked to imitate the professional broadcasters by asking, "How did I do?" and when she was off the air, she would toss her speech into the wastepaper basket with a flourish. She spoke of "deadlines," and said things like, "I've been working like a beaver," or "So much water has run under the bridge," or "I am working so that the chips fly from my fingernails."[17]

She spoke at fund raising events at Madison Square Garden, Carnegie Hall, the Brooklyn Academy of Music and similar arenas in other parts of the country—many times. She sat through more dinners and luncheons in hotel banquet rooms than she could bear, and she spoke at all of them.

Frightening stories of internments and concentration camps were reaching her. When Hans was at Harvard and she could speak to him when she wanted to, she managed to keep going, but after he left, her sense of isolation overwhelmed her. She was close to sixty, not very well, and alone in a strange country. She had already seen more of the United States than most Americans do in a lifetime, and she was in no mood to wander around museums. When she felt that she could no longer bear her empty apartment, she got out and walked. Wrapped in a long, dark cape, with a silly old hat on her head, she wandered around Brooklyn. The Botanical Gardens, Fort Hamilton, Prospect Park and the benches at the waterfront became her haunts. When she couldn't sleep, she would walk across the Brooklyn Bridge. Often she was the only one there and friends warned her that it was dangerous, but she said she wasn't afraid. When the United States entered the war, the bridge was closed to pedestrians and those walks were over, but by then she was haunting other parts of Brooklyn.

"I love Coney Island when there are next to no people there, as it is in the wintertime—the deserted amusement parks, the boardwalk and the ocean coming right in to the funny little world of playthings," she wrote a friend.[18]

When homesickness overcame her, she wrote long letters, never knowing if they would be received. She wrote to Ragnhild in Sweden, and relied on her to relay the news to the family in Norway. The mail to Sweden was also censored and she had to be careful. Since she didn't know what could create difficulties for her family, she typed her letters on business stationery some of the time, and wrote in longhand at other times. Sometimes she signed Berit or other fictitious names, and sometimes she didn't sign them at all—she switched back and forth from Norwegian to English. Although letters took weeks to be delivered, she always mailed them at the Hotel St. George because she was told that hotel mail was picked up more often. After the war, there were 87 letters from her in Stockholm and no one knows how many never arrived.[19] One batch, which was on a plane that was downed in Lisbon, arrived completely water-stained, long after the war was over.

She was lonely, but she believed that she had no right to feel sorry for herself. When she felt defeated, she forced herself to do something constructive. She would read to the sailors at the Scandinavian Club, or attend a meeting of the St. Ansgar's League. Sometimes, longing for company, she invited a few sailors to her apartment for a Norwegian meal.

One sixteen-year-old boy, who had gotten into trouble, stayed with her for a few days while she helped him out of a mess. She mothered him, took him to the movies, put his clothes in order and got him transferred to another boat. When she wrote to Ragnhild about it, she was proud that he had not known who she was. For him, she was just a kind, elderly lady. When he left, she wrote a story about a wounded Norwegian boy who vowed that he would write a beautiful poem about his country if he survived the war. The story ends with: *"Whether you survive or not, my boy, you have already written your poem."*

She didn't enjoy the company of some of the refugees. They felt too sorry for themselves. They were always bemoaning their fates, and there was too much backbiting—and she avoided Thomas Mann in particular.

When I asked Alfred Knopf if he knew why she had taken such a dislike to Mann, he tactfully said that he had never known that she hadn't liked him and then he told me the following story:

There was a fund raising dinner at which Mann was to be the guest of honor. Many distinguished people in government and the arts had endorsed it and contributed large amounts of money. After the event, Knopf discovered that Mann had arranged (before he agreed to appear) to receive a substantial percentage of the money that was raised for his personal use. Those who had made contributions were not told that they were contributing to his private funds, and Knopf was shocked. He insisted that Mann refund the money, but Mann said it had already been spent, and Knopf and several others reimbursed the committee for the money that he had taken. To avoid a scandal, the story was never publicized, but if Sigrid heard even a rumor about it, it would have been enough to make her stay far, far away from Thomas Mann.

When Alfred Knopf finished telling the story, he thought for a while and then said, "It would never occur to one to do for Sigrid what we ended up doing for Mann."

"Why is that?" I asked.

> *She would never allow anyone to do anything for her. She would never ask for anything from anyone—for herself. We did a great deal for Mann, even when we were very small and had no money. He sort of expected it. She wasn't the kind of person to whom you could even suggest such a thing . . . She wasn't as outgoing either. Mann was a lot easier to get along with. In a short time he was Tommy, and it was Tommy to the end. We were also close to Willa Cather. She was Miss Cather to her death, yet we were as close to her as we could be . . . She was close to Edith Lewis for years, yet they called each other Miss Cather and Miss Lewis. She was very, very formal . . . Sigrid Undset was ideal from a publisher's point of view.[20]*

Sigrid found it hard to sit through those fund raising dinners at elegant hotels where celebrities "were seated on high seats and everyone was given fruit salad, chicken* and ice cream," and the speeches went on forever. Why was this necessary in order to get people to donate money? If they understood the importance of being there, why couldn't their donations go to the cause and not for their food and entertainment? There was something obscene about having to serve people an expensive dinner in an elegant hotel in order to move them to donate money for those who were starving.

She was also uncomfortable with the yearly dinners given by the American-Scandinavian Foundation as a memorial to Alfred Nobel where

---

*   She was so sick of "chicken, chicken, chicken," she told Campbell Norsgaard, that she was afraid feathers would soon be growing out of her back.

she and other Nobel Prize winners were expected "to be on display." She met Pearl Buck there, and although they had a number of interests in common, (both had cared for sick daughters, for one thing), Sigrid does not seem to have warmed up to her in person.

It is almost impossible to track down all of the articles she wrote and the events she participated in. She spoke at a number of P.E.N. meetings, appeared at a mass meeting for the Emergency Committee to save the Jews of Europe, spoke at a meeting of The Gallery of Living Catholic Authors, for the Polish Institute of Arts and Sciences, for Free Norway, and at the 17th of May celebrations of her countrymen. On February 6, 1941, she lectured at Mount Holyoke College about Emily Dickenson.

Free Norway was organized at the end of 1941 so that Norwegian refugees could act jointly. She was its first president and remained an honorary officer. She had been a member of the Norwegian Federation in Norway. When it was Nazified, and its leadership began to urge Norwegians abroad to come home and help create "a great German State," she helped to move its quarters to the United States where it remained until the war was over.

Slowly, she began to find friends to her liking. One day, at a meeting at St. Ansgar's League, she met Dorothy Day again. They hadn't seen each other since they had shared a platform at the student's meeting the night before the invasion of Norway. Dorothy Day was the editor, publisher, vendor and general factotum of *The Catholic Worker* which sold for a penny a copy, had no board of directors, no foundation backing, took no advertising, and paid no salaries. Started in 1933, its stated goal was to realize "the expressed and implied teachings of Christ . . ."

> *God has once and for all assumed our humanity, and we cannot hope to know Him without also turning to our neighbors in love. Such love is not merely a passing glow, but something concrete and active. It means extending the fellowship, sharing bread with the hungry, clothing the naked, standing beside those who were outcast and persecuted.*[21]

Often compared to Catherine of Siena, whom she admired, Dorothy Day was a radical within the Catholic Church, and although she was a pacifist and believed in militant non-violence, and Sigrid felt that violence was necessary in order to defeat Hitler, they became good friends. Dedicated to alleviating the burdens of the poor and the oppressed, Dorothy Day set up over thirty Houses of Hospitality for hungry and homeless people. In a letter to Ragnhild, Sigrid wrote:

> *She is not in the least bit beautiful, but in her simple, nearly poor little party dress she was one of the most beautiful people that I have ever seen. Heroine and Saint, that is what one feels when one is close to her. She is worth the whole trip to America just to have met her again.*[22]

Sigrid visited her farm and they saw each other when they were able to find the time.

Another new friend with whom she had a great deal in common was Hope Emily Allen. On April 14, 1941, Sigrid wrote to her sister that she had met "a wonderful, strange and terribly sweet old lady," (actually, she was a year younger than Sigrid), who had a master's degree in Medieval Literature, having researched English mystics. It was she who had helped identify the memoirs of Margery Kempe about whom Sigrid had written *Margery Kempe of Lynn*, which had appeared in *The Atlantic Monthly* in 1939.[*]

Hope brought five cartons of notes about English mystics, and photostats of manuscripts from the British Museum, when Sigrid accompanied her on a vacation. "She is an authority in her field," Sigrid wrote to Ragnhild, "yet few in the U.S. except at universities know of her work. She has been to Sweden and many parts of Europe."[23] Sigrid was sure that she would have little rest with her because, like her school chum Emma Munster, Hope loved to look for birds and growing things and could run up and down the woods and ravines like a rabbit. "She always tempts me to go where there are no paths and we wade through brooks and through underbrush and get all scratched up." They spent several weekends together that winter, and they took a cottage at Lake Twitchell for a few weeks the following summer.

"We had a wonderful evening in my apartment while I sat in my armchair and Hope crept around on the floor among the bookcases and dragged hundreds of books out," she wrote to Hans.[24] Although every windowsill of Sigrid's little apartment was already filled with flowering plants, Hope sent her boxes of sweet-smelling blooms regularly.

Sigrid always tried to maintain an independent point of view. She could overstate her opinions but she tried to be fair. Although she hated the Germans, she led a campaign to get the Nobel Peace Prize for Carl von

---

[*]   Included in *Men, Women and Places*, Alfred A. Knopf, 1939.

Ossietsky, (a well-known pacifist and journalist), who was German, and she wanted Arnulf Overland to get the prize for literature, although his politics were too far to the left for her tastes, but in *Return to the Future*, the book she wrote a year after she came to the United States, she was in no condition to be fair. Her description of the invasion of Norway and her escape to Sweden was brilliantly written and did much to gain respect for the Norwegian people, but some of her reactions to her trip across Russia and Japan were so lacking in objectivity as to negate any point she was trying to make.

One can understand the emotional state she was in when she left Sweden immediately after being told that her son had been killed; one can share her fury at the Soviet Union for bombing Finland and becoming Hitler's ally, but some of her comments were ridiculous. When she and Hans arrived in Moscow, the Russians were trying to carry out their side of the bargain Stalin had made with Hitler. People were on the streets night and day because they were on work shifts around the clock. They were wearing flimsy clothing because there was a terrible heat wave. They looked grim because they were under pressure to fulfill quotas and many could not stomach the Pact. Sigrid had been to other major cities in Europe but all she could remember at that moment was her beautiful country which she had been forced to leave. The population of Oslo was less than 450,000. The little square at Karl Johan's Gate is, even today, the center of activity for the entire city, and one can still do little more there than get a drink, go to one of the few movie houses, see an occasional play or watch endless parades. The four million Russians who were crowded into a sweltering Moscow where only two million had lived before the war must have presented a frightening specter.

New York City, on a hot summer day, with or without a doubled population, might have had the same effect. But to deduce from that, that "Russia can afford to let children perish,"[25] or that all Russians looked alike, or that it was incredible that the drinking water had to be boiled, (what did she drink when she was in Paris?), or that she didn't like the way they cared for their cattle, (which she only saw from the train window), and to dismiss all Russian art in a piece, (when no theaters were open while she was there, and she visited no museums), was certainly not being objective. Hans went to a theater performance in Valdivostok, she wrote, and told her that the leading lady was old and cross-eyed. In *Jenny*, she had written that Norwegian folk art was "a wooden porringer with painted roses and some carving," which experts were calling "original and nationally Norwegian,"[26] but she criticized the folk art in Russia, without making it clear that it was folk art in general, and not the Russian kind in particular, that she didn't like.

She was distressed that the trains were filthy, there was no water to wash with, and the toilets didn't work—and one can understand her discomfort. (A 1984 article in *Amtrak Magazine*, described a Trans-Siberian trip that didn't sound much improved.)

She was relieved to be in a clean environment when they boarded the Japanese boat that took them from Valdivostok to Kobe,* and it was encouraging that she doesn't seem to have succumbed to her unfortunate fear of "Orientals"—but her prejudices were expressed in many other ways. After conceding that "there is hardly any non-European people which does not have the right to accuse the white race of aggression and exploitation,"[27] she worries that such oppressed countries might not know how to handle the freedom that Western countries were teaching them to fight for.

"When entire populations have the right to take part in deliberations about ways and means for their future development," men and women "whose most eminent gift is the ability to elbow their way forward, or trample their fellow citizens underfoot," might be allowed to do so unhampered.[28]

If she were referring to Nazis, then they were certainly a "European people," and not of a non-white race, and no people could "trample their fellow citizens underfoot" with more viciousness than they were doing.

She was certainly under extreme stress and her statements were more hysterical than logical. Surely she still abided by her Christian belief that the poor shall inherit the earth. Could she have decided that they shall inherit only what the few felt they were worthy of?

The book appeared in February 1942,** shortly after Pearl Harbor and after the Germans had attacked Russia. By then the Russians were our allies and the Japanese our foes, but *The New York Times* gave it a favorable front-page review in the Sunday Book Review section. The only thing it criticized was the section about Russia. Other critics were not so kind and when the book was published abroad, the Russian section was dropped completely.

Sigrid, like other successful artists, had been subjected to petty jealousies and backbiting from her peers, (her compatriots still snipe at her and Ibsen, just as Hans Christian Andersen is still maligned in Denmark) but they had more than her success to fuel their animosity. She had an abnormal child, a difficult husband and his children, and unpopular religion, and a defiant nature, and she was often forced to defend adversary postures that she might

---

* Mr. Norsgaard gave me a charming photograph of her in a kimono which he took when they were on their way to Japan.

** Published by Alfred A. Knopf.

not have taken if she had been in a more cosmopolitan environment. She often overstated a point or contradicted herself in ways that deserved the criticism of her contemporaries, but the moralistic tone used against her pushed her into positions that were more extreme than she might have taken in a more relaxed atmosphere.

She mellowed each time she went abroad and her years in the United States exposed her to so many people of different backgrounds and persuasions that she was able to ventilate some of her thinking and lose some of her prejudices as her stay continued.

CHAPTER XVII

THE OCCUPATION
1940-1945

By 1942, more news was trickling through about conditions in Norway. An airman from home visited Sigrid on his way to Free Norway training camp in Toronto and brought a message to be relayed to America—*not* to send food to Norway, (which was being done through the Hoover Plan), because the Germans were bringing their women and children there by the thousands and eating it all. They ate like locusts, and if they had more food they would bring in more people to feed and put more Norwegians out of their homes.[1] It was an especially unbearable situation because children were so undernourished that they were suffering from bleeding kidneys and dentists were afraid to pull infected teeth because the bleeding could be fatal.[2]

BBC asked her to appeal to Sweden on a program called *Unity of the Northern Countries* which she did, although privately she said that she couldn't imagine how that could ever be achieved again since Finland had become an ally of Germany, and "the Swedes were sitting on their glorious memories of the great days of old (as they have it in their national anthem)," while allowing trains to cross their country full of Norwegian laborers being taken to slavery in Germany, and labor leaders being taken to concentration camps. She knew, she said, that "plenty of the Swedes must feel their bottoms chilled sitting like that."[3]

She had a miserable Christmas. She caught a cold. Her teeth ached. There was no one for whom to cook special treats, and she spent the day alone, but a few days later she was informed that she was to be awarded an Honorary Doctor of Humane Letters Degree from Rollins College in Winter Park, Florida, and she cheered up considerably. The College had conferred degrees on President Roosevelt, Secretary of State Hull, Thomas A. Edison, Jane Addams, Maurice Maeterlinck and Anne O'Hare McCormick before her, and she felt honored to be in such illustrious company. John Marquand also received an honorary degree that day,* and both Hudson Strode, (who taught at the University of Alabama and was a longtime friend of Sigrid's) and Marjorie Kinnan Rawlings attended the ceremony. Sigrid gave one of the *Animated Magazine* lectures, and after it was over, both Strode and Rawlings invited her for extended visits. It was arranged that she would go to Rawlings first and to the Strodes after that.

"Do you know, one thing that makes us Europeans marvel is that America is so wonderfully rich in natural beauty," Sigrid wrote to Marjorie Rawlings,** when she accepted her invitation. Americans do "a lot of bragging (if you will forgive me for saying so) about the mechanicahal [sic—her spelling] and technical achievements of man on his continent, but they tell singularly little about the marvels of God's creation in the Western Hemisphere." She had never known what flowering dogwood, nor hemlock pines were like, and it was worth coming two-thirds of the way around the globe to have seen them.[4]

Marjorie Rawlings, who lived in an old farm house in Cross Creek, Florida, had recently married Norton Baskin who owned the Castle Warden Hotel in St. Augustine, and they were dividing their time between Cross Creek and an apartment they maintained at the hotel.

"The country is completely flat," Sigrid wrote to Ragnhild,

> . . . and the soil is white like ocean sand. What there is of stone is something they call coquela [sic] which is shells and sea particles that have been packed together into a mass. The whole seems to have been thrown up by the ocean. There are pines, bogs, peat and quiet rivers where the landscape becomes completely tropical with palms and stone oaks and all the trees are veiled with Spanish moss—a gracious grey moss with garlands around each twig and branch and vines that grow. All along the riverbanks white herons, fish and fat alligators lie sunning themselves. Marjorie, whom I had never met before, picked me up at the college and took me out to her orange plantation for which she worked nine years before it paid for itself, and now she has success as a writer and she is on top again. But the plantation is still her heart

---

* February 23, 1942.
** All of Sigrid's letters to American friends were written in English.

child. It is quite enticing. A couple of cottages and an old farmhouse in the middle of a clump of 1800 orange, grapefruit and mandarin trees. I can't describe what the fruit tastes like when it hangs on the trees until it is fully ripe, and a brown girl goes out every morning and picks what is needed for the day. One feels one has not tasted oranges before.

I don't know if you read the Yearling—it was published in Scandinavia last year. She took me out to the place where it was going to be filmed, but now they will film it in created surroundings in California. The family that looks after it has a dog breeding farm much like our hunting dogs with the same deep musical voices when they warn of approaching strangers.

They had lunch with us and warmed coffee over an open fire of dry leaves out in the woods, which plays an important part in the book. There is a lot of wildlife in the woods and masses of birds are over the lakes, but most of the people who live here are poor. There is a great difference between the tourists who go to the cities along the coast and those who scrape some kind of subsistence out of the soil.[5]

Marjorie Rawlings had a housekeeper called Idella Parker* who was a wonderful cook, and Sigrid got many Southern recipes from her. She was probably the first black person Sigrid ever befriended and it could only have been an enlightening experience for her. Idella made a deep impression on her and Sigrid never failed to send regards to her when she wrote to Marjorie.

When I approached Norton Baskin for recollections of Sigrid, he wrote, "Of all people I met through Marjorie, Madame Undset was the most fascinating in every way, and I am happy to do anything to help present her to the world as the wonderful woman she was."[6]

A number of Southern writers were Undset fans and wanted to meet her and although Marjorie tried to protect her privacy as much as possible, there were a few that Sigrid was especially eager to meet. Edith Pope and her husband Senator Verle Pope, (of Florida), came one afternoon. Mrs. Pope was so concerned about what she should wear and checked on what her husband was going to wear so carefully before starting out, that the Senator asked, "who is this that we are going to meet that is so important to you?"

---

*   In *Cross Creek* she is called Martha Mickens.

"The Senator was a great sports enthusiast but not well informed about literature," Mr. Baskin explained, "so when his wife told him it was Sigrid Undset, he asked, 'Who in the world is that?' Mrs. Pope thought for a while and then replied, 'In my league, darling, she is Babe Ruth.'"[7]

Sigrid also met the historian Hamilton Basso, and pleased him when she told him that her son Anders had been a Civil War buff, had adored Robert E. Lee, and had read two of Basso's books.[8]

After a few days at Cross Creek, they went to Mr. Baskin's hotel in St. Augustine. They arrived late and by the time they came down for dinner it was almost eight o'clock. Mr. Baskin served some drinks and he was so upset by the astounding reports of Nazi atrocities that Sigrid was relating to them, that he failed to notice how late it was getting. His restaurant was famous partly because of its chef, and the chef was a very independent man. He had a strict rule that he would not serve after eight o'clock, and when Mr. Baskin noticed the time, he rushed to the kitchen. The chef had been standing behind a door that was slightly ajar, listening to Sigrid, and when he saw Mr. Baskin approaching, he waved him off saying, "Please don't hurry her. The later the better. She is very interesting."[9]

Sigrid enjoyed the visit with the Baskins tremendously and after she left, Marjorie, like Dea and Nini before her, became Sigrid's confidante.

Before going to the Strodes', Sigrid went to Charleston to visit an old friend who was ill. "Meeting Don Sturzo was rather sad," she wrote to Marjorie.

> *I had not seen him since 1938 in London. I used to think when Mussolini wanted his head so much, it was only partly because it contained one of the finest brains that ever opposed him, but partly too, because this Sicilian looked just what Mussolini would have given anything to look like—an old Roman from some coin or bust. Now he looked very old and frail, sitting propped up with pillows in an easy chair in his hospital room—and his fiery brown eyes had become mild and soft with an expression of seeing something faraway all the time. But I am more glad than I can say, that I saw him—maybe I'll never see him again. And he seemed glad that I came.*[10]

From there she continued to Tuscaloosa, Alabama, where Hudson and Therese Strode lived. Hudson Strode had met Sigrid in Finland in 1939 and they had been corresponding ever since. He had recently written a book called *Finland Forever* which she had reviewed for *The Herald Tribune*.

The Strodes lived in a comfortable home with a beautiful garden, and Sigrid enjoyed the visit very much. Marjorie had given her a plant with little blue star flowers which she carried to Tuscaloosa from Cross Creek, and when she left she had additional plants to carry home from there. (Later, she took a gardenia plant, which Willa Cather gave her, to Hope Allen's when she visited her, because she couldn't leave it home and was very proud that it was blooming for the second year.) When she added her new plants to the oranges, mangoes and marmalades that began to arrive from Florida and the flowers that Hope was sending, her apartment smelled even sweeter.

She wrote two stories about that trip—*Beautiful America* and *Florida Waters*. * She never warmed up to California, which she found artificial and uninteresting, but she loved what she had seen of Florida and the South.

In April, Sigrid was asked to give a series of radio talks called *The Spirit of the Vikings*. She objected to the subject, but did it to please the radio station. It was surprising, she wrote to Marjorie, how much "that mouldy Viking romanticism" was still alive amongst Americans of Norwegian descent. The thing to be proud of, she said, was how quickly the Norwegians in the early Middle Ages outgrew that sort of thing. There were other developments, even then, about which one could be much prouder.[11]

Sigrid had always loved Finland and the Finns. In 1941, she wrote to Strode that to Nordic people, Finland had always been "the eastwall of Europe against Asia and Barbarism, and, as we still hope for a day when the barbarians of Germany may be conquered and a civilized Scandinavia resurrected, anything that can be done to strengthen Finland is of the utmost importance to all of us."[12]

When she reviewed Strode's book on Finland, Finland was occupied by the Russians and she had nothing but compassion for the Finnish people, but after the Germans invaded Russia and many of her friends in Finland began to defend Nazism, she was disgusted with them and felt sorry for her three foster children. She said that she knew that they were "between the devil and the deep blue sea."

"I guess in a fight with wolves, you side with the one who attacks the one you were bitten by,"[13] but she didn't like what was going on there. She also criticized those of her Swedish friends who had become Nazi sympathizers—calling them "the face lifters," (a quote from a newspaper

---

* Written for American periodicals, they were also published in *Artikler og Taler fra Krigstiden*, by Aschehoug in 1952.

story about a group of Swedish journalists who came to the U.S. to do a propaganda job for Hitler).[14]

In March, she wrote that the Nazis were encouraging the territorial claims of one Scandinavian country against another in order to create enmity between them.[15]

News of what was happening in Norway was reaching her now in greater detail and it was grim.

On May 27, 1942, she wrote to Strode that Gestapo officers were living in her house in Lillehammer.

> *Two of the men who manage the camp at Jørstadmoen (where the teachers were interned and tortured before they were sent on their death voyage to the North) are staying there with their females and young ones. I don't care a dam [sic] if I shall never get more than the grounds back again—indeed, I feel as if I should ever be scenting the stink of Deutschtum seeping from walls and floors, if I were ever to return to the house. But when I think of the Swastika flying from my flagpole, and the offal of humanity living in the rooms where my little girl died, and my children and I and our friends lived, I see red and feel as if the thirst for revenge must choke me. And just now things do not look good—and every month the German occupation of the European countries is prolonged means untold miseries for millions of people, and the craving for revenge mounts in all of us.*

The Rector of the University of Oslo was sent to do slave labor in Poland and Russia.[16] Then, the dreadful news reports began to include her family. Sigrid's twenty-four year old niece, Charlotte, who was an assistant at the Historical Museum and her fiancé, Martin Blindheim, who was a professor there, were arrested with the rest of the Museum staff. She was released after seven weeks, but Martin was sent to a concentration camp in Norway and then transferred to one in Germany. Charlotte's father, Sigge Thomas, also a professor, and Eilif and Ole Henrik Moe were in camps as well. Ole's older brother, Tycho, who had managed to escape, got to Canada, trained as a flier, and visited Sigrid before returning to flight in Europe. He was killed over Normandie in 1943. Sigrid wrote a beautiful story about him called *Hjemme pa Vaerskjei*, (Home to Stay).*

She was half-crazy with worry, and when the bombings started in London, she had that to keep her up nights.

---

* In *Artikler og Taler fra Krigstiden* published by H. Aschehoug, 1952.

Then, she got word that Sigge was released from the concentration camp, rearrested, freed again because of his health—and that he had died a few weeks later. She could bolster her spirits no longer. She couldn't imagine how Signe could bear it. In addition to everything else, her sister's financial situation had become life threatening. Sigrid rushed around consulting banks and embassy people until she managed, through friends in Sweden who had money in Norwegian banks, to send money to her family, which she in turn deposited through American banks. She didn't have much for her own needs, but every sacrifice she could make helped relieve her of some of her guilt for being safe. When Signe's youngest daughter, also called Signe, married a musician and composer who was of Jewish ancestry, she worried that someone might point him out to the Gestapo. When they had their first baby, she managed to get money to Ragnhild who was able to get a layette delivered to them from Sweden.

Her hatred of Nazis had become so violent that she was finding it hard to breathe and when she read that the British had bombed a Christmas celebration near Bergen, where the Germans were awarding medals to Norwegians for their cooperation during the invasion, and thirty-five women of the Quisling party had been killed, she rejoiced and wrote:

> . . . *nobody except perhaps their relatives were sorry about them . . .*
> *A Quisling was lynched at a meeting near Drammen . . . We have a*
> *Norwegian saying: "As you call out in the woods, you will be answered,"*
> *but it is rather awful to think, that our peaceful woods have been taught*
> *to echo in German to that extent.*[17]

The summer was a hot one in 1942, and when the Knopfs heard that Sigrid sat in a bathtub all day to soothe her prickly heat, they tried to persuade her to go to the Berkshires. They were music lovers and attended the Tanglewood concerts regularly, and they thought the area would interest her. She was not particularly interested in music, but she was longing to get out of the city, and when a Finnish friend suggested the Brookbend Inn, in Monterey, Massachusetts, she tried it.

It was a quaint old structure that was used as an art school during the winter, with a large, low-ceilinged living room that had a fireplace at each end. The building had been enlarged in stages with no two rooms at the same level, and Sigrid found it charming. The guests were unostentatious, the meals were wholesome, she could work in peace, walk in the woods, and see the Knopfs when they came up for the concerts, and she became very attached to the place.

When she had first come to the United States, she had deplored American complacency about the war, and when the Lend Lease Bill was being discussed in Congress, she quoted Roosevelt as saying, "I don't take money when I lend my neighbor my garden hose if his house is on fire,"[18] but after Pearl Harbor, she was pleased that the Americans were "red hot mad." They had accused the small countries of capitulating too easily, but now that they too had been taken by surprise, they understood how that could happen.

She had tremendous respect and admiration for President and Eleanor Roosevelt, and when Mrs. Roosevelt asked to see her and suggested, as she had other refugee writers, that she write about the children of her country, Sigrid was delighted to oblige. It was a brilliant suggestion because it gave the homesick refugees an opportunity to write about home and presented the American people with a better understanding of what their lives had been like before the war. Sigrid wrote *Happy Times in Norway*, the first of her three children's books published in America. It appeared in 1942* and was about the happy times in Lillehammer when her children were growing up and Anders and Mosse were still alive. *Sigurd and his Brave Companions* followed in 1943, and her version of the Norwegian folk tales that Jørgen Moe and Peter Asbjørnsen had collected, appeared in 1945. She also wrote a long introduction to a collection of stories by the Danish writer Steen Steensen Blicher which was published by Princeton University Press for the American-Scandinavian Foundation in 1945.

Many who knew Sigrid personally have mentioned her wit. Lillian Bragdon, who was the editor of her children's books at Knopf, told me that those in the office who didn't know Sigrid were in awe of her, but she lunched with her often, and found her easy to be with and very funny. They usually ate at a French restaurant where Sigrid would relax, have a drink or two, smoke cigarettes and tell wonderful anecdotes. One afternoon she came back to the office still smiling over something Sigrid had said. "That Sigrid has such a delightful sense of humor," she told a colleague. Several in the room were so unbelieving that they asked in union, "Are you speaking of Sigrid Undset?"

"She put you off, if you didn't know her," Mrs. Bragdon explained. "You had to know her to appreciate how gentle and approachable she really was."

---

*   Published by Knopf.

*   *   *

On May 23, 1943, Sigrid received an honorary Doctor of Literature degree from Smith College.

In June, Marjorie Rawlings wrote that her husband had volunteered for the American Field Service as an ambulance driver in India, and Sigrid comforted her that he would come home safely. There were wonderful sulfa drugs and blood banks and people were able to survive the war even if they were badly wounded.

She thanked Marjorie for alerting her to a book by Dr. Brickner which she reviewed for the Saturday Literary Review. In it he had referred to the Germans as paranoid. She agreed with him, she wrote to Marjorie, and added that she found that there was also a strain of "infantilism in the average German which expresses itself in an exceedingly nasty interest for what you Americans so nicely call 'bowel movements.'" It was conspicuous in their jests all the way back to the early Middle Ages, and they were producing some samples of this taste in Norway that could almost be called comical as well as gruesome. They also did things like that "in Tolstoy's manor in Russia, according to Maurice Hindus," she continued.[*][19]

In October 1943, she got word that Svarstad had died of cancer. She didn't know that he had been ill, and she was deeply upset. It wasn't until February that she was able to write about him for *Nordisk Tidende*.[**] Early that year, Willert J. Klass, a student at Canisius College, Buffalo, N.Y. sent Sigrid a highly laudatory thesis about her work which he planned to submit for a Master of Arts degree in the Department of English. It was called *Sigrid Undset—the Evolution of a Traditionalist*, and he asked for her comments. She returned it with many handwritten marginal notes in which she objected to almost everything he had written, including the term "traditionalist," calling much of it "childish," and "nonsense"—and she strongly urged him not to publish it.

In a letter which accompanied the manuscript,[20] she wrote:

> *Now to begin with I would say, the worst possible device, when you want to write about a litterary [sic] subject, is to stuff your pages with quotations from litterary [sic] critics, especially when your "authorities"*

---

[*]   A German preoccupation with excrement seems to have been usual even in Mozart's time. His letters are full of references to it.

[**]   A Norwegian newspaper published in New York.

are chosen entirely without a vestige of discrimination. Gustafson[.] is the only one to be taken seriously; of course he possesses a good deal of knowledge, as far as you can aquire [sic] knowledge by diligent reading, but very scant understanding of litterature [sic] as an art, as you documented in that awful piece of bosh that you have quoted on page 66. It's not much good to know a lot about music, if you cannot hear if an orchestra is playing Yankee Doodle or a Funeral March of Chopin. And, like most Americans of Scandinavian descent, his ideas about Scandinavian matters seem to us modern Scandinavians to belong to the time of our grandparents. But then, you too seem to work with categories unearthed in God knows which old curiosity shop.

In response to some of his groupings of what he considered "Historical novels," she wrote:

> *One may lump a river, a tea-kettle and a waterspout because water flows through them . . .*
> *No amount of knowledge will of course make a writer able to write a single living sentence. Knowledge can never be more than a tool . . .*

His study had little of interest for this biography, but since Sigrid corrected many oft-repeated errors, it is important to list them so that they may finally be laid to rest. She wrote: "I never owned a bit of lace!" (Myth has it that she had collected antique laces from convents in Belgium and France.) "The name of Lillehammer has nothing to do with Hamar and I never had anything to do with the ruins of Hamar, some fifty English miles further south." "I once took part in a pageant dressed in a frock of my grandmother's. I suppose the myth of me wearing 'Viking dress' originated when some shrewd newspaperman presumed the Viking ladies were dressed all in lace caps, mittens and lilac Barège."

(The image of her wearing Norse dress as she did her daily chores around Lillehammer is so unlike her that it is hard to understand how that myth started and why it was repeated in so many encyclopedias and biographical notes both here and in England. One begins to question the reliability of such sources when they repeat each other's errors over and over again.)

[.]   Alrik Gustafson, author of *Six Scandinavian Novelists*, Princeton University Press, published by the American-Scandinavian Foundation in 1940

He had written that "even before her conversion to Catholicism she had concerned herself with the reasonings of the scholastics," and she wrote, "No, I had not."

He wrote that when she was informed that she was to receive the Nobel Prize she told interviewers, "I have no time to receive you. I am studying scholastic philosophy!" (He credits *Review of Reviews* of January 1929, page 42, with this statement, but it had appeared in a number of other places as well.) Sigrid wrote, "You can't believe I said that. I'm not a perfect idiot, after all!"

Other errors which should be corrected are:

She had three children, not four. Parts of her house dated from 1500, and not from the year 1000. Bjerkebaek is near but not at a lakeside, and she did not develop her interest in history by doing research for her father. She was eleven years old when he died!

Knopf had sent Sigrid a picture of Willa Cather, and he introduced them to each other after Sigrid came to the United States.

"Willa Cather is simply one of the most adorable people I have ever met," Sigrid wrote to her sister on December 18, 1941[21]—and in a letter to Carrie Miner Sherwood, Willa wrote that Sigrid was

> . . . *all a great woman should be—on a giant scale. She is a wonderful cook, a proficient scholar and has the literature of four languages at her finger ends. There is nothing about wild flowers and garden flowers that she doesn't know, and she is able to make plants thrive and bloom in her very humble and gloomy little hotel rooms. Besides all this, there is in the woman a kind of heroic calm and warmth that rises above all the cruel tragedies and loss of fortune that the last three years have brought. She simply surmounts everything that has been wrecked about her and stands large and calm; she who has lost everything seems still to possess everything, and the small pleasures can still make her rather cold eyes glow with marvelous pleasure. She combines in herself the nature of an artist, a peasant and a scholar. She is cut out on a larger pattern than any woman I have ever known and it rests me just to sit and look at the strength that stood unshaken through so much.*[22]

Willa Cather was ten years older than Sigrid. She lived in a spacious apartment on Park Avenue and 62nd Street with Edith Lewis whom she had met when they both worked at *McClure's Magazine*. When Sigrid knew them,

Edith was working as a copywriter at J. Walter Thompson and she had been living with Willa for thirty-five years. They had a wonderful cook and Sigrid dined with them often.

There was much that the two authors could admire about each other. Both had supported themselves since they were young girls and both had started out believing that a person could accomplish anything with willpower. Both wrote about independent women and went through crises in their lives which led them to religious conversions and religious subjects,* and both were masterful in their descriptions of nature.

Willa championed the right of the creative personality to express itself in an insensitive society and felt that government controls in the hands of "the masses" would make it hard for an article to be "free," and Sigrid supported President Roosevelt's New Deal but feared that industrialization would destroy the family which was the most civilizing institution available to mankind. And—unfortunately—both had prejudices. Willa was anti-Semitic, and patronizing in her depictions of foreign born Mexicans and blacks, and Sigrid worried that the "backward" Oriental and African cultures would take over the world and lower the level of Western culture. Both could be caustic when annoyed and witty when they wanted to be, and as they grew older, both had the same kind of massive body structures and ideas about how to dress—but there their similarities ended.

Cather's characters are highly romanticized. Their passions are restricted to "giving themselves altogether and finally" to their art. Her women are inaccessible, disappointed in men, and lacking in sexual drive; while Undset had such a profound understanding of the passions, dreams and fallibilities of human beings, that her characters, regardless of the time in which they lived, are timeless and universal. Both were strong, exceptional women and they respected each other tremendously.

In a letter to Marjory Rawlings, on February 24, 1944, Sigrid described a visit she had from Michael Tilley, a young man she had known in Norway. His father, she explained, had been a British marine interned in Norway during World War I, and had married a girl from Lillehammer. His wife and three children were received in the Church on the same day as she was. His father fought the Germans in the recent invasion and had managed to escape, and the family had no idea where he was or if he was still alive, but the Germans wouldn't give up searching for him. Their house was under surveillance for

---

* Born into a Baptist family, Willa converted to the Anglican Church at just about the time that Sigrid became a Catholic.

three years. They tried to drive his mother crazy. Some days, Michael told her, they entered and walked through the rooms every few hours, swept the photographs off the tables, tore down the pictures from the walls and trampled them, smashed their furniture, and soiled the bedclothes of all the beds, even the baby's cot. How could people become so evil?

Michael had been under arrest for two months and had managed to escape, but his brother, Sigrid's godchild, "had been beaten with rubber truncheons so that both his kidneys came loose and kicked so that several ribs had been broken. The body of a girl had been found in the park with her breasts cut off and a fireman had been killed by having boiling oil injected into the urether [sic]." Their parish priest had been tortured and sent to Oranienburg, where he died.

Michael said he hoped that:

> Norway would be freed by an invasion and not by withdrawal—all of us do, those at home and we too. Because, if we cannot get even with some of them, and kill a lot of them in Norway, so many people will go mad, thinking of the things they have done to them or to their sons and daughters with no retribution that they can be eyewitnesses to. Our doctors say so too—they tell us, people must have revenge, and they must see the revenge, or else their brains will crack.[23]

She couldn't fathom what it could be like to live day in and day out in such an atmosphere. Those in the underground developed a special kind of closeness, she was told, which sustained them. What happened to people who reduced to ciphers, whose major activity was to be as invisible as possible? How could they accept such deprivations and indignities in silence?

The Germans stripped the country of everything of value, but left the population just enough to survive on because they were needed for work. After they were reduced to total passivity, they could be deprived of still more because by then they were being controlled with torture.

When the poet-parson Kai Munk died, Sigrid wrote to the Strodes,

> He was taken from his home a couple of days ago by four men of the Gestapo. Next day his bullet-riddled [sic] body was found in the forest outside Silkeborg. I do not think the dramas of Kai Munk would have made him immortal—now the Gestapo has seen it.[24]

The atrocities haunted her. She wrote to Marjorie that she was glad that if Anders had to die, at least he died fighting. The thought of the thousands who were being subjected to torture and humiliation, stripped and unarmed, was unbearable. How could a parent bear it? She had seen a newsreel of fighting at Monte Cassino, Italy, that afternoon and she remembered being there with Anders when he was twelve. He had had a glorious time playing football with the boys from the monastery school in the beautiful cortile between the church and the museum buildings. Nothing seemed to be left of the monastery except some walls—and there was not a trace of the church. It was heartrending to think of so many lives laid waste.

> . . . *farms built on terraces with soil carried upon the backs of men and mules, century-old olive trees, vines tended carefully through generations, fields in the valley made to render four or five crops a year. The sufferings of the people in the occupied countries, from bombing by their friends and looting and shooting by their tyrants is something appalling. And yet—the people who have come out from Norway lately say, they hope for an invasion—they must see the Germans be killed and taken prisoners or else the memories of these four years will drive many of those who have suffered the worst wrongs crazy . . . Heine speaks in one of his poems of the man with the bloody axe who dogged his steps through the nightly streets of Cologne and told him. 'Ich bin—die That (tat) von deinem Gedanken.' He (the deed) will follow each individual German for generations, I fear.*[25]

As the war progressed, she began to worry about the Quislings who were already trying to get out of future punishment by turning witness against their friends before it was too late. Once, "a lady called with an introduction from one of the Norwegian big shots," she wrote to Marjorie,[26]

> *Of all things, she wanted me to get into some sort of women's council that was to prepare the world peace after the war—that is, European women refugees who should make ready to advise their sisters who have been through Hell and German occupation. I am afraid I was terribly rude to her, when we return to our countries after this war we will just have to be very, very modest and abstain from all attempts to "lead" the people at home anywhere.*

---

* I am the deed in your memories. Heine's *Germany*.

Eleanor Roosevelt asked her to accept a secret assignment, which she executed with great devotion. The American Commission for the Protection and Salvage of Artistic and Historical Documents in War Areas had begun to prepare lists of national treasures, which would have to be protected when the allied forces freed a country, and Sigrid and Arne Skouen were asked to compile a list with exact locations of buildings, libraries, art collections and scientific centers which had to be saved in Norway. It had to be kept secret because if it got into the wrong hands, it could give the Germans a blueprint of what to bomb.

During a scorching summer, Sigrid sweltered daily on the subways and at the 42nd Street library in order to refresh her memory with history, travel books and maps and when those sources were exhausted she worked, during an equally hot spell, in Washington with various archives. The finished report was 28 mimeographed pages.

When the news was good for a few days, she would make plans for going home—she would clean her house, wash her curtains and prune her plants—but when the news was bad, she neglected everything.

Christmas, after Hans left, was always a bad time for her, and in 1944, she had a rash which the doctor thought might be contagious. Afraid to infect any of her friends, she bought a little tree but was too depressed to decorate it. Not wanting to allow herself to get too despondent, she pulled up the blinds so that she could see the city lights, and read Dickens' *A Christmas Carol*. Later, when beautiful napkins arrived from the Strodes, and a Christmas hamper filled with goodies came from Marjorie and Norton, she was ashamed to have allowed herself to get so low. She wrote to Marjorie that she had once won a book as a prize that was called *Jack and the Christmas Hamper*, but she had never seen a hamper before.[27]

When the war seemed to be coming to an end, people began to say that revenge was inhuman and mercy should be shown to Germany—and she couldn't bear it. It seemed obvious to her that countries which had been invaded had to be helped before a thing could be done for the aggressors and she was stunned when she discovered that everyone didn't agree with her. Rex Stout, of the Writers' War Board, asked her to write how she felt to regional newspapers—and he gave her a list of them. The "America Firsters" were campaigning for mercy, and she began to get letters begging her to pray, as a Christian, that they would be forgiven. The perpetrators of each atrocity would have to ask God for forgiveness on his own, she wrote. She could only pray for justice for those whom they had injured. Now that the war was ending, she feared that all of the Quislings would be saying that they had "only followed orders." "Nobody is more clever than the Germans at complaining and asking for pity—when they do not precisely have the power to pose as Herrenvolk,"* she wrote in *Return to the Future.*[28]

The Germans were taking hostages and burning and destroying everything as they withdrew. Hospitals, churches, cattle, boats (even row boats), were burnt.

> *Boys I have known since they were toddlers that came in crying from my garden to ask me to help them with their pants, have been killed by slow torture of the most incredibly obscene kind, some are maimed for life, and still more kept as hostages. I freely confess, it would be all right with me if every single German man, woman and baby perished and the world could be purged of the master race.*[29]

"When I think of the millions of mothers all over the world who had once been happy and known no evil while they cared for their children," she wrote to Hans in 1943, "I think that nothing can ever stop my hatred."[30]

Sometimes, after working hard all day, when she was particularly lonely and depressed, she would call Arne Skouen at his Greenwich Village apartment and say, "We must have a meeting of the Authors' Association," and he would ask, "The usual or a peace meeting?" "Peace meeting," he wrote, meant that she had had a bad day and he was to bring a pint of bourbon. He would get the pint, take a subway and go to her regardless of the hour. They would have a few drinks, have a good talk, and she would feel better and go to bed.[31]

When I was researching this book in Norway, most people spoke of Sigrid with what bordered on awe, but there were some who tried to dissuade me from writing about her. At the Authors' Association, I was asked why I didn't choose someone else. They had "better writers." Was I sure I wanted to write about a Catholic—others asked. Did I know that all through the war she was living in luxury while they were fighting, and that she had become an alcoholic while she was away? I asked everyone I interviewed in the United States about that and they were all equally shocked at such a question. Lillian Bragdon said she would have a drink or two at lunch—not more—and none if she had an assignment to fulfill later. Alfred Knopf said she could have a drink or two to be sociable, but he never saw her affected in any way by drink. Arne Skouen, who was with her more than anyone else, wrote that he too had heard such talk when he got back to Norway but had

_____

*   A master race.

never seen her inebriated. She could never have fulfilled such an incredible number of assignments if she had been drinking, he said, and she was such a conscientious soldier that she would never have allowed anything to interfere with her ability to do her best work.

When President Roosevelt died,* she was as devastated as most Americans, and spoke at a memorial meeting extolling his greatness, but in a letter to Marjorie, she wrote that "America, Britain and the Scandinavian countries won't realize before it's too late, that the ideas we held to be 'selfevident truths' [sic] were never selfevident and never truths to anybody but ourselves."[32]

In San Francisco, on April 25, 1945, she was part of the group that wrote the governing treaty for the Charter of the United Nations that was being established. Fifty nations attended. She said that the document they produced was not perfect—but the American Constitution had not been perfect in the beginning either. It had needed to be improved as the years went by.

In a letter to Ingeborg Møller, Sigrid wrote that she was "sorry that Americans saw Norwegians as clumsy, good-natured oafs, with good hearts and their pants hanging down, who once in a while opened their clenched teeth to utter a few rune inscriptions and were always dancing around in folk costumes in village squares."[33] She was particularly revolted by *The Song of Norway* which was playing to packed houses on Broadway. "It was the most horribly vulgar nonsense. The music was a stew of 300 different Grieg songs. To Solveig's song, a lady, who was the Maiden of Norway, danced in a costume that would not have been acceptable on a beach."[34]

Her mood became more cheerful as the war seemed to be coming to an end. The news from home was very moving. There is "exuberant rejoicing and yet an order and a self-discipline," she wrote to Marjorie on May 25th, 1945, "and at present at least, a unity among all groups and parties and classes undreamt of before."

No family had been exempt from prison camps and torture chambers. The head of one of the largest private banks was carried home after being tortured and "will probably never be able to move a hand or a foot, as every joint had been crushed in arms, legs, feet and hands." Both of his sons were killed while in the Norwegian Air Force. A few weeks before the liberation, one of the leading psychiatrists had been shot as a hostage. Such things did a lot to unite a nation.

---

*   April 12, 1945.

Arnulf Øverland, Norway's greatest living poet, was recovering in a hospital in Sweden, after having spent three years in Sachsenhausen, and he was already writing about his prison experience.

> *The most hateful thing was, to him, the mixture of sadism and a pretense to humanitarian considerations: the doctors told the Gestapomen that a women in the fifth month of her pregnancy could very well stand examination, but out of regard for her condition she ought to be given a stool to sit on, when she was being whipped.*[35]

Now that it was almost over, Sigrid wrote to Marjorie, people couldn't understand how they had managed to survive on bread made of bark, peatmoss and potato peel, rotten herring and turnip with no fats, potatoes, fresh fish, meat, milk, eggs or flour.

> *The planned assassination of the occupied nations by way of starvation, disease and planned filthiness is not such a spectacular crime as the murders in the camps and the torturing to death and shooting of prisoners, but it has hit every man, woman and child in the countries which have been invaded. And never a sign from any of the Germans—soldiers, officers, or civilians—that they disapproved. So it seems, the 'good German' has to be written off together with the dinosaurs, passenger pigeons, and the great auk and other extinct specimens of animals.*[36]

German problems were deep-rooted, and she felt they could not be handled as they were after the First World War. The allies couldn't just get rid of the bad leaders and trust that the rest of the people would then go back to being normal. She believed that the German people were riddled with psychopaths and would have to be treated by doctors, and she hoped that Germany would be occupied by the victorious nations so that they could be prevented from murdering each other when they didn't have the Jews and the people of the occupied countries to murder.[37]

In *Return to the Future*, she had written that if the Nazi policy that only the strongest in the race should survive, had been carried out in the past, then "neither Swift, Newton, Darwin nor Hans Christian Andersen, (all sick people) would have had a dog's chance to live and carry out his life work. Of course, Hitler or Goebbels either, or our own Quisling."[38]

In a letter to Hans, she wrote: "One thing I'm certain about, Germany and Germans and all that we mean by that must be crushed to nothing if there shall be any hope for better days, and if anything can be created on the ruins, I don't know."[39]

The Russians have been behaving "like angels in the North of Norway," she wrote to Marjorie,

> . . . where they have taken some of the towns, helping the people to make shelters of sod, lending them tents, sharing their rations with a population that was thrown out of their houses and hospitals and farms without being permitted to carry off a thing, before the Germans put everything to the torch, even rowboats and stacks of peat, and killed all the animals. But, if the Russians behave so wonderfully well, they certainly have an intention . . . however much we may admire their war achievements, and some sides of their system. We Norwegians would not be happy for a long time under a system that would impose on us laws from the outside.[40]

She was ecstatic when she got word that Ole Henrik had been released from the concentration camp and was recuperating in Sweden. Charlotte's fiancé, Martin Blindheim, who had been sentenced to death, was exchanged for a German officer at the last minute. They planned to marry as soon as he got home.

She knew that she would miss America, but she couldn't wait to get back. She began to plan for the future. She didn't think she would ever want to live at Bjerkebaek after the Germans had besmirched it. Maybe she would take a small flat in Oslo near her widowed sister. When the refugees got home, she repeated often, they would all have to live in the background, modestly, and let those who had suffered decide how they wanted their countries rebuilt. It would have to be under the leadership of those who had fought and suffered. She couldn't imagine how the reconstruction could be managed. The fishing industry had been destroyed because of the scarcity of gas, the destruction of their boats, and the mining of the harbors. They had always needed it in order to import the foodstuffs and fertilizers they depended upon. After years of malnutrition, they would probably face outright starvation.

Actually, she had started preparing for her trip home shortly after she arrived, buying things at sales that she knew they would be short of after the war. Her apartment was filled with boxes and crates of blankets, linens, housewares and clothing. She started to get typhus, typhoid, diphtheria and smallpox shots long before the war was over. Although periodically there were serious setbacks, she wanted to be ready when the time came. Hans, who had become a Second Lieutenant, wanted her to meet him in London so that they could go home together, but transportation would be difficult to obtain, and she wrote that she would take what she could get and, if necessary, meet him in Norway.

When she received word that Norton Baskin was home and recuperating from tropical dysentery, and that *The Yearling* would be shot in Florida and not in "a fabricated Hollywood studio," she was delighted. She and Marjorie were in such good humor that they were exchanging jokes.

Sigrid wrote about an inebriated man who sat on a streetcar in an occupied country mumbling, "Well, there is only one man, only a single man, who is responsible for this horrible war." Passengers tried to silence him, but he kept on repeating it over and over again, "One man—just one man did all this to us." A German heard him and took him to Gestapo headquarters.

"Who were you complaining about on that streetcar?" he was asked.

"Why, Winston Churchill, of course," the drunk said, innocently.

The officers laughed, called him a good man and released him. When he got to the door, he turned and said, "Say, who did you think I was referring to?"[41]

She promised Knopf that she would write a history of Norway for young people, as sequel to her autobiographical novel, *The Longest Years*, and maybe a biography of Linné when she got home, and she had contracted with another American publisher to write a biography of Catherine of Sienna. She said it was too soon to write about the war. One needed perspective for that, and she wasn't interested in continuing *Madame Dorthea*. Writing about the past wasn't possible for her anymore.

In June, in a letter to the Strodes, she wrote that fifteen thousand Quislings had been rounded up in Norway and they would have to be tried and punished. The younger ones would be sent to reformatories—and all that would cost money. The country was stripped of everything.[42]

> *I feel some apprehension about going home, they have suffered so terribly, they have been so efficient and unflinching in their resistance to the invaders—and so many of my friends and the young people, friends of my boys, the youths who used to come to my house to dance or play bridge or something, are no more—But it is going to be wonderful too, to see again my country and to meet my own people . . .* [43]

It is after all, rather strange to be about to leave America. I have come to love so much here, have found such dear and true friends—and of course, I have lived in Brooklyn longer than any other place outside Norway—almost five years, think of it. And I have simply acquired a kind of local patriotism for this borough—when you come to know it, it is so intensely human and exceedingly interesting. Lovely too—some places—the other night I went to say goodbye to some friends who live in what is now a very low neighborhood, but they have had their old house for more than 35 years, and it is a wellworn, truly homely home—and behind the old brick house with the tall steep stoop is a lovely back garden and the 'tree that grows in Brooklyn,' the ailanthus, makes the space between the two old streets, the backyards like a young wood. We sat in the garden, trying to keep cool in the heatwave we are plagued with at present, and the moon was behind the leaves, and it was really the loveliest retreat, hidden away behind all those old, drab houses. I have never seen anything like this in Europe, I mean these hidden gardens in the midst of a sordid part of the great city.[44]

An American-Norwegian cultural association was going to be set up, she wrote to her American friends and Norwegians would be coming to the United States to study. In the past they had gone to Germany, but

. . . the record of the German university teachers, the medical profession and the other German intellectuals is about the most disgraceful in the picture of universal German degradation. Those doctors who worked out the biological warfare, the horrors of the prison camps, or just acquiesced in the starvation and overworking of slave laborers and prisoners seem to me the lowest of the low.[45]

They could never again respect German scholarship and science.

Finally, after five years in exile, she found a way to get home. Since no other transportation was available, she took a job as a stewardess on the freighter Montevideo and sailed on July 21, 1945. On the boat she met Gerda Evang, a left-wing friend who had worked in the health department before the war, and they had a wonderful trip together. Since the ship was carrying precious cargo of things required for needy people at home, she took only what she could carry and left the rest to be shipped when it would be possible.

Before she left, she distributed all of her plants amongst her friends with a little note attached to each on how to care for it.

As a going-home present, Marjorie and Norton sent her the equivalent of 4,250 Norwegian crowns which they had collected from their friends for the rehabilitation of displaced Norwegians, and she was delighted to be bringing that home.

CHAPTER XVIII

THE LONG LONELINESS IS OVER
1945-1949

The trip home was wonderful, she wrote to Arne Skouen on August 12th—the weather was perfect all the way. A pilot got on near Bergen to help them navigate through the mined harbor and by 6a.m. on July 30th, 1945 they were in Oslo. Standing straight and tall, heavier and much grayer than when she left, she showed the stress of the past five years as she searched the faces on the pier. Then she saw Signe, "Little" Signe, and Gunvor Hjerkinn (Anders' fiancée), waving frantically to get her attention. She sighed. Everything would be different now, but it was good to be home.

Her first words were: "Have you heard from Hans?" after which she asked how Martin and Ole Henrik were. Hans was back and would no doubt be there any moment, and both Martin and Ole Henrik were recuperating and doing as well as could be expected. Martin, whose ankle had been crushed under torture, would probably be lame for the rest of his life. He and Charlotte were to be married at the end of that week. "Little" Signe's son, who was eight months old, was fine.

Then came the surprise that "almost knocked her off her feet." One of Signe's twin daughters, Sigrid, had recently married the well-known psychiatrist Trygve Braatøy! Sigrid remembered him as much older than her niece, (thirteen years, to be exact), and a radical who had often differed with her at meetings of the Norwegian Authors' Association. She respected him as an intelligent and honorable man, but it would be a while before she would feel comfortable with him as a member of the family.

There was little time to ask about others before she was surrounded by reporters who were clamoring to know how she felt about the death sentence for traitors. "The Bible says, 'Authority shall not carry the sword in vain,'" she said, and it was her opinion that in extreme cases the death sentence was justified.[1] Then Hans came running toward her and she rushed to embrace him. They hadn't seen each other for four years and she refused to answer any more questions.

Hans looked fine, but the others had aged painfully. At Signe's house she distributed the first installment of the gifts she had brought. Since she could only bring what she could carry, there was silk underwear, nylon stockings, nice smelling soap, shampoo, sewing materials and tea. She had heard that during the war, Little Signe had offered to send her cousin Ulla her orange evening gown in exchange for a bread knife, so she also brought bread knives and kitchen utensils. Blankets, bed linens, and other bulky items would come as soon as space became available on a ship. "I know how it feels for young girls to have to wear worn-out underclothes for such a long time," she explained, "so that was my first priority."[2]

For days she basked in being with her family, weeping over what they had been through and listening to how Hans had fared in London, but she couldn't postpone going home forever. Hans hoped to finish his studies at Cambridge or the Sorbonne, but in the meantime he had registered at the University of Oslo and she was returning to Bjerkebaek alone.

Fredrik Bøe came for her just as he had in the past. His car was different and he had aged like all the rest, but she was glad to see her old friend again. Anders was gone and there would be no rides with Mosse anymore, but she would be in her own home at last.

"So must they feel who rode towards their homes knowing that the houses lie there burnt to ashes and cold charred wood . . ." she had written long ago when Kristin Lavransdatter returned home after seeing two of her sons off to a monastery, knowing that the rest needed her no longer.[3]

She had been warned that the devastation at Bjerkebaek would upset her, but nothing could have prepared her for the sight that took her breath away. Her beautiful birch trees had been shaved to the ground and a paved parking lot, like a shiny billiard ball, stared her in the face. Her garden was a mass of brambles and weeds, and remnants of some of her most treasured belongings were heaped in a towering mass of rubbish behind the house. The interior, which she was told had taken four women a week to clean up, seemed eerier still. Stripped of books, bookcases, pictures and furniture, it was an empty shell. Like a slap in the face, she was struck with how much that was dear to her would never be there again. She was an old woman at sixty-three, alone in an empty house.

Her former housekeeper, Thea Morgenstuen, had married Fredrik Bøe. At first, they had been allowed to remain at Bjerkebaek, they told her, and had managed, with the help of friends, to save some of her belongings, although the Germans had photographed everything inside and out as soon as she left, but in 1942, the Gestapo took possession of the estate and the Bøes were forced to leave. By the time Sigrid returned, they had four-year-old twin sons, and since housing was rationed, and she would not be allowed to occupy more than part of her house, they had applied for permission to share it in return for cooking and caring for her.

She had already been told that Ole Henrik had sneaked out some of her botany books before he was arrested—including a work of Linné's that had been published in 1741, and an old picture of the author dressed as a Laplander with a bouquet of *Linorea* in his hands. Ole Henrik had remembered her excitement when she had found them in an old bookstore, he told her later.

His father had been more daring. He had been packing her most valuable books, (leaving paperbacks, novels and encyclopedias, which were replaceable), when two Gestapo officers caught him in the act. Asked what he thought he as doing, he had reacted quickly and said that the books had been borrowed from the King's scientific collection in Trondheim, and the university library in Oslo, and they wanted them back. When they didn't believe him, he suggested they call the chief librarian (whom he knew) to check. One of the officers picked up the phone and called, and although the bewildered librarian was not aware of what was going on, he thought for a moment and said, "Oh, of course, the books in Madame Undset's house belong here. They are part of our national archives." Fortunately, the officers didn't want to create an issue over things upon which they set little value, and they allowed the boxes to be shipped to the libraries. Later, the books were repacked in small parcels and hidden in various basements and attics and she would have them back soon.

When the two most despised Gestapo men moved in they had had the trees cut down, the parking lot put in, and a small prison camp built on the grounds. She was lucky, she wrote to Marjorie, that her house lacked central heating and what they considered "comfortable furniture" so they only kept some of their interpreter and "tarts" with them.[4]

Her former housekeeper's sons were charming and funny but of course very different from pre-war children—the things they have heard and seen. The other day, when they overheard their mother telephoning a florist about a wreath for a dead child, one of the boys asked, "But mommy, my daddy said all the Germans have left Lillehammer. How could Mathinson's baby be dead?" [5]

Her father's writing table, the bookcases and anything else of wood had been used for firewood and truckloads of perennials from her garden had been carted away to be sent to Germany.[6] In the attic she found crates filled with her belongings, addressed to destinations in Germany, which they had not had time to ship before they were forced to leave, but none of the table silver, china, glassware, blankets or linens (except some embroidered tablecloths, which her housekeeper had sneaked out) remained. After the Germans left, refugees from the North were housed there, but they had returned to the burned-out sites of their homes as soon as they were permitted to do so.

"I wanted to tell you how I disposed of the money you gave me," she wrote to Marjorie.

However, except for one third, which I gave together with a contribution in my own name to a foundation for the education of children whose parents have been killed . . . I have not been able to do anything with the rest. I am going to give all, I think, to the work of re-building our northernmost three provinces, where the Germans destroyed everything with true German thoroughness,—some 60,000 people are living in basements of their burnt out houses, in caves and old mines, hundreds of miles above the Artic circle. But, the difficult thing is to get materials, and I had hoped maybe I should be able to get a license and buy some household goods and clothes in Sweden where some money is due to me,—then the money would be very useful, when the people can get materials for re-building their homes, the orphanages and old people's homes which were destroyed. This little town, Lillehammer, has adopted a town Lebesby—on the very shores of the Arctic—or rather, the people of Lebesby, for of the town absolutely nothing is standing, and not as much as a single fishing boat has been spared. And the people of the North cling to their homes, or the sites of their homes. They had been evacuated by force by the Germans (in crowded ships where babies were born and died and the small bodies thrown overboard, and the weaker perished by the dozens), but as soon as Norway was free they rushed home and now they refuse to budge.—They are different from other Norwegians—more emotional and fantastic, adventurous and full of fun, and very often the handsomest people I ever saw. But different—as maybe is natural for people who, with some exaggeration, live through a winter night of three or four or five months and a summer's day of the same length. The North is the real land of the Midnight sun, you know—I never saw the Midnight sun until 1930, when I voyaged beyond the arctic circle.[7]

The Knopf staff sent some blankets, and on November 14, she wrote to Lillian Bragdon:

They were a godsend . . . The work of building up the country proceeds rapidly in some directions, in other directions nothing has been done or can be done at present—the housing situation is very bad, and you cannot build when you have no materials. The Germans took everything and prevented us from manufacturing anything for our own use. The food situation is good. We have bread, meat, some fish (the fishing fleet is in a very bad state, or else we would have fish in abundance), milk (but no butter, no cheese and very few eggs, because the cattle were in a bad state, having been fed wood pulp for years, so all the milk we get must be used au naturel, nothing can be spared for dairy produce until next summer) . . . It really is instructive to learn, how cause and effect work in the whole structure of the economy—you cannot get this, because you lack that, nails for instance. (I brought a small box of nails with me from America, they are a most precious store to be distributed among my friends by the half-dozen.) On the whole, we never knew how we used to depend on all those tiny items which we took for granted, and which now are entirely missing: pins and needles, nailbrushes and toothbrushes, real soap, (we get something made up from a herring oil and lye, very useful, but with a terrible stink), elastics, zippers,—in short, all the things I used to buy at the Five-and-Ten stores in America and which became treasures over here,—I bought a supply but I might very well have brought with me ten times more for my friends. The worst however is the lack of footwear and the difficulties for people to get clothing,—and of course, without rationing cards you cannot buy a thing (except flowers, books and

*paintings.) So the Norwegian publishers have a swell time, whatever
they publish, even the worst trash, is sold out in no time at all.*

To the Strodes, she wrote that all they published were American "best
sellers, of crazy adventures and the love interests put on top, hot and sweet
and plenty of it, like chocolate sauce and ice cream. But it is misleading, when
people take these things for an expression of American literary life."[8]

The Knopf staff exchanged Christmas presents each year, but they
decided to send presents to Norway instead. They found a company that
would guarantee delivery, and shipped a huge box of nails, hammers, tools,
cigarettes, pots and pans, canned foods, face tissues, and many of the small
items that Sigrid had mentioned in her letter.

Marjorie Rawlings and Norton Baskin also sent packages regularly from
Macy's and Frazer Morris. In her letters of appreciation Sigrid mentions the
arrival at various times of sugar, tea, coffee, rice, seeds, dried fruits, soap,
English cheeses, canned fruits, candy, as well as a subscription to *Time*
magazine, which she had especially asked for. The Strodes kept her supplied
with nylons and books. Blanche and Alfred Knopf also sent books—and
she, of course, shared all of those wonderful gifts with her neighbors, family
and friends.

After the first few months, she begged her American friends not to send
so much. Although it was nice to have some variety, they had enough to eat
and fuel enough to keep warm. Compared to other countries that had been
occupied, they were well off. What they lacked were construction materials,
clothing, shoes and electricity. The gifts were deeply appreciated but their
generosity embarrassed her because she had no way of reciprocating. Her
dollar earnings had to be deposited directly to Norwegian banks because
dollars were so badly needed, and there was little that one could buy with
Norwegian money except pottery . . . "Armies of girls have gone into pottery
making, calling themselves arts-and-crafts women and making ugly things
which break when you look at them, which really is a good thing," she wrote
to Marjorie,[9] so she dug into her possessions and sent jewelry and whatever
else she still possessed to her friends and her newly wed nieces.

It wasn't material things that she missed, she would gladly "do without,"
it was the human losses that were so hard to bear. Her house was full of
memories and it was only when she was home that she finally faced just
how poor she had become. Not only Anders and Mosse were missing—her
mother, Svarstad, Signe's husband, Nini Roll Anker (who had died in 1942

on Sigrid's 60th birthday), Fredrik Paasche, Anders Whyller and many others were gone. She was grateful that she still had Hans, but he had his own life to live and spent little time with her. Almost every family in Lillehammer had been maimed by the loss of one or more of its members. Many had been tortured and had died horrible deaths, or were so broken that they would never be the same. Her friend, Helene Frøysland, had lost her son Helge in a way that haunted all who had known him.

Helge, who was twenty-two, "secretly left home some days after Christmas in 1943," she wrote to Marjorie, on November 24, 1945.

> *. . . and for more than a year he lived up in the mountains, above the timberline, in a cave where they dared not have a fire, because of the smoke, spending their days and nights in sleeping bags (and later in fur coats that were sent up to them) while they were sending secret radio messages to our army in England and receiving and hiding the armament that was dropped by airplanes for our home forces. It was a life like the lives of the outlaws of old, but Helge and his companions were used to mountaineering and skiing since they were tiny boys.*

He managed to send his mother a message occasionally and a little tea and candy that had been dropped from English planes. Then Helge and a few of his companions encountered a group of Russians in the woods who claimed to be escaping prisoners. After they fed them and gave them some clothes, the Russians, who were working for the Germans, turned them over to the Gestapo. They were tortured for eleven days but wouldn't give away their hiding place. Finally, some of the group managed to fight their way out, but since Helge was tied to a tree, he couldn't get away. After the fighting was over, when the snow had melted in the mountains, the survivors searched and found his mangled body. Unable to live with the memory, his mother died shortly after he was buried,—but there were some "happy endings."

> *Ole Henrik . . . was taken prisoner in 1943, tortured, given solitary confinement for seven months, then concentration camp in Norway, then Sachsenhausen—and he is back again, and the rumor that they had destroyed his hands (he is a pianist) was untrue. He is sane in body and mind—only very much more mature than his 26 years.*[10]

Another "happy ending" was that her niece's fiancé, who had been sentenced to be beheaded, had miraculously remained alive, because his captors "were so busy beheading Poles and Russians who knew too much that the five Norwegians, who sat chained to the fortress of Brandenburg, had to wait."

"He is one of the handsomest men I ever saw," Sigrid continued. He married her niece and was living with her sister "on next to nothing," while they were both continuing their studies—she on her dissertation and he were he left off, though he was easily fatigued and often fell asleep suddenly.[11]

(Unfortunately, not everyone was so brave. A number of people in Oslo believe that Svarstad had become an apologist for the Germans during the occupation and reported that he had been ostracized by many before he died. Kjeld Rasmussen, who was a schoolmate and close friend of Hans', told me that "Svarstad and my father had formed a club of two dedicated to hating the Jews long before the Nazis arrived." Gunhild believed that her father found it easier to cooperate with the Germans than to fight with them, but he would never have helped those who had killed his beloved son.)

On October 26th, shortly after Sigrid returned to Norway, the Norwegian Authors' Association celebrated its 50th Anniversary by honoring a number of their outstanding writers. Sigrid was led to the platform with the rest of the honored guests, but was not mentioned. Old jealousies and hostilities had flared up again. She was resented for not having suffered with them during the war, and she, herself, felt guilty about it. Although she had been made a life member, she decided to leave the work to younger writers and stopped going to meetings.

When she could, she came to Oslo to see Hans, her stepdaughters and her sister's family. She was especially fond of her nieces, and since all three of them had recently married, each invited her to dinner, so that she could become better acquainted with their spouses. All went well until it was time to visit the Braatøys.

"Little" Sigrid made a delicious dinner and Dr. Braatøy did all within his power to entertain his aunt, but as Charlotte described in *Moster Sigrid*, Sigrid sat like Queen Victoria when she was supposed to have said, "We are not amused," and nothing they could think of could get a conversation going. Then, knowing that her aunt was interested in stories about the supernatural, the hostess hit on a way to get her involved. In Kalundborg, the Gyths believed that a monstrous yellow dog always appeared to one of them when someone in the family was about to die, and she told Sigrid that one Sunday afternoon, in 1944, she had seen a large, yellow dog crossing the living room in the half-darkness. She was terribly frightened, of course, and told Gunvor Hjerkinn about it. A few days later, her father, who had been ill since his second release from the concentration camp, had a turn for the worse, was taken to the hospital and died.

Sigrid had been lost in thought while she was telling the story, but at the word "died," she burst out with, "Nonsense, Sigrid! That dog has never been outside of Kalundborg." Everyone started to laugh and they enjoyed the kind of evening they had always had when Aunt Sigrid was at her best. Trygve, who had just about given up on her, was bowled over by her playfulness and humor. A lively debate about parapsychology and Freud (whom Charlotte Blindheim says Sigrid detested) and Øverland's lyrics, (which they all loved) developed, and it continued well into the night.[12]

When Sigrid left the United States she was full of energy and eager to do her part in the postwar reconstruction. Working for the Royal Norwegian Information Services, she had heard only about deeds of heroism, and according to Arne Skouen, she was ready to "dress herself in sackcloth and ashes,"[13] take a back seat, and follow orders. She couldn't imagine what it was like to be hungry all of the time, deprived of one's rights, and too frightened to fight back. She imagined that people lived like moles in the hope that if they didn't make waves, they wouldn't get into trouble, but she wasn't prepared for the numbers who had toadied to the Nazis by betraying their neighbors for the slightest advantage for themselves. Disillusioned in life and their fellow men, people were too cynical and tried to care about politics and the future. They just wanted to get back to some kind of normalcy and their apathy astounded her.

Borghild Krane, in her biography of Sigrid, quotes a letter which Sigrid wrote to Hans Aanrud on December 20, 1948:

> *I have to admit that I think the world has become sad now. When I was in America during the war, I felt I was doing something useful and I was looking forward to the future—not that I expected that it would all be wonderful at once, or that the old times would ever come back, but I hadn't expected that the new times would be so bloodless and sapless. After so much blood was wasted the people are tired and anemic.*[14]

There was no fight left in them and they weren't interested in creating a better world.

Trials of traitors and collaborators were going on, and the press was full of their dreadful deeds. The two subjects most on everyone's minds were:

Should there be a death penalty? and What shall we do about the Atom Bomb? Pacifists were saying that people should not allow themselves to be whipped into a militaristic stance because of the existence of the Bomb, and Sigrid said, "that was wishful thinking all over again."

On November 23, 1946, she wrote an article for *Verdens Gang* called *This is No Time for Pollyannas** in which she said that it was important to be armed in order to protect the peace.

> *Can they not or don't they dare to see, those who speak of disarmament, what it cost the world when some nations neglected to arm themselves while others were planning to take over the world? . . . How many years has it prolonged the war when those countries who really believed that peace is better than war, were not armed to defend the peace? I remember the childish distrust of 'the military' from my childhood in Ragna Nielsen's school, when Ullman and Bjørnson dreamt about a Norway 'without a single lieutenant.' It is incredible that there is still anyone outside of the psychiatric clinics who can believe such things.*[16]

Dr. Braatøy answered her on the 27th, in the *Dagbladet,* with an article entitled *Women and Compulsory Military Service.* "People like Sigrid Undset, the generals, and Arnulf Øverland—yes, even Arnulf Øverland," were already preparing for a new war. Were they now going to mobilize women and children? What about the Atom Bomb? And why was she slandering defenseless patients in psychiatric clinics?

Sigrid answered with an article called *Military Service*, and the family was embroiled in a public debate.

Signe was irritated with her son-in-law. Sigrid had not meant to denigrate his patients. He had taken her too literally. She meant that only someone in a psychiatric clinic could believe a thing like that—the way one says, "You'd have to be crazy to believe it."

Newspaper readers were delighted with the family dispute which was being aired in the press, but it wasn't long before they were all friends again. Sigrid invited each of the new couples to Bjerkebaek and put herself out, as only she could do to entertain them. When Charlotte and Martin came up,

---

*   A title she borrowed from *The New York Herald Tribune* which a friend had sent her.[15]

she took them to see the ruins in Hamar and they visited the Stav churches*
in Valdres.

"It is amazing how one can manage when there are shortages," she wrote
to Marjorie. "The other day my son broke one of the chain knobs in the
bathroom." There were none to be had in all of Norway, and a friend suggested
turning the problem over to someone who had been in a concentration camp.
"They make anything from nothing, and could probably make you a knob
of wood or metal." To keep from brooding, people in concentration camps
discovered abilities they had no idea they possessed. But it wasn't shortages
that worried Sigrid.

> It's rather the future in a wider sense that I think worries us,—the
> world is certainly very far from being at peace still, and I don't think
> the outlook is any too bright. America too seems to have troubles enough
> of her own, and there is the atomic bomb of which we have just seen
> the debut . . . And Germany and Russia are still the dark horses—or
> Germany at least is unchanged, and I believe Russia too is getting
> more and more like old Russia with her policy of ruse and jockeying
> for power. As to the Germans—can you imagine, I and a lot of my
> acquaintances are getting letters from Germans asking for help, also for
> help to get into Norway and get a situation here, or for other things.
> But of course they all insist, they were never Nazis—This nephew of
> mine I mentioned even got a letter from one of his jailers, a torturist,
> who tells him how much he liked him and admired his courage—and
> can we not now be friends and could he not help him to get off with
> a light sentence and afterwards acquire Norwegian citizenship and a
> situation as a trainer of prizefighters? And lots of love and sympathy
> for those boys he helped to thrash and kick, but only because he had to
> obey orders, as he really liked them so much.[17]

When Hudson Strode wrote that he was coming to Norway (in 1946),
Sigrid warned him not to rely on the old honesty of the Norwegians.

> For five years it has been good sport and a patriotic achievement
> to cheat and steal from the Germans what they had taken from us, but
> now the generation that grew up perfecting themselves as master thieves
> is not so easily turned into honest citizens of the old style. That's what

---

* Old wooden churches from the 11th, 12th and 13th centuries.

*war always does to a nation . . . good people are very worried about
the deterioration of the morals of the young.*[18]

"Indeed the outlook is none too bright anywhere in this uprooted world,"
she wrote to Marjorie in November.

> *It's hope for the best and be prepared for the worst, though the
> worst is probably too bad to be imagined. I do hope, exactly because
> the outlook is so grim and the fear so universal, that those who have
> been made responsible for the future of all of us may really persevere
> until they have found a way leading out of the mess. I have seen just
> about enough of world history, I can do without being the contemporary
> to much more. But then, I have still one son left—. and I was never
> able to feel that other people's concerns were no concern of mine . . .
> if no new disasters occur, we shall be able little by little to create the
> conditions for as perfect a society as is to be expected in a world of not
> very perfect human beings. Our Labor Government is doing a good
> job . . . Of course, a lot of the restrictions and encroachments of the
> government control in every aspect of life have been introduced as an
> emergency measure but really are here to stay.*[19]

She continued to praise the labor government for doing a good job in
the reconstruction, but, in time, she found them a little naïve. "Our Labor
Government and their employees," she wrote to Marjorie,

> *. . . are nice capable men in a way. Most of them have come forward
> by way of the Trade Unions where they held important situations, but
> governing a country and running the whole economic life is another
> thing, and it becomes more and more evident, they have taken upon
> themselves a lot of jobs where they are just amateurs and bungle a
> good deal.*[20]

The situation in Finland was terrible.

> *During the war, hundreds and hundreds of Finnish children were
> sent to Sweden and taken care of in Swedish homes, of course mostly by
> well-to-do people. Now the poor kids must return to their own parents.
> But in many cases they don't remember a single word of Finnish. And
> they have been used to having a room of their own, their foster parents*

had cars, they got all they wanted of candy, toys, nice clothing and good food. And they turn stiff with horror and disgust when they return to a cottage where ten or twelve persons live in two rooms, two or more children sleeping in one bed, their parents take over their lovely clothes to share with younger sisters and brothers, and they have only coarse food and not much of it. Some they had to return to their Swedish hosts, who were willing to adopt them . . . certainly the consequences of this war are far from being conquered—on the contrary, new problems develop every day.[21]

She was still being bombarded with letters from Germans who wanted "to go on as if nothing was the matter,"

. . . this slight misunderstanding between us—they think I ought to do something,—write and explain how innocent were really the greater part of the poor Germans. In the meantime we are still trying Gestapo men and Quislings who are guilty of torturing and murdering Norwegian civilians and soldiers and the tragedies of the concentration camps are being threshed over and over again at each trial. In this small town we have a Russian churchyard, a cemetery where 986 Russian slave workers are buried. The first of them came in 1942, to work at the fortifications they built all over the valley. Of these Russians, some 20 were killed outright, the others died of starvation, cold and overwork. Many of the people here tried to help them, smuggling food and bits of clothing,—a boy who used to work in my garden was arrested, with his father and mother because they had given food from their small farm to some escaped Russians. The boy died in Sachsenhausen, the mother in Ravensbruck, only the father is back again now. I don't think anybody except the most fanatical communists trust Russia as a political power more than we trusted Nazi Germany. But the Russians as individuals were very much liked, partly because they were so cruelly treated, partly because they bore their sufferings bravely, were polite and charming when they managed to contact the Norwegians.—But, the letters many of them promised to send their Norwegian friends never arrived, and it is whispered that those prisoners of war who did see too much of how other nations live, have been sent to Sibir to disappear . . . Lillehammer was a resort of capitalistic millionaires, as every family lived in a house of his own, with an orchard and flower garden.[22]

For a person who tried to be fair and was never one to feel that the problems of others were no concern of hers, the contradictions around her were overwhelming. Needing clear issues to fight for, the events were making her ill. She could not reconcile her religious belief in serene acceptance with her passionate intellectual conviction that constant vigilance, and even violence, was sometimes necessary to keep one part of mankind from taking too much advantage of another. If wrongdoers were not punished, what would keep others from repeating their deeds?

She began to question everything she had ever believed. Criticism from Catholics had lessened some of her religious ardor, and she had attended church less frequently when she was in America. She went more regularly after she got home, but nothing was the same anymore.

She had promised Knopf a number of books before she left, but she wasn't enthusiastic about any of them. She needed money and she had a commitment from an American publisher for a biography of Catherine of Siena, and it was that which she decided to write.

"She had always written as a moral action, and she couldn't see a point of view for herself," Arne Skouen wrote. "Her wild hate of the enemy was too strong for her to be able to forgive,[23] yet she knew that 'hate and thirst for revenge are sterile passions.'"[24]

"The old artist's fate is never a happy one," she had written when Olav Dunn died in 1939. "To feel the force of the imagination weaken, the hand become uncertain, and the temperature of one's mind begin to sink—that is always hard to take."[25]

"Since Anders died," she wrote to Ingeborg Møller on April 23, 1947,

I have felt that I'm not firmly bound to this earth. It isn't a weariness of life, or anything like that, I have much to live for—but always I feel that whatever I do, is something I'm doing while I wait.

In December 1946, she reviewed a book by Ingeborg Møller called *The Twelve Apostle Sages*. The two women had been friends for years and lived near each other, and since they were both lonely and neither had enough to do, they formed "an exclusive club for two" which met once a week, first in one, and then in the other's house, to discuss the Golden Age of Denmark. The hostess on a given week chose the topic to be researched for the following week. It was a sad "make-work" activity for two lonely old ladies.

Sigrid was short of money and she was worried about Hans' future. "Thea," she wrote to the Strodes, "says the boy is clever enough if he would only pull himself together and do one thing at a time instead of skipping from one kind of work to another."[26] After a year at the university, he had written an article about the Norwegian constitution which was published and he left school determined to become an author. His article "was very keen and well written, too, but I wish he would think of getting his degree,"[27] she wrote to Marjorie. He was twenty-seven and had a lot of studying to catch up with, and so far, other than the four years when he was in the army, he had earned nothing and had no way of supporting himself in the future. All of the young people close to her were completing their studies and getting on with their careers. Ole Henrik, who had suffered so much, had just appeared as a pianist at his first concert since the war and had played magnificently. She had been so proud of him that she had cried. Charlotte Blindheim had a job at the Museum of Oslo and had already given birth to a son.

When Svarstad died, he had left the house in Kampen to Ebba, what was left of his father's estate in Ringerike (which he had inherited when his mother died), to Gunhild, and some money to each of his children—including Hans. Since he wasn't attending classes, Hans decided to use the money he inherited from his father to arrange an exhibition of his paintings. It was very successful and he talked of touring it abroad. He was also planning to write a biography of his father and to go back to school to study law, but nothing came of his plans. He had lost two years of school, his inheritance was spent, and he was in debt. Sigrid was still supporting him and had to pay his debts. He had no direction and was depressed, and she worried about him.

Her late husband, she wrote to Marjorie in December, was not a bad man, and he was a fine artist, but, somehow, everything he touched became blighted.

Ebba, who attended college for a while, decided to leave her job and use her inheritance to become a schoolteacher. "She is forty-four years old, and not very bright," Sigrid continued, "and has run into debt to such an extent that I don't think she knows herself how much she owes." She had helped her several times in the past and would probably have to do so again. Her stepson Trond was forty, and believed that he spoke to his dead brother Anders every night. The only one who had turned out right was Gunhild. "She is married, a sensible, hardworking girl and a good mother. She invested her modest inheritance in fixing up the summer house she got from her father, kept her husband, who is a ship's engineer, hidden so that he had not to said for the Germans, (he was in a Norwegian harbor when the invasion came), fed herself and her family on the produce of the place during the famine years, and had always a little to help others with too."[28]

After Sigrid's books had been collected from their hiding places, she reread some of Cather's and Rawlings' work and wrote to each of them that knowing them and having seen how and where they lived, had enhanced her pleasure in the second readings. To Willa, she wrote that she had unearthed a picture of her which Knopf had sent. It was "a little broken and soiled, but all the more dear to me." On April 24, 1947, she was writing a letter to Cather when a telegram arrived that she had died. Deeply upset, she wired Edith Lewis how sorry she was.[*29]

> *Spring has come at last—or is it hot as in the middle of the summer. The birches overnight became veiled in green and our Norwegian cousin of the chokecherries will be covered with clusters of white flowers in a couple of days. To get my garden put in order I have engaged a gang of young boys sentenced for treason to terms of penal servitude (the man who did for me in the garden on his free watches is a watchman in their camp outside of Lillehammer). It feels a little like using chain gangs—though the boys of course are very well treated, they look strong and healthy working naked to the middle—a couple of them are very goodlooking fairharied Norwegian youngsters, and the whole thing seems so pitiful—and meaningless. How could those nice-looking clean-limbed country lads let themselves be trapped into Quisling's guards or into the German-organized Regiment Nordland and go and fight for the Germans in Russia? The camp where now our traitors are sitting was the scene of obscene tortures of Norwegians during the war.*[30]

Those prisoners upset her deeply. She couldn't stop thinking about them. How would it help anyone if those young men, who should have been in schools and had already lost seven years of their lives, did penal labor in her garden? Yet, how could anyone forgive them for helping the beasts who had tortured and killed so many? People who did such things had to be punished or they, and others like them, would do it again. What should a caring person do? What was right and what was wrong? Now there was the Atom Bomb and no one knew what would happen next. She was reading Count Ciano's diaries and they were utterly terrifying.[31]

---

[*] According to Borghild Krane, there once were seventeen letters at Bjerkebaek from Willa Cather.

In March, forty Swedish writers and scholars who had heard that her silver had been stolen by the Nazis, presented her with a silver table service for twelve—and—in the spring, Laurence W. Beilenson, a Hollywood lawyer, and the director John Cromwell, optioned the movie rights to *Kristin Lavransdatter* and were considering Ingrid Bergman to play Kristin.

Shortly after Sigrid's 65th birthday, King Haskon presented her with the highest award her country bestowed—the Grand Cross of the Order of St. Olav—"for eminent services to literature and the nation." It was an honor as important to her as her Nobel Prize and the Pro Ecclesia Et Pontifice award from the Pope. She also received the Icelandic Folk Award, the Danish Freedom Order and the Norwegian War Participation Medal.[32]

The honors and gifts pleased her tremendously, and the possibility of a movie relieved her of some of her worries about Hans' future,* but she was not feeling well, and early in June she had a medical checkup.

The doctor found nothing and recommended a rest. Since rest was what she had too much of, her sister decided a change of scene would be more helpful, and she and a friend accompanied her on a car trip to Trondheim. She didn't get any better, and in September, she checked into a hospital for a more thorough examination. The x-rays showed nothing. The elasticity of her organism seemed to have given out, the doctor explained. Perhaps rest would bring her back to health. Hans came up for short visits, but she was alone much of the time. She enjoyed the Bøe twins, especially the one who reminded her of Anders, but for company she turned more and more to the nuns in Hamar.

She got a permit to have her roof repaired, and stayed in Oslo for a few months to research Catherine of Siena. In November, she wrote to Professor Strode that she was on the last Chapter and had gone through 400 of Catherine's letters and her Dialogue. "I think she is one of the strangest and most gifted women who ever lived, but doing her life is not easy when you are no saint yourself."[33]

She had begun to question so many of her strongly felt and oft-stated theories, that her biography of St. Catherine began to take an unexpected direction. Under torture people were capable of incredible acts of bravery and self-sacrifice, but when left to their own devices, they could not get along with their brothers and were even less ready to make sacrifices for strangers. With her strength ebbing, disillusioned in the power of religion to influence

---

*   The movie was never made, but Mr. Beilenson continued to renew that option and it helped provide some income for Hans through the years.

human behavior, (Hitler had made her realize that one couldn't leave the future of mankind to God alone), fearing that governments, education, and political maneuvering wouldn't help, there was nowhere to turn for solutions. Humanity was hopelessly headed towards its destruction, and the only thing one could do was to pray for some kind of magical intervention from unknown sources. Catherine of Siena was a simple, illiterate girl who had devoted herself to the poor and was supposed to have succeeded in uniting the Church, (at the time when there was a French Pope in Avignon and an Italian one in Rome), by speaking directly to her "Bridegroom in Heaven," who appeared to her regularly and instructed her on what to do. The descriptions of her highly erotic ecstasies, her epileptic seizures, and the miracles she was supposed to have performed, miracles which the greatest thinkers and most important leaders of the Church were incapable of creating—had changed what was supposed to have been a biography of a saint, to a feverish and often unintelligible final statement from a broken, sexually undernourished, disappointed woman.

Father Hallvard Rieber-Mohn, O.P., a Dominican priest in Oslo, who is the author of a book about Sigrid called *Sten Pa Sten*, (*Stone by Stone*), wrote an article honoring the 100th anniversary of Sigrid's birth: "*Catherine of Siena* does not belong among her more meaningful works . . . Her Christian mysticism turned her into Norwegian literature's first (and only) hagiographer."

Then, as if she weren't depressed enough, *Catherine of Siena* was rejected by the publisher.[*] She was a Nobel Prize winner and author of thirty-nine books. To have the 40th rejected was an unbelievable experience. When they had promised to do the book, the publisher wrote, they were under the impression it was to be an historical biography, but the manuscript which she had submitted was totally different. It was a blow that she was not in a condition to handle. She had truly reached the moment when "midnight shakes the memory as a madman shakes a dead geranium."[34]

In an effort to keep going, she went to Denmark with Ingeborg Møller. They visited the Thorvaldsen Museum and planned to see the places they had researched, but she suffered a stroke and Alice Lyttkens and her husband, who were vacationing nearby, had to come care for her. It was

---

[*] There seems to be a difference of opinion as to who the publisher was. Some say it was Doubleday and Doran, others that it was Farrar, Straus and Cudahy It was published posthumously, in Norway in 1951— and in the United States by Sheed and Ward in 1954.

not severe and she was able to go home, but she had a more serious attack in Norway and was sent to the neurological center of the Riks Hospital for observation. She recovered from that too, and Hans took her to the fjords for a few weeks.

On October 28, 1948 she wrote to Marjorie that she was upset by what was happening in Czechoslovakia. (She was referring to the strange death of Jan Masaryk and the Russian takeover of Czechoslovakia.)

"Who will be next?" she asked Hudson Strode when she wrote to him on February 29th. Everyone was concerned about the Russians. Most of the socialists in the Norwegian government were old-time socialists, not communists, and they were just as unhappy about the possibility of a takeover as everyone else. Nothing had changed. They were right back where they had started. If things got very bad, she wanted Hans to leave the country. She was too old to go anywhere anymore. Her niece, Sigrid, and her husband were going to America where Dr. Braatøy had been invited to work at the Menninger Institute in Topeka, Kansas.[35]

In December, she complained that the government was building athletic fields, railway stations, and public buildings, but housing was still not available. Her nieces and their husbands and babies were still forced to live with parents, while "lamentation letters" were arriving regularly from Germans who "seemed to have howled themselves into getting much more than their one-time victims. At least they complain because they get too little of things which we never see at all."[36]

"Sometimes I feel terribly old, having lived through two world wars and remembering the quiet and comfortable times before the first," she wrote to the Strodes. "It is really too much world history for one person to witness."[37]

But the fight was not quite out of her yet. Early in 1949, the Knopfs sent her *Burke's Politics* which they had just published and a flicker of her old enthusiasm returned. She began to reread Burke.[38]

During the first week of June, she developed a kidney inflammation. There was no intercommunicating system at Bjerkebaek, and she suffered alone for several hours before Thea discovered how sick she was. Her doctor was away, so she was taken to the hospital in Lillehammer. Since she had had kidney infections before, no one realized how serious it was, and her family was not informed. She asked for her priest, but he too was away. The prioress at St. Torfinn's clinic sent Sister Xavier to keep her company. She was with her all night, and in the morning of June 10th, Sigrid convinced Sister Xavier to go to Bjerkebaek for a rest. Shortly after she got there, word came from the hospital that Sigrid had died. She was alone in the end. An unfinished essay on Burke was in her typewriter.*

Sigrid's body was brought home and laid out where Mosse had lain, and on June 14th, after her family and friends had arrived, she was taken to St. Torfinn's Church in Hamar. Bishop Jacob Mangers, of Oslo, conducted the services. Martin Blindheim and Ole Henrik Moe led the honor guards who carried her casket. Hans, flanked by his two aunts and his Danish relative, Clara Hasselbalch, followed and the nieces, friends and relatives came after them. Sigrid's body was taken to the Mesnalian churchyard where she was buried next to her son and daughter. The Storting voted that her burial was to be at the expense of the State, but in Lillehammer life went on as usual. No one would have guessed that their most illustrious neighbor had died.

Her gravestone, as she instructed reads: *Ti se jeg er Herrens tjennerrine* (You see, I am a handmaiden of God), a quote from *Kristin Lavransdatter*.[39]

After she died, Peter Egge wrote:

> *If, at the end, the value of a human life can be measured by its ability to give to others, then Sigrid Undset was the most valuable person I have known. She lived to give, give, give proudly and quietly without asking for anything in return. But she had enough to pour from. Her heart was always full, because its sources never went dry. She was lonely, as a genius is always lonely in spite of friends and world renown. Hers was a fighting life, on the inner front, with the fear of silent defeats and the glory of secret triumphs, and that struggle was the wellspring of her genius.*[40]

In *Kristin Lavransdatter*, Sigrid wrote that at the end, Kristin

> *. . . had come to look out over her life in a new way: as when a man comes up on a height above his native place where he has never climbed before, and looks down from it into his own dale. He knows each farm and fence, each thicket, the gully of each beck; but he seems to see for the first time how these things all lie on the face of the land . . .* [41]

Sigrid never reached that point, or achieved such peace. Her religious beliefs should have been a comfort to her in the end, but that doesn't seem to have been enough. She died bewildered and alone.

---

* Published later in *Tidens Tegn*.

NOTES

Abbreviations

Krane	*Sigrid Undset* by Borghild Krane
Minn Venn	*Minn Venn Sigrid Undset* by Nini Roll Anker
A Woman's Point of View	*Et Kvinde-synspunkt*
SU Writes Home	*Sigrid Undset Writes Home* by Arne Skouen
HS	Hudson Strode
MKR	Marjorie Kinnan Rawlings
Dea	Dea Hedberg
Nini	Nini Roll Anker
Ragnhild	Ragnhild Undset Wiberg, Sigrid's sister
Hans	Hans Benedict Svarstad, Sigrid's son
Moster Sigrid	*Moster Sigrid* by Charlotte Blindheim

ENDNOTES

CHAPTER I—THE BEGINNING

1. *The Longest Years* (Alfred A. Knopf, N.Y., 1935) 13
2. Ibid., 128
3. Ibid., 129
4. Ibid., 11
5. Ibid., 127
6. Ibid., 267
7. Ibid., 11
8. Borghild Krane, *Sigrid Undset* (Gyldendal Norsk Forlag, Oslo, 1970), 14
9. The Longest Years, 11-12
10. Ibid., 15-16
11. Ibid., 12
12. Ibid., 49
13. Ibid., 51
14. Ibid., 51
15. Ibid., 39
16. Ibid., 292
17. Ibid., 41
18. Ibid., 43
19. Ibid., 43
20. Ibid., 125
21. Ibid., 208-209
22. Ibid., 70
23. Ibid., 84
24. Ibid., 85
25. Ibid., 87
26. Ibid., 89

[27] Ibid., 150

[28] Ibid., 150

[29] Ibid., 150

[30] Ibid., 150

[31] Ibid., 105

[32] Ibid., 106

[33] Ibid., 222

[34] Ibid., 222

[35] Ibid., 221

[36] Ibid., 233

[37] Ibid., 161

[38] Ibid., 239

[39] Ibid., 250

[40] Ibid., 277

[41] Ibid., 326

[42] Ibid., 288

CHAPTER II—YOUTH

[1] Stanley Kunitz & Howard Haycroft, 24

[2] Krane, 16

[3] Ibid., 20

[4] Letter to Dea Hedberg, January 18, 1899—most letters to Dea also in *Kjaere Dea*, (J.W. Cappelens, Forlag A.S., Oslo, 1979), and in the university library, Oslo, 14

[5] Ibid., February 2, 1899

[6] *The Longest Years*, 264-267

[7] Letter to Dea, 2/2/1889

[8] Ibid., January 2, 1889

[9] Ibid., November 6, 1901

[10] Ibid., April 3, 1900

[11] Ibid., October 29, 1900

[12] Ibid., June 23, 1901

[13] Ibid., January 2, 1901

[14] Ibid., January 2, 1901

[15] Ibid., February 25, 1901

[16] Ibid., November 6, 1901

[17] Ibid., November 6, 1901

[18] Ibid., November 6, 1901

[19] Ibid., November 6, 1901

[20] Ibid., March 8, 1902

[21] Ibid., March 8, 1902

[22] Ibid., April 23, 1902

[23] Ibid., December 19, 1902

[24] Ibid., May 9, 1903

[25] Ibid., May 9, 1903

[26] Ibid., June 7, 1903

[27] Ibid., June 7, 1903

[28] Ibid., October 28, 1903

[29] Ibid., October 28, 1903

[30] Ibid., October 28, 1903

[31] Ibid., April 18, 1904

[32] Ibid., May 28, 1904, also Krane, 138

[33] Ibid., June 1, 1904

CHAPTER III—"BECOME SOMETHING, DARLING…"

[1] Andreas H. Winsnes, *A Study in Christian Realism*, (Sheed & Ward, N.Y., 1953), 34

[2] Letter in Aschehoug files, also in Winsnes, 35

[3] *Fru Marta Oulie*, (Aschehoug & Co., Oslo, 1906), 37

[4] Ibid., 82

[5] Ibid., 6

[6] Ibid., 3

[7] Ibid., 80

[8] Ibid., 129

[9] Letter to Dea, May 28, 1907

[10] Ibid., September 4, 1908

[11] Ibid., December 22, 1908

[12] Ibid., March 8, 1909

CHAPTER IV—LOVE—"NOT PALE, TIRED, GREY-WEATHER DREAMS"

[1] *Gunnar's Daughter*, (Alfred A. Knopf, N.Y., 1936), 63-64

[2] Ibid., 216

[3] Ibid., 227

[4] Ibid., 252

5   Ibid., 258-259

6   Letter to Nils Collett Vogt, January 9, 1909, also Krane, 28

7   Ibid., 1/9/1909

8   *Jenny* (Alfred A. Knopf, N.Y., 1921), 40-41

9   Ibid., 96

10   Ibid., 28

11   Ibid., 15

12   Ibid., 261, 263

13   Letter to Nils Collett Vogt, February 3, 1909, also Krane, 29

14   *Jenny*, 87

15   Ibid., 97

16   Nini Roll Anker, *Min VennSigrid Undset*, (Aschehoug & Co., Oslo 1946), 9

17   Ibid., 10

18   Ibid., 10

19   *Vaaren*, (*The Spring*), (Aschehoug & Co., Oslo 1914) 31

20   Ibid., 32

21   *Min Venn*, 11

22   *Ungdom*, (*Youth*), (Aschehoug & Co., Oslo, 1910 an 1957), quote from *Credo*, (free translation), 9

23   *Jenny*, 172

24   Ibid., 62

25   Ibid., 87

26   Ibid., 87

27   Ibid., 44

28   Ibid., 118

29   Ibid., 130

30   Ibid., 157

31   Ibid., 204

32   Ibid., 62

33   Ibid., 264-265

34   Ibid., 290-291

35   Ibid., 284

36   *Min Venn*, 12

37   Ibid., 13

38   Ibid., 13

39   Letter to Dea, January 18, 1912

40   Ibid., October 2, 1912

CHAPTER V—MARRIAGE

[1] Letter to Nini, 10/5/1912
[2] Ibid., 10/5/1912
[3] Ibid., July 29, 1912
[4] Ibid., July 29, 1912
[5] Ibid., July 29, 1912
[6] Ibid., July 29, 1912
[7] Ibid., July 29, 1912
[8] Ibid., July 29, 1912
[9] Leonard S. Woolf, *Beginning Again*, (Harcourt Brace 1963), 94-95
[10] Letter to Nini, July 29, 1912
[11] Krane, 38
[12] *Min Venn*, 19
[13] Ibid., 19
[14] Ibid., 18
[15] The New Columbia Encyclopedia, (Columbia University Press, N.Y., 1975), 357
[16] *Four Stories*, (Alfred A. Knopf, N.Y., 1959), 7
[17] Ibid., 7
[18] Ibid., 202
[19] Ibid., 204-205
[20] Ibid., 239
[21] Ibid., 245
[22] Ibid., 246
[23] Letter to Dea, October 2, 1912
[24] Krane, 142
[25] *Et Kvinde-Synspunkt*, (*A Woman's Point of View*), (Aschehoug & Co., Oslo, 1919), 4; also in Samtiden, *Some Reflections on the Suffragette Movement*, by Sigrid Undset, 1912, 538-556
[26] Ibid., 6
[27] Ibid., 7
[28] Ibid., 8
[29] Ibid., 20
[30] Ibid., 21
[31] Ibid., 21-22
[32] Ibid., 22
[33] Ibid., 26
[34] Ibid., 27

[35] Ibid., 28-29
[36] Ibid., 30
[37] *Min Venn*, 21
[38] Letter to Dea, December 21, 1912
[39] Ibid., December 22, 1912
[40] Ibid., December 21, 1912
[41] Letter to Nini, February 19, 1913, also in *Min Venn*, 25

CHAPTER VI—SKI

[1] Letter to Dea, May 9, 1914
[2] Ibid., May 9, 1914
[3] *Min Venn*, 28-29
[4] Letter to Dea, May 11, 1914
[5] *A Woman's Point of View*, 49
[6] Ibid., 44
[7] Ibid., 61
[8] Letter to Nini—*Min Venn*, 29-30
[9] *Min Venn*, 28-29
[10] Ibid., 32
[11] Ibid, 33
[12] Ibid., 34
[13] Letter to Nini, October 1915

CHAPTER VII—SINSEN

[1] Letter to Nini—*Min Venn*, 36
[2] Ibid., 37
[3] Ibid., 37-38
[4] *Min Venn*, 38
[5] Letter to Nini, May 21, 1916, also Krane, 45
[6] Laurens van der Post, *Yet Being Someone Other*, (Hogarth Press, London, 1982), 186
[7] Letter to Nini, also in *Min Venn*, 41-42
[8] Ibid., 41-42
[9] Ibid., October 22, 1918
[10] *Min Venn*, 39-40
[11] *Images in a Mirror*, (Alfred A. Knopf, N.Y., 1938), 225-226

[12] *Four Stories*, 73
[13] Ibid., 77
[14] Ibid., 98

CHAPTER VIII—LILLEHAMMER

[1] *The Stranger*, (*Den Lykkelige Alder*), (Aschehoug & Co., Oslo, 1908), 89
[2] *Min Venn*, 48
[3] Ibid., 49
[4] Letter to Nini, July, 1919
[5] Ibid., July, 1919
[6] *Min Venn*, 52
[7] Letter to Nini, August 28, 1919
[8] Ibid., December 8, 1919
[9] Ibid., December 8, 1919
[10] *Min Venn*, 52
[11] Letter to Nini, January 17, 1920
[12] Ibid., May 10, 1920
[13] Ibid., May 10, 1920
[14] Ibid., May 10, 1920
[15] Interviews with Gunhild Svarstad Andreasson, March & April, 1981

CHAPTER IX - A WOMAN'S POINT OF VIEW

[1] *A Woman's Point of View*, 68
[2] Ibid., 70
[3] Ibid., 72
[4] Krane, 170-171
[5] *A Woman's Point of View*, 93
[6] Ibid., 93-94
[7] Ibid., 94
[8] Ibid., 96
[9] Ibid.,98
[10] Ibid., 98-99
[11] Ibid., 100
[12] Ibid., 101
[13] Ibid., 102
[14] Ibid., 103
[15] Ibid., 105-106

[16]   Ibid., 105-106
[17]   Ibid., 106
[18]   Ibid., 109
[19]   *Tidens Tegn* (periodical), April, 1919
[20]   Charlotte Perkins Gilman *A Man-Made World or, Our Androcentric Culture*, (Charlton Co., N.Y., 1911), 136
[21]   *A Woman's Point of View*
[22]   Ibid., 134-135
[23]   Ibid. 132-133
[24]   Ibid., 57
[25]   Ibid., 128-129
[26]   Ibid., 130
[27]   Ibid., 135
[28]   Ibid., 163-164
[29]   Ibid., 167
[30]   Ibid., 167
[31]   Ibid., 168
[32]   Ibid., 168
[33]   Ibid., 170
[34]   Will Durant, *The Age of Faith*, (Simon and Schuster, N.Y., 1950), 585
[35]   *A Woman's Point of View*
[36]   *Return to the Future*, (Alfred A. Knopf, N.Y., 1942), 211-212

CHAPTER X - KRISTIN LAVRANSDATTER

[1]   *Min Venn*, 54
[2]   Krane, 53
[3]   *Jenny*, 87
[4]   Ibid., 89
[5]   Arne Skouen, (*Sigrid Undset Skriver Hjem*, (*Sigrid Undset Writes Home*), (Aschehoug & Co., Oslo, 1982), 22
[6]   *Min Venn*, 57
[7]   Ibid., 57-58
[8]   Letter to Nini, August 8, 1920
[9]   *Kristin Lavransdatter*, 73
[10]   Ibid., 33
[11]   Ibid., 105
[12]   Ibid., 3
[13]   Ibid., 266

14   Ibid., 267
15   Ibid., 268
16   Ibid., 269
17   Ibid., 270
18   Ibid., 271
19   Ibid., 272
20   Ibid., 272
21   Charlotte Blindheim, *Moster Sigrid*, (Aschehoug & Co., Oslo, 1982), 53
22   *Kristin Lavransdatter*
23   Ibid., 356
24   Ibid., 407
25   Ibid., 408
26   Ibid., 459
27   Ibid., 460
28   Ibid., 562
29   Ibid., 794
30   Ibid., 794
31   Ibid., 794
32   Ibid., 794
33   Ibid., 796
34   Ibid., 800
35   Ibid., 845
36   Ibid., 846
37   Ibid., 847
38   Ibid., 847
39   Ibid., 580
40   Ibid., 848
41   Ibid., 849
42   Ibid., 850
43   Ibid., 850
44   Ibid., 854-855
45   Ibid., 855
46   Ibid., 988
47   Ibid., 997
48   Ibid., 1006
49   Ibid., 1044
50   Ibid., 837
51   *Min Venn*, 59-60

CHAPTER XI—HAPPY TIMES

[1] Letter to Nini, July 12, 1924
[2] Ibid., July 12, 1924
[3] *Moster Sigrid*, 10
[4] *Min Venn*, 64
[5] *Moster Sigrid*
[6] Alice Lyttkens, quoted in *Moster Sigrid*, 31
[7] Letter from Ulla Wiberg Day, July 1, 1983
[8] *Min Venn*, 75
[9] Taped interview with Alfred A. Knopf, N.Y. March 30, 1983
[10] *Moster Sigrid*, 24
[11] *Happy Times in Norway*, (Alfred A. Knopf, N.Y., 1942), 28
[12] Ibid., 90
[13] Ibid., 185
[14] Letter to Nini 6/8/1923
[15] *Happy Times in Norway*, 191-192
[16] Ibid., 171
[17] Letter from Gunhild Svarstad Andreasson, August 24, 1981
[18] *Moster Sigrid*, 38
[19] Ibid., 41
[20] Ibid., 41
[21] Isaac Dinesen, *Letters from Africa*, 1914-1931, (University of Chicago Press, 1981); Letter to Mary Bess Westenholz, March 30, 1928, 359
[22] *Kristin Lavransdatter*, 401-402
[23] *Happy Times in Norway*, 57-58

CHAPTER XII—THE MASTER OF HESTVIKEN

[1] *The Burning Bush*, Part II of *The Winding Road*, (Alfred A. Knopf, N.Y., 1932), 345
[2] Letter to Nini, January 10, 1921, Krane, 59
[3] Ibid.
[4] Quote from Edvard Bull's *Nation and Church in the Middle Ages* in *A Study in Christian Realism*, Andreas H. Winsnes, 99
[5] *The Master of Hestviken*, (Alfred A. Knopf, First Plume Printing, March 1978, USA), 629

6   *Kristin Lavransdatter*, 1018
7   *The Master of Hestviken*, 143-144

CHAPTER XIII—THE NOBEL PRIZE

1   *The Longest Years*, 4
2   Ibid., 4
3   Ibid., 4
4   Ibid., 6
5   Olav Lagerkrantz, *August Strindberg*, (Farrar Straus Giroux, N.Y., 1984), 368
6   Interview with Ole Henrik Moe, April 1981
7   Ibid.

CHAPTER XIV—THE THIRTIES

1   *America* (periodical), June 13, 1942
2   *The Wild Orchid*, Part I of *The Winding Road*, (Alfred A. Knopf, N.Y., 1931), 281
3   *The Sign* (periodical), April, 1929
4   Ibid., July, 1929
5   *The Catholic World* (periodical), April 1938
6   *Ida Elisabeth*, (Cassell & Co., Ltd., London, 1933), 13
7   Ibid., 15
8   Ibid., 17
9   Ibid., 48
10 Ibid., 122
11 Ibid., 125
12 Ibid., 133
13 Ibid., 273
14 Ibid., 274
15 Ibid., 231
16 Ibid., 335
17 *Morgenblatte* (periodical), December 9, 1936, also Krane, 98
18 *Dagbladet* and *Aftenposten* (periodicals), November 28, 1938, also Krane, 98
19 Interviews with Kjeld Rasmussen, March and April, 1981
20 *Ida Elisabeth*, 154
21 Interview with Kjeld Rasmussen
22 Ibid.
23 Interview with Gunhild Svarstad Andreasson
24 Interview with Sigrid's nieces

25   *Men, Women and Places*, (Alfred A. Knopf, N.Y., 1939), 47

26   Ibid., 44

27   Ibid., 40

28   Ibid., 51-52

29   Ibid., 52-53

30   *Moster Sigrid*, 3

31   Ibid., 8

32   The Gyth Family Tree, 196

33   *Madame Dorthea*, (Alfred A. Knopf, N.Y., 1940), 39

34   Letter to Nini, January 18, 1940; also Krane, 100

35   Ibid., October 30, 1927; also Krane, 90-91

36   *A Woman's Point of View*, 82-83; and *Return to the Future*, 219

CHAPTER XV—WAR

1   *Moster Sigrid*, 45

2   Ibid., 48

3   *Kristin Lavransdatter*, 849

4   *Return to the Future*, 9

5   Interview with Ole Henrik Moe, April 1981

6   Ibid.

7   Ibid.

8   *Return to the Future*, 17

9   Ibid., 19

10   Ibid., 19-20

11   Ibid., 20-21

12   Ibid., 21

13   *Tromsø* (periodical), April 24, 1940; also Krane, 105

14   *Return to the Future*, 8

15   Ibid., 33

16   Ibid., 33

17   Ibid., 34

18   Ibid., 77

19   Interview with Ole Henrik Moe, April 1981

20   *Return to the Future*, 66

21   Ibid., 55

22   Ibid., 56

23   Alice Lyttkens, *Live and Let Live*, (Bonnier, Sweden, 1980), quoted in *SU Writes Home* by Arne Skouen, 15

24 *Return to the Future*, 66
25 Ibid., 73-74
26 Ibid., 74
27 Ibid., 75
28 *Nordisk Tidende* (periodical); also *SU Writes Home*, 92
29 *Return to the Future*, 65
30 Ibid., 68
31 *Moster Sigrid*, 83

CHAPTER XVI—AMERICA

1   *SU Writes Home*, 11
2   Interview with Alfred A. Knopf, March 29, 1983
3   Interview with Carol Brandt, March 31, 1983
4   Letter to Hans, January 2, 1941
5   Interview with Carol Brandt, March 31, 183
6   Interview with Alfred A. Knopf, March 29, 1983
7   Ibid.
8   Ibid.
9   *SU Writes Home*, 49
10 Krane, 114
11 *SU Writes Home*, 11
12 Interview with Campbell Norsgaard, July 20, 1981
13 American Newspapers; also Krane, 108-110
14 Interview with Sigrid's nieces in Oslo, March and April, 1981
15 *SU Writes Home*, 7-8
16 Ibid., 11-12
17 Ibid., 41
18 Letter to Marjorie Kinnan Rawlins, April 24, 1942
19 *SU Writes Home*, 18-19
20 Interview with Alfred A. Knopf, March 29, 1983
21 Quote from *Introduction* by Robert Ellsberg, XVI in *By Little and By Little*, (selected writings by Dorothy Day), (Alfred A. Knopf, N.Y., 1983)
22 Letter to Ragnhild, March 8, 1941; also *SU Writes Home*, 80
23 Ibid., August 11, 1944; also *SU Writes Home*, 85
24 Letter to Hans, August 23, 1943
25 *Return to the Future*, 128
26 *Jenny*, 173
27 *Return to the Future*, 201-202

[28] Ibid., 198

CHAPTER XVII—THE OCCUPATION

[1] Letter to Hudson Strode, March 19, 1941
[2] Ibid., June 1, 1943
[3] Ibid., November 24, 1941
[4] Letter to Marjorie Kinnan Rawlings, January 19, 1942
[5] Letter to Ragnhild, March 9, 1942; also *SU Writes Home*, 87
[6] Letter from Norton Baskin, March 10, 1983
[7] Telephone interview with Norton Baskin, March 17, 1983
[8] Ibid.; also letter to Hudson Strode, September 19, 1939
[9] Ibid., March, 1983
[10] Letter to MKR, March 5, 1942
[11] Ibid., April 24, 1942
[12] Letter to HS, January 12, 1942
[13] Letter to Ragnhild, December 18, 1941; also *SU Writes Home*, 114
[14] Ibid., September 19, 1942; also *SU Writes Home*, 117
[15] Letter to HS, March 19, 1941
[16] Ibid., September 26, 1942
[17] Ibid., February 14, 1952
[18] *SU Writes Home*, 53
[19] Letter to MKR, June 28, 1943
[20] Letter to Willert J. Klass, August 3, 1943
[21] Letter to Ragnhild; also *SU Writes Home*, 79
[22] Letter to MKR, February 24, 1944
[23] Letter to HS, January 4, 1944
[24] Letter to MKR, June 2, 1944
[25] Ibid., April 24, 1942
[26] Ibid., January 6, 1945
[27] *Return to the Future*, 34
[28] Letter to MKR, December 13, 1944
[29] Letter to Hans, March 23, 1943; also *SU Writes Home*, 76-77
[30] Ibid., 104
[31] Letter to MKR, September 17, 1943
[32] Letter to Ingeborg Møller, September 12, 1942; also *SU Writes Home*, 123
[33] Letter to Ragnhild, June 5, 1945; also *SU Writes Home*, 107
[34] Letter to MKR, May 25, 1945
[35] Ibid., May 25, 1945

36 Letter to HS, March 8, 1943
37 *Return to the Future*, 129
38 Letter to Hans, December 4, 1943; also *SU Writes Home*, 73
39 Letter to HS, January 6, 1945
40 Ibid., May 25, 1945
41 Ibid., June 17, 1945
42 Ibid., July 1, 1945
43 Ibid., June 17, 1945
44 Ibid., June 17, 1945
45 Ibid., June 17, 1945

CHAPTER XVIII—THE LONG LONLINESS IS OVER

1 Krane, 120
2 *Moster Sigrid*, 13
3 *Kristin Lavransdatter*, 946
4 Letter to MKR, November 24, 1945
5 Ibid., November 24, 1945
6 Letter to HS, December 1, 1945
7 Letter to MKR, November 24, 1945
8 Letter to HS, March 15, 1947
9 Letter to MKR, March 29, 1949
10 Ibid., November 24, 1945
11 Ibid., November 24, 1945
12 *Moster Sigrid*, 90
13 *SU Writes Home*, 132
14 Letter to Hans Aanrud, December 20, 1948; also Krane, 121-122
15 Letter to MKR, November 19, 1946 (footnote)
16 *Moster Sigrid*, 91
17 Letter to MKR, July 3, 1946
18 Letter to HS, July 15, 1946
19 Letter to MKR, November 19, 1946
20 Ibid., February 17, 1947
21 Ibid., January 15, 1944
22 Ibid., January 15, 1947
23 *SU Writes Home*, 146
24 *Return to the Future*, 210
25 *SU Writes Home*, 147-148
26 Letter to HS, March 15, 1947

27 Letter to MKR, July 3, 1946
28 Ibid., December 3, 1947
29 Krane, 111
30 Letter to MKR, May 12, 1947
31 Ibid., May 12, 1947
32 Krane, 130
33 Letter to HS, December 14, 1947
34 T.S. Eliot, *Rhapsody on a Windy Night*
35 Letter to MKR, October 29, 1948
36 Letter to HS, December 2, 1948
37 Ibid., February 2, 1949
38 Letter to MKR, May 26, 1949
39 *Moster Sigrid*, 81 (*Kristin Lavransdatter*, 1045)
40 Ibid., 100
41 *Kristin Lavransdatter*, 1006

Made in the USA
San Bernardino, CA
24 September 2013